Public Relations Programming and Production

Public Relations Programming and Production

E. W. BRODY

1988

PRAEGER

New York
Westport, Connecticut
London

HM
263
.B67
1988

For Margaret and Powell

Library of Congress Cataloging-in-Publication Data

Brody, E. W.
  Public relations programming and production / E.W. Brody.
    p. cm.
  Bibliography: p.
  Includes index.
  ISBN 0-275-92677-X (alk. paper) ISBN 0-275-92682-6
(pbk. : alk. paper)
  1. Public relations. I. Title.
HM263.B67 1988
659.2—dc19
87–24626

Library of Congress Catalog Card Number: 87–24626

ISBN: 0–275–92677–X
ISBN: 0–275–92682–6 (pbk.)

First published in 1988

Praeger Publishers, One Madison Avenue, New York, NY 10010
A division of Greenwood Press, Inc.

Printed in the United States of America
(∞)
The paper used in this book complies with the
Permanent Paper Standard issued by the National
Information Standards Organization (Z39.48–1984).

10 9 8 7 6 5 4 3 2 1

Contents

List of Figures

Preface

Public relations practice involves multiple functions that have been in a state of flux for decades. Mass media publicity was practitioners' primary objective in the early years. The bulk of their work involved packaging and delivery of information to the mass media.

In the latter decades of the twentieth century, very different conditions prevail. Practitioners are involved in multiple organizational activities. They are responsible for environmental assessment, identifying and elaborating emerging trends, and defining alternative responses for organizational managers. They are accountable for programmatic results in the form of constituent behaviors rather than merely the volume of media exposure their efforts generate. They apply sophisticated research techniques before, during, and after public relations efforts to enhance their efficacy and measure results.

While message preparation and delivery thus has come to occupy a less prominent role in public relations practice, these functions nevertheless have grown more complex and more demanding. Several factors are responsible for the change. First, channels of communication available to practitioners have multiplied. Second, media audiences have declined quantitatively as communication channels have increased in number. Finally, communication channels have become progressively more specialized in content and more oriented to narrow audiences.

Public relations practice thus requires more messages prepared for more media serving smaller audiences to achieve results that once could be accomplished through mass media publicity. These circumstances are attaching new importance to the technician role in public relations. Practitioners during the 1960s and early 1970s almost exclusively entered the profession as technicians. They served largely as apprentices, ultimately progressing to counseling and management. Newcomers to the profession continue in large part to be technicians but the new complexities with which they deal increasingly make them equal partners in a multifaceted profession.

This trend has been accompanied by change in the academic curricula that prepare students for public relations practice. Public relations education once largely was confined to undergraduate degree programs. Increasing practice complexity in recent years has been accompanied by parallel curricular change. The knowledge and skills required of practitioners has grown beyond the capacity of baccalaureate studies. More and more postsecondary educational institutions are offering master's degree programs in public relations and detailed recommendations as to their content have been prepared by the Commission on Graduate Public Relations Education.

This book thus was designed to meet the needs of two groups. Its content is oriented primarily for use in graduate courses in public relations programming and production. It also was developed for use as a reference by practitioners whose educations predate the development of contemporary complexity in public relations programming and production.

The content of the pages that follow is a distillation of knowledge acquired during more than two decades of public relations practice and a half dozen years of teaching and writing as a member of undergraduate and graduate university faculties. Some is original. A great deal more is a product of assimilation and synthesis of ideas and techniques developed by others and tested in practice situations.

Neither programming nor production in public relations is undertaken in a vacuum. The nature of these processes requires that they be carried out in specific organizational contexts. The earlier of the chapters that follow thus are dedicated to contextual matters. They explore the environments in which organizations function and the manner in which they must respond to environmental change. They also address the organizational as well as the professional responsibilities of public relations practitioners.

The later chapters deal with the specifics of programming and production. They relate programmatic concerns to the needs of clients and employers before proceeding to examine the complex sets of communication channels at the practitioners' disposal.

Neither this book nor any other is an individual product. Each contains the thoughts of many others, garnered from multiple sources. Innumerable colleagues in public relations practice and in education thus have contributed knowingly and unknowingly to this work. Their thoughts have been supplemented by many others stimulated by the challenging questions of undergraduate and graduate students.

Authorship also requires another ingredient: the indulgence and support of colleagues and their organizations. I am most indebted to the College of Communication and Fine Arts and the Department of Journalism at Memphis State University for the freedom and support they extended. Dean Richard

R. Ranta and Drs. John DeMott and Dan L. Lattimore have been most supportive.

Colleagues in other institutions and in the Public Relations Society of America also have contributed to what follows. I am especially obligated to Professor Bill L. Baxter of Marquette University for the comments he provided while reviewing the manuscript.

These contributions and those of the editorial staff of Praeger Publishers, especially Alison Bricken, were essential in bringing this work to completion.

1

New Realities

Organizational success in recent years has become a function of ability to adapt to changing circumstances. Social, technological, and economic changes in the United States and around the world are exerting mounting pressure on organizations of all kinds. Public relations departments and consultancies are no exception. The scope of public relations practice has changed and continues to change. Several components have been added to the traditional practice model. The relative importance of model components in achieving success has changed dramatically; and public relations practitioners have changed as well.

Contemporary public relations programming and production practices for these reasons are far different than once was the case. Both are more complex and demanding although in different ways. Programming has expanded in depth and breadth, encompassing organizational reality as well as stakeholder perception. Production has grown to embrace a multiplicity of new media and techniques, all of them more demanding of practitioner expertise.

With increased complexity and sophistication, programming and production literally have been redefined. Redefinition brought with it a new set of terms descriptive of modified processes.

Mastery of public relations programming and production processes requires practitioners to understand the nature and scope of these changes. Each of them bears directly on both processes and the measurable results expected today by employer and client alike.

SCOPE OF PRACTICE

Public relations historically has been cast as an art or craft that deals primarily with communication. During the past decade it has become much ✶

more. In seeking to engender accommodation between organizations and their constituent groups, public relations practitioners increasingly have become involved in changing realities as well as perceptions.

The realities in question are both internal and external. They involve those environmental events and trends that impact organizations and their stakeholders and the actions that organizations take in response to stimuli originating in their environments.

Environmental Assessment

Events and trends are monitored through a process relatively new to public relations called environmental assessment. Two components are involved: scanning and monitoring. Scanning requires ongoing examination of organizational environments to identify events that may signal the start of significant trends. Monitoring involves watching the development of those trends. Their breadth, depth, and speed of development all may be significant in organizational planning. The process applies to two sets of environments: internal and external. The external are the suprasystems of which organizations are a part. The internal are the subsystems of which they are composed.

Organizational Environments

Organizations, like individuals, mold and are molded by their environments. The process is adaptive and ongoing. While occasionally appearing confrontational or revolutionary, as in heated political campaigns or labor disputes, it is essentially evolutionary in nature.

Organizational-environmental relationships are complex. Organizations are molded by the natural, technological, human, political, socioeconomic, and market environments in which they function. Their behaviors are equally influenced by their internal environments: psychological, social, political, and technological.

The natures of organizations and environments are primary determinants of organizational directions and of the goals and strategies that guide them. Those who succeed in public relations programming must recognize and understand the relational dynamics involved.

PRACTICE MODEL COMPONENTS

Practitioner need for understanding placed environmental assessment with research, planning, communication, and evaluation as a basic component of public relations process. Some consider environmental assessment a component of what has been called issues management. Close examination shows it differs from contemporary public relations practice only in that its advocates consider it pertinent only to problems with which government ultimately may become involved. Public relations practitioners argue that what has been called "issues management" long has existed in the form of governmental public relations.

Perception and Reality

The debate has been more a matter of semantic than real differences and has served only to becloud the development of environmental assessment as a component of public relations practice. Also largely unnoticed in many quarters has been another basic change in public relations. Practitioners now deal directly with organizational realities as well as stakeholder perceptions.

In earlier days, the emphasis was on communication. Organizational policy, procedure, and action were taken as "given." The public relations function involved casting those factors in the most favorable possible light. Today public relations deals with realities as well as stakeholder perceptions. The emphasis has shifted from communication to behavior; to insuring that the organization meets its social and political as well as economic responsibilities.

The change is significant. Public relations once was defined as "doing a good job and getting credit for it." Practitioners then were involved primarily in achieving the latter objective. They now are equally concerned with the former. They apply information gathered through environmental assessment in a series of steps.

Information Applied

First existing and prospective organizational impact is assessed. Then alternative responses are defined. Finally public relations practitioners recommend specific courses of action. The public relations process thus has become (a) environmental assessment, (b) research, (c) delineation of alternative responses, (d) counseling management in terms of the alternatives, (e) communication, and (f) evaluation.

Except in the case of communication, most of these elements remain little changed other than in level of sophistication. Communication involves a sender, a message, a channel or medium, and a receiver. Message and medium traditionally have been public relations' primary concerns. Contemporary practitioners recognize, however, that communication is controlled by receivers. Receiver characteristics thus have become predominant in message development and channel selection. Their needs, desires, and perceptions have assumed preeminence in the communication process. Organizational policy, procedure, and posture, once accepted as "given" by public relations practitioners, have become variables.

PRACTITIONER ROLES

Organizational evolution has been paramount in the development of practitioner roles, which have changed in keeping with the evolution of the public relations process. Where they once served primarily as technicians in communication, they now are counselors to management. Communication is fast becoming a secondary, perhaps even a tertiary, function among senior practitioners.

Appropriate organizational action often must precede communication. Public relations practitioners thus are required to do more than see that their organizations obtain credit for responsible behavior. They play a major role in insuring that organizations behave responsibly. They serve as social analysts and organizational consciences as well as communicators.

During the transitional years, those who practiced public relations necessarily became professionals in the true sense of that word. They assumed responsibilities beyond those that traditionally bind employer and employee.

They came to participate in developing policy and procedure rather than accepting without question the wisdom and propriety of employers or clients. They began to serve as organizational consciences in an era in which ethics and morality too often were sacrificed on the altars of economic or political expediency.

THE ORIGINS OF PROFESSIONALISM

Professionalism in public relations arguably has developed more out of pragmatism rather than idealism. Survival among contemporary organizations is a function of their willingness and ability to meet the demands of multiple stakeholder groups concurrently. Better informed and increasingly critical, these groups have been imposing ever more stringent definitions of economic and social responsibility on every organization. Organizations fail to respond at their peril.

Decline in the U.S. automotive industry is a striking example of the consequences that await organizations that neglect or ignore constituent needs. Only time will tell whether automakers can recover from decades during which the interests of employees and customers were sacrificed in favor of managers and shareholders. Adversarial employee relations policies and emphases on horsepower and body style rather than efficiency and quality produced predictable results.

Organizations that would succeed today must respond to the needs of employees, consumers, and communities in which they operate as well as of shareholders and managers. Neither "the public be damned" nor "any color they want as long as it's black" will suffice. Organizations are interdependent components of complex societies. Accommodation with all stakeholder groups is prerequisite to their long-term survival.

Problems in Public Relations

Development of these conditions produced radical change in formulae for public relations success. Practitioners in every industry were faced with enhanced accountability for their work. Cost-conscious employers and clients demanded measurable results. Stakeholder groups with which they were concerned became progressively more skeptical and cynical. Media audiences fragmented as channels of communication proliferated.

Successful public relations programming in these circumstances came to require more than mastery of media and messages. Organizational performance acceptable to all stakeholder groups became a vital component of the public relations process. Unfortunately, neither organizations nor their managers readily became acclimated to these conditions. Vestiges of the "public be damned" era remained in the closing years of the twentieth century. Senior managers experienced no little difficulty in adjusting to the demise of the age of buccaneering free enterprise. Their juniors, in hot pursuit of "the good life," triggered a series of scandals in Wall Street and elsewhere that contributed to public skepticism and cynicism and compounded public relations tasks.

The New Standard

Public relations practitioners in these conditions had no choice but to become involved in organizational performance as well as communication. They found themselves forced to speak out on the development of organizational policy and practice as well as communication of the outcomes.

"Is it right?"
"Is it fair to all concerned?"
"Who will benefit or suffer?"

These and other questions that address the morality and ethics of organizations more and more came to be primary concerns of public relations. Practitioners, out of practical necessity, were forced to become involved in decision making. As organizational improprieties became progressively less defensible, they increasingly were forced to serve as ombudsmen for stakeholder groups.

The New Professionals

In the process, and without conscious effort, public relations became a profession. The change hardly was altruistic. Public relations programming in behalf of organizations that failed to discharge their social responsibilities was becoming an exercise in futility. Public relations failures endangered practitioners' economic health.

The net result, nevertheless, was development of what had been the missing dimension in the professionalization of public relations: adherence to moral and ethical standards and primary commitment to the public good.

Other accepted components of professionalism, including an expanding body of specialized knowledge and accredited academic curricula, already were in place. By the mid–1980s, practitioners were coming to accept the need to meet other demands that traditionally attach to professional stature. A Public Relations Society of America Task Force on Professionalism had become a standing Committee on the Future of Public Relations. The committee appeared to be moving toward mandatory continuing education and recredentialing programs. Perhaps most important, professional standards were governing public relations practice.

PROFESSIONALISM AND PROGRAMMING

Professionalism and pragmatism together require that public relations programming begin with organizational policies and practices rather than messages and media. Performance, in other words, has become more important than perception. The former must precede the latter if public relations programs are to succeed.

The essence of performance is doing what is right. The latter phrase refers not only to the organization but to its several stakeholder groups. "Right" can be more difficult to define but is readily demonstrable. Johnson & Johnson Company, for example, was "right" in withdrawing Tylenol from retail outlets when cyanide was discovered in several packages in the early 1980s. Volkswagen of North America was equally wrong a few years later in denying the existence of mechanical problems in the wake of a rash of uncontrolled acceleration incidents in Audi automobiles.

Performance and Results

Results demonstrate the wisdom of Johnson & Johnson's tactics and the failure of Volkswagen's strategy. Tylenol quickly recaptured most of its earlier market share after being reintroduced with tamper-resistant packaging. Audi sales had declined by 25 percent before Volkswagen acceded to governmental pressure and recalled its vehicles for mechanical modification.

Similarly contrasting circumstances developed in the employee relations of USX Corporation (formerly U.S. Steel) and Federal Express Corporation during the same period. USX's long-standing adversarial relationship with its unions led to an extended strike while the company was seeking to cope with major economic problems. At about the same time, Federal Express discontinued its ill-fated ZAP Mail venture without incident.

Professional Standards

The same principles have encouraged development of professionalism among public relations practitioners. Like most professions, public relations is populated by a relatively tight-knit group. Practitioners, educators, and even the so-called head hunters in public relations know one another personally and by reputation, especially at senior levels. They know each other's clients, employers, professional expertise, and ethical standards.

The latter factors are especially significant. Most public relations positions are filled by individual referral rather than by advertising. Personal reputation is a strong factor in the process. High personal and professional standards thus become essential to those who would progress in public relations. As in the case of organizations, they are judged by their behaviors.

PROCESS REDEFINED

Value judgments also are rendered in keeping with practitioner mastery of the public relations process. With change in the process has come new terminology that tends to confuse all involved.

"Plan," "program," "project," and "process" are words often attached to "public relations." Each has a clear meaning in the abstract sense that has become somewhat distorted when linked to "public relations." The latter term is no less ambiguous. Dozens of individuals and organizations have attempted to develop concise definitions without noteworthy success.

Public relations here refers to the process through which organizations seek to achieve accommodation with stakeholder groups over issues of mutual concern. Stakeholder groups are those sets of individuals that may be impacted by organizational action or inaction or whose actions or inaction may impact the organization. The process includes planning, programming, and execution of a set of projects.

Planning and programming are less readily defined; the terms have been ambiguously applied. Planning here refers to the ongoing, cyclical process through which practitioners establish public relations goals and objectives supportive of organizational goals and objectives. Programming refers to the process through which sets of specific projects are developed in terms of individual stakeholder groups. The multiplicity of such groups with which practitioners must deal was well illustrated by Ronald Goodman of Des Moines in a brochure for his counseling firm (see Figure 1.1).

There thus evolve stakeholder-specific employee relations programs, shareholder relations programs, and such. Two factors contribute most to their success or failure. One is practitioner reliance on fact as opposed to assumption. The other is knowledge of human beings and the manner in which they receive and process messages. Both must be understood before successful planning and programming can begin.

Figure 1.1. The complexity of organizational relationships is depicted graphically in this illustration from a counseling firm brochure. After Kurt Lewin, Topological Psychology and "Field Theory," University of Iowa and MIT Research, 1963–64. Copyright 1977, Ronald Goodman & Company, Inc., Des Moines, Iowa. Reprinted by permission.

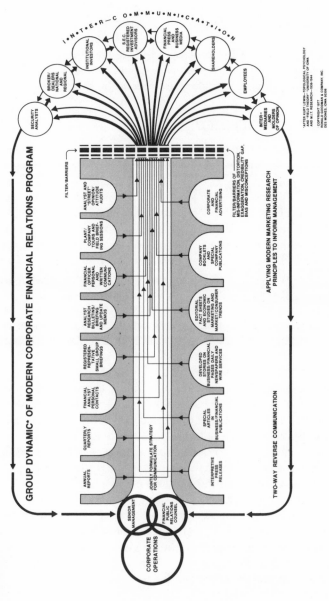

Beginnings of Programming

Public relations programming, in keeping with contemporary standards, must begin with responses to several critical questions:

1. Where do we stand? What do our research and information gathering processes tell us about our standing with our several stakeholder groups?
2. Where are we going? What are our organizational objectives? Will they produce equitable outcomes for our stakeholders? Will all of them share in the benefits of what we do?
3. What contingent problems do we face? What social or economic trends are apt to create difficulties for us? What actions can we take to minimize their impacts?
4. What actions should we take to achieve our objectives; to move forward to the benefit of all involved?
5. What messages should we send to our constituents to assure their understanding and support of our actions, and how shall they be transmitted?

Programmatic differences. Organizational responses to these questions establish parameters within which public relations programs must be developed. The questions themselves are as significant as resulting programs.

Public relations programs traditionally have been developed in support of organizational goals and strategies. The propriety and legitimacy of the goals and strategies have been assumed to be morally and ethically acceptable or, at worst, defensible.

Such assumptions always have been tenuous at best. They may have been functionally viable from a public relations perspective in earlier times but they meet this test no longer. Contemporary stakeholders are quick to challenge institutions as well as organizations. They are as prepared to contest the legitimacy of actions undertaken by the president of the United States as those of a mere organizational executive.

Programming essentials. Successful public relations programming therefore now requires stakeholder concurrence at all levels. Organizations are judged not merely on the quality of their products or services but on the morality of their behaviors and the equity of the results.

Ideally, the results of organizational undertakings would produce benefits equitably distributed among owners, managers, employees, shareholders, and communities. Organizations' efforts in a perfect world would be understood and accepted as achieving these objectives.

Absent such perfection, public relations professionals must deal first with organizational realities and only later with communicating them. Whether in organizational or counselor practice, they must assume ombudsman and consultant roles. They must see to it that the interests of all stakeholder groups are expressed in organizational deliberations. They must assure that senior managers understand the impact of prospective decisions on those groups and their implications as to organizational public relations.

BEGINNING THE PROCESS

Public relations programming begins with organizational objectives. More precisely, it begins immediately after objectives have been set. Few organizations today would have the temerity to advance socially unacceptable objectives. Many encounter difficulties, however, in establishing strategies that conform to moral, ethical, and social standards.

Consider, for example, an issue that has preoccupied many organizations in the United States for a decade or more: productivity. Many an organization has used a variety of techniques in efforts to enhance productivity. Many have installed computers, robots, and other technological devices to supplant manual labor.

PROGRAMMING AND PRODUCTION

Conditions internal and external to the organizations that public relations practitioners serve also have complicated what once were two relatively simple professional functions: programming and production. Programming has been complicated by expanded professional roles coupled with extensive social and economic change. Production has grown increasingly complex with the development of new technologies and their application in creating new channels of communication.

Both processes require greater bodies of knowledge and more diverse skills than once were adequate if not sufficient to public relations practice. They nevertheless are processes that can be systematically learned and applied.

Thomas Edison once defined success as consisting of 99 percent perspiration and 1 percent inspiration. Success in public relations programming and production is achieved in similar fashion. Knowledge, systematically applied, is its primary component. Creative brilliance plays a minor role.

Public relations programming is a process applied to individual organizations and their constituencies in specific circumstances. Organizations, constituent groups, and their environments thus are public relations programmers' primary concerns. No two are alike. The programming process, however, is uniformly applied. It involves ten variables:

1. The nature of the organization involved
2. Organizational environments
3. Organizational goals
4. Public relations goals
5. Constituencies involved

6. Constituent motivators
7. Constituent behaviors—existing and desired
8. Message content necessary to induce desired behavior
9. Channels through which messages can be communicated
10. Mechanisms to measure behavioral change

Nature of Organizations

Organizations are readily characterized. The basic categories are for-profit and not-for-profit. The former deal with production, distribution, or sale of products or services. The latter are governmental, quasi governmental, political, or charitable.

"Political" is used here in a generic sense to describe individuals who gather in groups to influence the behavior of others. The term is equally applicable to chambers of commerce, political action committees, and labor unions.

Political behavior, however, is not confined to organizations. It arises in individuals and families as well and is both accepted and understood by those who succeed in public relations.

Organizational Environments

The term "organizational environments" refers here to external conditions within which organizations function as well as internal factors with which they must deal. External conditions include a broad range of elements that exert influences that vary with the nature of the organization. Those involved directly or indirectly in agriculture, for example, are sensitive to climatic conditions. Capital intensive organizations are similarly sensitive to conditions in the financial marketplace. Those in regulated industries must be concerned with legislative and regulatory matters.

Internal factors are more consistent across organizations but nevertheless vary in influence level. Working environments are more a concern in manufacturing than service businesses, for example, in context with the regulations of the Occupational Safety and Health Administration. Employee safety concerns vary in like context. Where production processes are automated, however, organizations may be less sensitive to change in the labor marketplace.

Organizational Goals

Goals and strategies vary across organizations. They are influenced by a host of factors. The nature of individual organizations and contemporary environmental circumstances are major determinants. Individual and organizational chronological factors also play a part. Younger organizations guided by entrepeneurial leaderships tend to exhibit behaviors far different than those arising among their mature, conservatively led counterparts.

These factors exert a strong but indirect influence on public relations programming. They play a major role in determining organizational strategies. These, in turn, influence public relations program priorities. The priorities of a young organization in a high technology industry, for example, will differ considerably from those of a long-established firm in a mature industry. Financial public relations and employee relations are apt to be among the high tech firm's high priority items. Customer relations tend to be more important among organizations of the latter sort.

Public Relations Goals

Public relations is a process through which organizations seek to achieve accommodation with their constituencies. Public relations units fill—or should fill—mediating or facilitating roles in this process. Their primary responsibility is developing levels of mutual understanding sufficient to support accommodation. Resulting programs and processes must be designed accordingly in keeping with organizational objectives.

A new concept. This concept of public relations requires departure from traditional practice patterns. Where practitioners once were responsible primarily for disseminating organizational viewpoints, today they must provide for two-way communication between organizations and constituent groups. They must gain organizational understanding of constituent needs as well as constituent understanding of organizational needs.

There are major differences, of course, between understanding, acceptance, and support. The complexities of contemporary society render the latter element elusive. It often appears and well may be beyond reach. Understanding and acceptance, however, usually are achievable goals.

Differing perspectives. The concept of social responsibility amply illustrates the latter point. It suggests that organizations are obligated to the communities of which they are a part. It offers little guidance, however, as to the extent of the responsibilities involved.

Given acceptance of the social responsibility concept by a for-profit organization, senior management is faced with multiple painful choices. Organizational resources always are limited. Shareholders, employees, managers, and consumers of the organization's products and services each have legitimate claims on those resources. Shareholders seek greater dividends and enhanced securities prices. Employees and managers want higher compensation and benefit levels. Consumers demand better products and services. Each group's needs must be met if the success that produced current earnings is to be perpetuated.

Conflicting demands. The collective desires of the groups involved inevitably exceed available resources. The dollars available can be expended only once. Parties to the decisions universally declare they seek only "fairness" and "equity." They can be expected to accept senior management decisions only where two conditions are met. First, decision makers must be adequately informed as to constituent viewpoints. Second, constituent groups must be knowledgeable as to to the views of others involved, including those of the decision makers. The public relations unit must accept responsibility for producing required knowledge levels.

Successful discharge of this obligation requires considerable knowledge of the organization as well as existing and contingent constituencies. The latter groups can be especially troublesome. In some cases, their appearance can be readily forecast. In others, they seem to form spontaneously around issues that the organization is powerless to anticipate.

Constituent Groups

An organization's existing constituencies are readily identified. Primary among them are customers, prospective customers, and employees. Among not-for-profit organizations, users or prospective users of services or facilities often can be substituted for the former groups. Others may be specified easily or only with some difficulty. In publicly owned manufacturing businesses, they will include existing and prospective shareholders and suppliers. Current and future donors might be added to the constituent lists of fund-raising organizations. Governmental agencies—legislative and administrative—are involved in both cases.

Developing lists of constituent groups may be most readily accomplished where the term "stakeholder" is substituted for "constituent" or, to use an increasingly outmoded term, "public." Stakeholders are simply groups of individuals who have a stake in the organization. They include each and every group that may be negatively or affirmatively impacted by organizational action of any kind.

The resulting list necessarily will be incomplete. Exhaustive lists can be compiled only by those with sufficient foresight to anticipate every contingent event. Recurring rumors during the mid–1980s concerning the purportedly "satanic" nature of Proctor and Gamble's crescent moon and stars trademark, for example, involved the giant consumer products company with multiple religious groups. Ultimately, the firm found it necessary to abandon the trademark.

None can successfully anticipate every event that may influence relationships between organizations and their constituencies, but many can be identified. Others can be forecast with considerable accuracy. They are most readily anticipated where public relations practitioners proceed on two assumptions:

1. Anything that can go wrong will go wrong.
2. History repeats itself.

Three Mile Island. Assumption 1 should have encouraged operators of nuclear power plants to anticipate Three Mile Island as well as subsequent public reactions. Assumption 2 suggested further disasters, as in the case of Chernobyl and others that ultimately may occur.

The same assumptions would have suggested potential for the two major disasters that befell the U.S. manned space flight program. Others well may follow.

At the other end of the predictability scale are population changes arising out of known demographic trends and the ultimate depletion of natural resources. The aging of the nation's population will continue for the foreseeable future. A major manpower shortage will occur during the late 1900s and early 2000s. Fossil fuel supplies ultimately will be exhausted.

Environmental assessment. To discharge their responsibilities successfully, public relations units must continuously monitor developments in organizational environments and among their constituencies. The process involved is called "environmental assessment." As described earlier, it consists of "scanning" to identify events that may signal trends significant to the organization and monitoring those trends.

Constituent Motivators

Many trends important to an organization and its public relations counselors are far less obvious than those specified above. Life-styles in the United States, for example, have been changing in recent years and appear apt to continue to change. While disposable consumer products generally have grown in popularity, for example, the reverse has been true in the automotive sector. More and more buyers are demonstrating a willingness to pay premium prices for dependability and durability rather than speed and style.

Social change. Family structures and behaviors have been changing in similar fashion. Single-parent households have been multiplying. Increasing numbers of women are opting for careers The elderly are not only increasing in number but in longevity and prosperity. Each of these and many other trends ultimately will change U.S. society and require organizational response.

They also will change individual priorities and, with them, the relative strength of factors that motivate individual actions. Single parents are more concerned with child care facilities than others. Women preoccupied with careers look far more favorably than others on convenience and time-saving devices. The elderly are concerned about secure neighborhoods and health care. In each case, motivational factors influence organizations as well.

Organizational change. Tomorrow's organization may find it necessary to provide day care facilities for children and the dependent elderly in order to attract workers. Maternity leave may become parental leave, required for males as well as females. Change in the nuclear family already has induced legislation requiring employers to extend health care benefits to divorced spouses and widows. These and other changes inevitably will occur to create new and different constituent needs requiring innovative organizational response. Individual organizational success well may depend upon the alacrity with which changing constituent priorities are recognized and met.

Constituent Behaviors

The success of public relations programs is measured in the behaviors of specified constituent groups. They are designed to produce change; to induce support for a point of view or purchase of a product or service. They succeed only to the extent that desired behaviors result.

Behavior is induced by stimuli contained in messages. Message content must address the needs of both organizations and recipients. It must demonstrate organizational responsiveness. It must show recipients that their interests and those of sponsoring organizations coincide. It must convince them that accommodation is preferable to confrontation.

Where these goals are accomplished, behaviors change and objectives are achieved. This assumes, of course, that underlying organizational actions justify necessary constituent understanding, support, and action.

It also assumes messages are (a) carefully crafted to reach constituent groups and (b) transmitted through channels that reach those groups. Neither of these prerequisites is readily accomplished.

Message Content

Public relations practitioners once were preoccupied mainly with the design and delivery of messages. Their then-prevailing assumption was: messages delivered and understood produce desired results. Few today believe this is the case.

Messages, they recognize, must be designed to engage the interest of specific audiences in terms meaningful to their members. This means they must be delivered in understandable language and contain appeals that will trigger desired responses.

Where issues are involved, these reactions occur only when organizational performance warrants support and where community of interest has been established. Knowledge of organizational constituencies, as indicated earlier, thus becomes a component of the message design process. It is no more important, however, than the communication channels to be used.

Media Selection

Synthesis and transmission of messages is not equivalent to communication. Receipt and understanding are essential to complete the process. They can occur only when channels are selected with considerable care.

The ability of mass media to capture substantial portions of any population increasingly is open to question. Network television audiences have been fragmented by cable channels. Daily newspaper circulation in many markets has been declining as the *New York Times, Wall Street Journal, USA Today,* and others gain readers. Total magazine circulation has grown, but the growth has been produced more by explosive growth among special-interest publications than otherwise. During 1986, the *Reader's Digest* yielded circulation leadership in the magazine world to *TV Guide.*

These circumstances are compounded by other factors. The videocassette recorder, for example, enables working women to return home to soap operas rather than the evening news. Computer utilities are gaining increasing attention. Much of it may represent losses to competing information sources. The public relations practitioner thus is confronted with mounting media audience problems. They are soluble, but not without difficulty.

Measuring Change

The cyclical nature of public relations programming requires constant measurement of results. Only where accurate data concerning program-induced change is available can public relations efforts be fine-tuned for optimum results. Change can be measured in several ways and at varying costs. Repetitive survey research is often used to the extent that budgets permit. Practitioners otherwise seek out existing indirect indicators of results.

Programming should begin with research. The attitudes and opinions of stakeholder groups toward organizations, their policies and their programs must be known before effective programs can be developed. Relatively costly survey research usually is applied to meet this need. Surveys subsequently may be repeated to measure progress but less expensive alternatives often are employed. Change in numbers of customer complaints and employee turnover rates, for example, are relatively accurate indicators of attitude and opinion in those groups.

IN SUMMARY

A new set of realities has developed over the past decade in public relations practice. Social, technological, and economic changes that have impacted every organization have generated new demands on the public relations function and public relations practitioners.

They have been forced to become involved with organizational realities as well as communication processes. They have found it necessary to monitor through environmental assessment the ongoing changes that may require organizational response through action or communication.

Environmental assessment has become a component of the public relations process as organizational expectations of public relations practitioners have

changed. After identifying events and trends of organizational concern, practitioners are expected to delineate alternative responses and recommend those
that will best serve their employers or clients.

In the process they assume the ultimate attribute of professionalism. They
become advocates of organizational ethics or morality. They accept and adhere primarily to socially responsible rather than organizationally imposed
standards of conduct.

These standards require that public relations programming begin with organizational policies and practices rather than after-the-fact communication.
Performance rather than publicity has become the key to public relations
success.

The change in standards is reflected in the public relations practice, now
defined as a process through which organizations achieve accommodation
with stakeholder groups. Planning in public relations then involves establishing
public relations goals and objectives consonant with those of the organization.
Programming refers to developing sets of projects to reach specific stakeholder
groups.

Social, technological, and economic complexities require that public relations professionals approach planning, programming, and production with
more knowledge and skills than earlier had been necessary to practice success.
Professionals must be knowledgeable in the nature of organizations, their
goals, and the strategies they establish to achieve them.

Contemporary public relations processes must establish two-way rather
than one-way communication with constituent groups. They must recognize
and accommodate to changing definitions of social responsibility. They must
focus on constituents or stakeholders as well as organizations. Their needs,
motivations, perceptions, and behaviors all must be taken into consideration
in determining organizational policy and procedure, message content, and
media selection.

2

Process and Pitfalls

Success and failure in human endeavor are products of knowledge and assumptions. Potential for success increases with knowledge and declines with assumptions. For failure, the reverse is true. The road to disaster invariably is paved with tenuous assumptions.

Assumptions play a role, to a greater or lesser extent, in public relations programming and production. These processes deal with six sets of variables: organizations and their problems, stakeholder groups, message content, communication channels, time factors, and costs. They can be accepted as perceived by public relations practitioners or as validated by research.

The former approach creates almost unlimited potential for erroneous assumptions. Public relations practitioners are no less fallible than other humans. They tend to assume others are much like themselves. In the absence of contrary evidence, they expect others' knowledge levels and perceptions of reality to be similar to theirs.

This human tendency exists despite the fact that it goes counter to all logic. Most individuals are aware that they come from diverse socioeconomic and educational backgrounds. These alone are adequate to assure substantive differences among groups and individuals. These differences are compounded by variation in perspective and perception across age groups, geographic groups, sexes, and other characteristics, creating considerable diversity.

Diversity, however, does not imply homogeneity. Individuals of varying backgrounds are not evenly distributed in any population. Organizational stakeholder groups are no exception. Diversity across managerial, worker, shareholder, and customer groups is expected. It is no less prevalent within these groups. Public relations efforts that assume otherwise at best fall short of realizing their potential. At worst, they are unmitigated disasters.

These conditions require that practitioners understand more than the term "public relations" generally implies. They must be conversant with human behavior; knowledgeable in how people function. They must understand the nature of communication and the manner in which ideas are disseminated, adopted, and acted upon.

OF HUMAN NATURE

Humans have been viewed over the years from one of two basic perspectives. In one they are active creatures, attempting to enhance the likelihood that some events will transpire and that others will not. In the other, they are passive organisms, reacting instinctively or intuitively to external forces and playing no part in molding their futures.

The passive perspective, which arguably continues to prevail in the social and behavioral sciences, has a number of strong advocates. They range from Harvard behavioral psychologist B. F. Skinner to Sigmund Freud. Skinner has argued that actions are predetermined by the history of individual conditioning in specific environments. Freud contended that human personality is a product of the interplay of instinctive forces limited by social constraints.

In the active view, humans are seen as playing active roles in gaining understanding of events and messages and in directing their actions. In this concept, as psychologist Isidor Chein (1972) pointed out, individuals comprehend external realities by selectively interpreting messages from their environments. They are seen as active elements rather than passive responders to external stimuli.

Creating Understanding

Humans thus synthesize understandings of their worlds, examining objects, events, and actions they perceive as significant and as requiring explanation. As Swanson and Delia (1976) pointed out, "The person actively builds understanding; understanding is not poured into the head of a passive person."

Individuals instead take what might be called an anthropological approach to their environments. They seek out order or organization to induce understanding. They organize their worlds into personally and socially meaningful systems or constructs and interpret events or situations in those contexts.

These concepts are vital to public relations programming in that individuals live in perceptual fields which for them constitute reality. Two factors are especially important here. First, perceptual fields are not viewed by individuals as constructions of reality; they *are* reality. Second, the perceptual field is a constructed, organized world. As such, it tends to be receptive to congruent thoughts, ideas, and concepts but resistant to the incongruous.

Self-Concept

Central to the perceptual field is the notion of self-concept: what persons believe about themselves. Self-concept has been described as a sort of map that individuals consult to achieve self-understanding, especially when under stress. The perceptual field and self-concept direct perceptual behavior.

Perception and interpretation, the components of perceptual behavior, are selective processes. Individuals select the messages to which they respond and interpret them in keeping with their perceptual fields and self-concepts.

Selection and interpretation are influenced by several factors. Preeminent among them are individuals' perceptual constructs, self-concept, and perceived goals and needs. The sense they make of their worlds, as Swanson and Delia pointed out, therefore is individual and personal:

Each person lives only his own life; he knows the world only through his own personal system of interpretive schemes. Subjective experience, thus, in a very genuine way is private. It is the possession of only the single experiencing person.

Some predisposition toward uniformity is created in most individuals, however, through their membership in formal or informal groups.

People in Groups

Groups and organizations superimpose their values, beliefs, life-styles, mores, and folkways upon those who would be members. Compliance with group and organizational norms is part of the price of membership. In practical terms, group standards are integrated over time into individuals' perceptual fields. Their reactions to events, situations, and messages thus can be predicted in part on the basis of group membership.

Stakeholder groups are paramount in public relations programming. These groups are defined by common interests. Their goals, needs, and situational requirements at least in part govern their perceptions and, therefore, their communication behaviors. Group behavior is considerably less predictable than individual behavior, however, as a result of member diversity. While membership requires a level of conformity, other factors may predominate at any given moment.

These factors can be categorized as internal and external. Groups often are internally fragmented. Their members also vary in the extent to which they are prepared to follow. Fragmentation is most readily observed in labor unions. The perceptions of rank-and-file membership, local leadership, and national leadership often are at variance with one another, especially in situations such as contract negotiations. Rank-and-file members view these as pocketbook issues. Local leaderships often are primarily concerned with the impact of alternative outcomes on their ability to gain reelection. National leaderships tend to be most interested in building local memberships—and dues revenues—regardless of the outcome of the negotiations.

Variation in Commitment

Variation in individual commitment most frequently arises out of membership in multiple groups, each with its own standards. It is most evident in professions that prescribe hierarchies of loyalty. The "public" welfare invariably is presumed paramount in such groups. Loyalty to professional organizations generally is conceded second ranking while pocketbook issues follow. Physician members of animal welfare organizations thus presumably would hold the advance of medical research more important than efforts to limit vivisection. Their self-concepts and perceptual constructs would tend to lead them away from the group's norms.

Further variation among individuals is generated by membership in other groups or categories. Many if not most of them have been identified or synthesized through a diverse set of typologies. Arguably best known among them is psychologist Abraham Maslow's hierarchy of needs. Maslow suggested that individuals are primarily motivated at any given moment by the extent to which their needs have been satisfied. Those preoccupied by physiological needs—food, clothing, and shelter—are unlikely to be significantly influenced by the need for self-actualization. The physiological needs are lowest in Maslow's hierarchy; self-actualization is highest.

Critical Typologies

Other typologies also are important to public relations practitioners. Perhaps most significant among them is the values and life-styles (VALS) typology developed by Arnold Mitchell and his colleagues at the Stanford Research Institute (now SRI International). Their typology divides Americans into four major groups with nine life-styles and identifies the central concerns of each group (see Figure 2.1)

The VALS typology and the central concerns of members of the several groups involved parallels a set of categories identified by public relations counselor Patrick Jackson as to adoption of new concepts, ideas and products. In this context, Jackson told the 1985 conference of the Public Relations Society of America in Detroit, individuals can be classified as innovators, early adopters, early majority, majority, and laggards.

In general, he said, socioeconomic and educational levels, mass media usage, social participation, and occupational expertise are highest among innovators and lowest among laggards. While innovators may adopt a new concept or idea in less than five months, laggards may require more than 30 months. Jackson's data are suggestive of the level of difficulty that public relations practitioners face in modifying attitude and opinion.

Figure 2.1. Adapted from Arnold Mitchell, *The Nine American Lifestyles: Who We Are and Where We Are Going.* New York: Macmillan, 1983.

VALS Lifestyles and Central Concerns		
Group	Lifestyle	Central Concern
Need-driven	Survivor	Survival
	Sustainer	Sustaining and Solidifying gains from survivor stage and hopefully extending them
Outer-Directed	Belonger	Belonging, being accepted by others, fitting into a closed, sharply defined, local network.
	Emulator	Breaking free of the local network to make it as an individual within the major system, emulating leaders of the system.
	Achiever	Achievement, success, leadership and power in the major system.
Inner-Directed	I-Am-Me	Breaking free of outer-directed patterns and discovery of inner self.
	Experiential	Living intensely, vividly and experientially, so as to widen and deepen the inner experience.
	Socially Conscious	Societal issues, especially those affecting the less material qualities of life.
Combined Outer and Inner-Directed	Integrated	Melding outer and inner perspectives so as to combine the best of the two into higher-order views.

Still other typologies have been defined in marketing, management, and organizational settings. Shoppers have been defined as early adopters, appearance-conscious, carefree, traditional department store, and apathetic. Management styles been labeled Theory X, Theory Y, and Theory Z. Organizational members have been styled as Organization Man, Jungle Fighter, Craftsman, and Gamesman. From time to time, almost any typology can be of benefit to public relations practitioners seeking to better understand the nature of groups with which they are attempting to communicate.

COMMUNICATION

The typologies identified above are important in public relations for a simple reason: Each is an indicator of the extent to which any message may be received and accepted at any time. What once was believed to be a rather simple process now is known instead for its complexity. Audiences once were considered universally responsive. Ideas, knowledge, and motivations were considered readily transferable from sender to receiver. Anticipated results were expected to follow.

Fallacies in all of these concepts have been demonstrated through research. Rather than being universally responsive, audience members generally can be categorized as active, informed, and latent. The latter group, largest of the three by far, is unaware of any need to act or change. The aware group, also of significant size, recognizes the need but is not inclined to act. Only the small active group is prepared to do something.

The bulk of the nation's population, says Jackson, spends most of its time in front of a television set with a beer can in one hand and a remote control device in the other, "and hasn't entertained a new idea in 20 years." Pragmatically, the idea may have been discarded on receipt or rejected during what has become known as the adoption process.

Audience Variables

Researchers have identified several audience variables that may interfere with receipt and assimilation of messages. They include demographic factors, reference group membership, personality variables, and the significance of messages to recipients. Selective exposure, perception, and retention also may intervene.

Demographic elements include age, race, sex, education, occupational status, and place of residence. Attitude and opinion have been demonstrated to vary with these factors.

Reference groups are the formal or informal groups with which message recipients identify. They may be occupational, fraternal, political, or otherwise.

Personality variables include such factors as intelligence, self-esteem, tolerance for ambiguity, and authoritarianism.

Significance involves the notion of self-interest or perceived utility—what otherwise has been called the "what's in it for me factor."

Intervening Variables

Other intervening elements in communication include three by which individuals control or alter messages directed to them: selective exposure, selective perception, and selective retention. Selective exposure is the phenomenon through which individuals seek out some messages but avoid others. Selective perception is a predisposition on the part of recipients to see what they want to see or are prepared to see. Selective retention is the process by which the human mind sorts out messages, some to be retained indefinitely, others never to be recalled again.

Even where messages survive all these tests, they may be abandoned by recipients at any point in what has come to be called the diffusion process—the five steps through which new ideas are adopted:

1. Awareness, in which individuals become aware of ideas but lack details.
2. Interest, in which they obtain facts, develop interest, and envision possibilities.
3. Evaluation, a period of mental trial and weighing of alternatives leading to a trial.
4. Trial, which involves experimental use on a small scale; application or testing of the idea, practice, or product.
5. Adoption, in which ideas, practices, or products that have proven themselves worthwhile are adopted for large-scale or continued use.

Communication is a complex process. Potential for success in any given circumstance is limited by multiple intervening variables. Diversity in audiences or stakeholder groups is but one of them. Others include messages, channels of communication, complexity in the communication process, and source credibility.

Limits on Success

Source credibility, like the adoption process, restricts practitioner potential for success at any given moment. The concept applies to mediated and nonmediated communication; to the mass media with which public relations traditionally has been involved; and to intrapersonal information sources. Mediated information plays a role in the adoption process, Iowa State University researchers found in exploring source credibility, but its strength varies across the five phases of the adoption process (see Figure 2.2).

Most significant to public relations practice in Bohlen and Beal's research is the decline in effectiveness of the mass media after the information phase of the diffusion process. More personal sources—individuals and opinion leaders—become dominant as need for psychological support supplants need for information. These conditions in part explain the relative strength of mass media in agenda setting and their relative weakness in influencing decision making. They similarly illuminate the relative strength of public relations in creating issue awareness and its relative weakness in inducing behavioral response.

Surgical Approach

These circumstances require a surgical approach to public relations practice and, especially, to public relations programming and production. Accurate

Figure 2.2. From Joe M. Bohlen and George M. Beal, "Factors in Adoption of Farm Practices," paper presented to the 13th National Conference, Public Relations Society of America, November 1960.

Sources of Influence in Introduction of New
Agricultural Products and Processes

Awareness	Information	Evaluation	Trial	Adoption
1. Mass Media	Mass Media	Neighbors & Friends	Salesmen	Neighbors & Friends
2. Government Agencies	Salesmen	Salesmen	Neighbors & Friends	Salesmen
3. Neighbors & Friends	Government Agencies	Government Agencies	Government Agencies	Government Agencies
4. Salesmen	Neighbors & Friends	Mass Media	Mass Media	Mass Media

diagnosis of the problem is vital. Practitioners must obtain every scrap of information available concerning their organizations, the nature of organizational problems, prevailing stakeholder attitude and opinion, and available communication channels. Then, and only then, are they equipped to proceed with minimum potential for failure.

Complexity in problems and stakeholder groups makes failure more likely than success in the absence of adequate diagnostic procedures. If knowledge ever can be equated with power, it is in circumstances such as these. As value in real estate is produced by location, location, and location, success in public relations is generated through research, research, and research.

The products of information-gathering in public relations provide the foundation for programming and planning. The processes involved must be undertaken with all the precision exercised by the surgeon in diagnostic testing. Precise test results permit accurate diagnoses. They identify the sources and extent of disease. They provide direction for the course of treatment and indicate which medical or surgical procedures should be used. The same principles apply in public relations. Knowledge of the problem and of the nature and perceptions of stakeholder groups permit practitioners to synthesize messages and select delivery channels to produce necessary change.

The latter processes have declined in relative importance over the years in public relations practice. Message synthesis and delivery require care in handling but the processes involved largely are mechanical in nature. Craftsmanlike use of the language is essential, for example, but brilliance is unnecessary and may be counterproductive. The purpose of communication is information delivery. Anything that distracts the recipient, including brilliant prose, should be avoided rather than encouraged. The same principle applies in use of delivery channels. The medium cannot be permitted to become the message. Graphic design in publications must enhance rather than distract from message content.

A PROCESS APPROACH

Armed with adequate knowledge of the areas discussed above, public relations practitioners are prepared to proceed with planning, programming, and production. Information-gathering in several forms is central and critical to all these processes. Organizational problems must be precisely diagnosed. Stakeholder groups must become intimately known rather than merely identified. Messages must be crafted to produce desired responses in multiple groups without contradicting one another in word, substance, or implication. Appropriate delivery channels must be selected from a set increasing in number and declining in audience size. All of these steps must be successfully completed within usually demanding time and economic constraints.

Planning

Planning is a five-step cyclical process. It consists of fact-finding, research, programming, communication, and measurement. Data gathered in the fact-finding and research phases of planning also constitute a point of beginning for the programming process.

The latter process involves developing a set of programs through which messages are delivered at predetermined times to produce measurable behavioral change in specific stakeholder groups. Measurement enables practitioners to "fine tune" plans and programs; to make changes in strategies, messages, and communication channels to enhance subsequent results.

Public relations practitioners need not be researchers as such. Necessary primary research often is assigned to qualified research organizations. Practitioners must be sufficiently conversant with the process, however, to handle fact-finding and secondary research, define objectives for primary research, and apply resulting data.

Programming

Fact-finding and research conducted in the planning process also are the first of ten steps in public relations programming. Collective results permit construction of a detailed overview of organizations, stakeholder groups, and communication needs. Steps in the programming process thus include:

1. Fact-finding
2. Research
3. Developing an overview

4. Establishing objectives
5. Defining stakeholder groups
6. Selecting communication channels
7. Developing messages
8. Creating strategies and timetables
9. Establishing measurement criteria
10. Developing a budget

There is no magic in the number of steps or in the words used to describe them. They establish parameters for a process, however, which is increasingly important in public relations practice. Organizational problems, special interest stakeholder groups, and channels of communication have been multiplying at a rate that demands a process approach. Organizational overviews thus become necessary in defining needs or problems.

Specific needs provide guidance in establishing objectives. Clearly stated objectives facilitate defining stakeholder groups and identifying channels of communication through which each is most accessible. This knowledge in turn is essential in fashioning strategies to influence each group as well as programmatic timetables, measurement mechanisms, and appropriate budgets.

INFORMATION-GATHERING

Information required in public relations practice is obtained through four processes: scanning, fact-finding, secondary research, and primary research. Scanning or "pulse-taking" requires "management by walking around," as it is called, to assimilate impressions of the organization as a whole. Fact-finding in large part involves gathering all existing published information concerning the organization and its stakeholder groups. Secondary research consists of obtaining and analyzing survey or other reliable data in the same context. Primary research usually involves obtaining original information through surveys or other techniques.

The three processes are applied collectively rather than individually in planning, programming and—to a lesser extent—production. Data they yield are applicable in all of the areas specified above.

Scanning

Any research effort that ignores a set of seemingly superficial indicators of organizational "health" is unnecessarily weakened. Observation and listening in the course of carefully designed walking tours can and will provide a wealth of subjective but nevertheless helpful information.

Observation involves examining the organization's facilities and equipment.

Their condition is a strong indicator of morale. The countenances of personnel are no less valuable.

Collectively, these factors are indicative of morale and productivity. They are amenable to elaboration through casual conversation with those involved. The coffee shop, cafeteria, and other places where employees gather during meals and break periods can be especially productive to the careful listener.

Fact-Finding

Personal impressions then can be validated and expanded through a multifaceted fact-finding process. It requires examining the organization, its products, markets, stakeholder groups, and competition, as well as communication objectives and strategies. The latter include marketing, advertising, and sales promotion as well as public relations. Consistency in messages emanating from organizations is vital to avoid disharmony and confusion among stakeholder groups.

Organizational missions, objectives, and strategies are equally important in public relations practice. The public relations program must be supportive of organizational efforts in these contexts.

Each organizational element requires close examination. Is the organization committed, for example, to equitable treatment of stakeholder groups? Are employees, managers, shareholders, customers, and communities regarded and treated as equally important to organizational success? Do they perceive themselves as equally valued? Are organizational resources equally allocated among them?

Stakeholders were selected deliberately for examination in the paragraph above. More than a few organizations are prone to grandiose statements concerning their commitments to stakeholder groups. Their actions too frequently belie their words. Where this is the case, conscientious public relations practitioners quickly invoke an overly simplified but nevertheless significant definition of public relations: doing a good job and getting credit for it. Such circumstances require intervention. Managements must be told directly albeit gently that performance is the first and essential step toward public relations success. Deeds must conform to words or changes must be made.

Ethical and practical realities necessitate such intervention. Misleading messages are ethically wrong and inevitably lead to failure in public relations. Neither outcome is acceptable to those who would succeed in public relations practice.

Formal Research

Techniques applied in formal research are no less complex than in information gathering. Both primary and secondary research usually are used in public relations. The former involves traditional survey techniques. The latter

consists of an assessment of available data that may contribute to understanding the organization, its stakeholders, and its problems.

Secondary research usually precedes primary. It is more readily and less
expensively accomplished and provides insights useful in developing primary
programs. Secondary research requires accumulating all available data concerning organizations and stakeholders. A host of sources is accessible and
all should be used to provide as complete a picture as possible.

A great deal of secondary research can be accomplished within the organization. Personnel records, for example, yield considerable data concerning
employee demographics, seniority, attendance, turnover rates, and so on.
Considerable shareholder information also can be obtained from organizational records.

Basic community data are accessible through the Bureau of the Census.
Demographic, socioeconomic, educational, and occupational information is
available for every census tract in the nation. In most instances, it also is
broken down by U.S. Postal Service ZIP codes. Indicators extracted from this
basic data set then can be superimposed over several of the typologies described earlier to provide several informative extrapolations. The VALS and
Bohlen and Beal typologies can be especially helpful.

Resultant information then can be used in determining the nature and
extent of necessary primary research. Secondary data may be adequate for
some stakeholder groups but more usually is necessary in dealing with primary
constituencies in terms of any specified organizational problem or need. The
primary purpose of the research process is defining organizational problems
and needs although it provides data applicable in developing messages and
selecting communication channels as well.

ESTABLISHING OBJECTIVES

Public relations objectives in any organization are a function of organizational objectives. The latter must be examined in terms of the interests and
concerns of stakeholder groups. Public relations techniques then are applied
to support the organization in achieving its objectives.

Public relations objectives should be designed to meet several criteria. First,
as indicated above, they should relate to overall organizational objectives.
Second, they should be improvement-oriented. Third, they should be sufficiently specific to permit measurement of results. Finally, they should be
achievable.

Presented in capsule form, these steps appear simple and readily accomplished. Seldom is this the case. Inertia and inherent preference for the status
quo create major obstacles to change inherent in organizational objectives.
Public relations objectives involve, in order of difficulty, (a) creating awareness, (b) informing, (c) educating, (d) reinforcing attitudes or behaviors, or

(e) changing attitudes or behaviors. Numbers of group members responding as communicators desire grow fewer as difficulty increases.

In general, organizational stakeholders examine prospective change in keeping with self-interest. Their primary question: What benefits or problems will the proposed change create for me? Their concerns usually are readily anticipated. With adequate research data, messages and channels of communication can be specified.

DEFINING STAKEHOLDER GROUPS

Precise analysis of stakeholder groups is critical to success in public relations. The process begins with a simple step but then grows complex. The first step: Set aside the term "general public." There is no "general" public in public relations. Then, define the stakeholder groups that affect or are affected by the organization.

As indicated earlier, employees, managers, shareholders, and customers necessarily are among them. From this point, however, complexity compounds. Manufacturers' customers, for example, seldom are ultimate consumers. Their products may may pass through the hands of distributors, wholesalers, retailers, or all three before reaching the end user. Each is a stakeholder group. Indirectly, their shareholders, managers, and employees also are involved.

An alternative and often appropriate approach to stakeholder development involves first identifying organizational functions and then specifying groups involved. Those enumerated above, for example, are party to the distribution function. The manufacturing function, in like manner, would include employees and suppliers. Secondary groups would include employees' families as well as suppliers' shareholders, managers, and employees.

Stakeholder identification generally involves specifying categories of stakeholders. Subgroups or components then must be identified before they can be regrouped in order of importance in relation to the problem or program at hand. The planner also must identify opinion leaders and others, such as media gatekeepers who might be termed "intervening" groups. They also become stakeholders.

The process also may include examining group overlap. Individuals often are members of overlapping groups. Employees, for example, also may be shareholders. This component of the process is critical where organizations' communication functions are not closely coordinated. Conflicting message problems then may arise.

CHANNELS OF COMMUNICATION

Public relations practitioners traditionally deal with mass media in communicating with organizations' stakeholder groups. This approach is increasingly anachronistic in an era of media proliferation and audience fragmentation. In some cases it arguably never was most appropriate. Employees and shareholders, especially the former, are examples of groups that only inappropriately can be addressed through mass media. They are otherwise more accessible and more readily engaged.

Nonmediated Communication

Mediated communication is inherently inferior to other forms. Every communication channel that has been or can be applied in public relations, save one, is less than optimally productive. The one—for which all others are less efficient substitutes—is one-on-one, face-to-face conversation between individuals. Small group meetings, large group meetings, and auditorium-style presentations are progressively less desirable approaches, but nevertheless deserve priority consideration. Only when these alternatives have been used or discarded as impractical should mediated communication be considered.

This rationale in recent years has produced increasing organizational interest in inducing greater managerial communication skills. Interest has been in evidence in several forms. Senior managers in the thousands have been trained in a variety of personal communication skills. They range from "on camera" training for those who deal with the mass media to training in the conduct of small group meetings for middle managers.

In any and all circumstances, organizational spokespersons at every level should be recruited, trained, and made a part of the public relations program. Only where this objective has been accomplished should other communication channels be considered.

Mediated Communication

Other channels fall into two categories: controlled and uncontrolled. Controlled channels include newsletters, brochures, and audio-visual presentations. They permit careful message preparation, precise timing, and pretesting of messages. They also tend to be less credible owing to perceived bias, and more expensive. Uncontrolled channels include news releases, news conferences, and media interviews. Their attributes include objectivity, lower practitioner time demand, and lower cost. These are offset by increased potential for error, variation in timing, and inability to pretest messages.

Communication channels vary in terms of cost, time, and audience selectivity as well as control. These factors must be considered collectively rather than individually in selecting appropriate channels. Where mass media are involved, circulation and audience data can be especially misleading. Public relations practitioners must focus on numbers of stakeholders within groups rather than total group size.

MESSAGE DEVELOPMENT

The product of the information-gathering process is critical to message synthesis. Messages destined to be received and acted upon share several critical characteristics. They are developed in light of prevailing attitude and opinion among stakeholder groups. They reflect organizational realities. They convey concepts that will encourage change in attitude and opinion to reflect reality.

In most cases, the concepts can and should be reduced to key words. These should be both appealing to stakeholder groups and used repeatedly across multiple media to hammer home the key points involved.

STRATEGIES AND TIMETABLES

Strategies are to communication channels in public relations what musical scores are to members of a choir. They tell individuals involved what to do and when to do it. They orchestrate multiple messages to assure a harmonious flow of information to produce optimum audience response.

Strategies usually are synthesized in two parts. The first is a brief policy or strategy statement that defines primary objectives and organizational (as opposed to communication) actions to be taken to achieve them. The second is a listing of communication efforts to be made, including a list of channels to be used for each. They are accompanied by timetables that specify sequences of events and communication efforts and identify individuals responsible.

MEASUREMENT AND BUDGETING

Levels of difficulty that practitioners encounter in establishing criteria for measurement of public relations results are a function of program objectives. Where they are expressed specifically or where desired outcomes are defined precisely measurement is not difficult. Where either of these criteria are neglected, the reverse is true.

Sales volume, employee turnover rates, and number of manufacturing defects, for example, all are amenable to measurement. In addition, they are measurable in most organizations through already-recorded data. The measurement system need not require additional record keeping.

Indirect Measurement

This also can be the case where it is necessary inexpensively to measure "the immeasurable." Employee morale, for instance, can be precisely measured only through repetitive surveys. Public relations practitioners and senior managers usually have little difficulty, however, in agreeing that employee absenteeism and tardiness are relatively accurate indicators of morale levels. A difficult-to-measure variable thus can be rendered economically amenable to monitoring.

The Budget Process

Economics, always a component of business management, is most in evidence in the public relations budgeting process. Budget development in terms of a free-standing program rather than an annual departmental situation involves "pricing out the program."

Detailed price tags must be attached to every component. They must include all costs involved. Labor, fringe benefits, and other overhead must be specified together with any and all production and out-of-pocket costs for each component of the proposed program. Production cost factors should be based on multiple vendor estimates rather than practitioner "guesstimates." At all times, "no unpleasant surprises" should be a cardinal guideline in budget preparation.

Data generated in the process permit senior management to calculate the value of anticipated results against the costs involved. Where both factors are in evidence, they also enable practitioners to rank order various components as to their relative value to the program.

PRODUCTION PROCESSES

Scheduling is the key to success in producing communication vehicles in public relations. Vehicles or channels are nothing more than containers in which messages can be delivered. They must be selected with care during the planning process to assure messages will be received. Thereafter, however, relatively little creativity or judgment in most cases is necessary to their completion.

Timely delivery and receipt of appropriate messages are the primary criteria in channel selection and message development. To the extent that graphic and electronic techniques may enhance receipt and assimilation of content, creativity may be a factor. Otherwise, the processes are wholly mechanical in nature.

Production has been complicated in recent years through the development of new communication channels. Videotape has come of age. Satellite and computer-based communication systems are becoming more common. More traditional communication channels, such as television and magazines, also have increased in number and diversity. Public relations practitioners thus find production tasks increasing in number and diversity. Computers increasingly are used to monitor and control developmental processes, however, softening the impact of more complex production requirements.

Alternative production techniques applied to the several communication channels used in public relations will be discussed in subsequent chapters.

IN SUMMARY

"Planning" and "programming" have been used almost interchangeably in public relations. The former refers here to the ongoing, cyclical process through which practitioners establish public relations goals and objectives. Programming refers to the process through which sets of projects are developed and scheduled to attain goals and objectives.

Successful public relations programming requires knowledge of the manner in which humans form their perceptions of the world and handle the process of communication. This knowledge and the results of extensive information-gathering processes form the bases of successful public relations plans and programs.

Planning is a five-step cyclical process consisting of fact-finding, research, programming, communication, and measurement. The fact-finding and research components of the planning process also constitute the beginnings of the programming process. Resultant data permits construction of a detailed overview of the organization, its stakeholder groups and its communication needs. The 10-step planning process thus includes:

1. Fact-finding
2. Research
3. Developing an overview
4. Establishing objectives
5. Defining stakeholder groups
6. Selecting communication channels
7. Developing messages
8. Creating strategies and timetables
9. Establishing measurement criteria
10. Developing a budget

There is no magic in the number of specified steps. Almost all are amenable to some combination or subdivision. Fact-finding and research might be combined as "information-gathering." The research component, on the other hand, might be subdivided to include its primary components. These are primary and secondary research, the latter consisting of analysis of existing data.

Public relations objectives are established in keeping with research data and organizational goals and strategies. The nature of the objectives permits identification of stakeholder groups involved. Group characteristics in turn suggest which communication channels will be most productive.

Channel selection is increasingly troublesome in public relations for several reasons. Perhaps first among them is a tendency in the profession to deal almost exclusively with mediated communication. Individual, small group, and large group communication on face-to-face bases often are equally if not more important. Mediated communication channels, controlled and uncontrolled, are substitutes for human channels and must be employed accordingly.

Messages to be conveyed through all of these channels must be developed in keeping with recipient need. They should reflect organizational realities and encourage change in recipient attitude and opinion to reflect those realities. They also must be consistent across both stakeholder groups and communication channels used.

Channel use is programmed in keeping with public relations strategies and timetables. Strategies include statements of organizational objectives and actions to achieve them. The latter are lists of planned communication efforts and channels to be used for each. They are accompanied by timetables setting out both sequences of events and individuals responsible.

Measurement and budgeting are separate and distinct but equally important processes. Measurement is based on precisely expressed programmatic objectives. The extent to which they are achieved constitutes evidence of success. Budgeting requires attaching price tags to each component of the plan. They must include all costs involved. The role and results expected through application of each component should be included in order that comparative values can readily be established.

When budgets have been approved, production begins. Scheduling, now often handled by computer, is the key to production success. All components of the process must be oriented to support message delivery and comprehension.

ADDITIONAL READING

Bohlen, Joe M., and George M. Beal. "Factors in Adoption of Farm Practices," paper presented to the 13th National Conference of the Public Relations Society of America, November 1960.

Chein, Isidor. *The Science of Behavior and the Image of Man*. New York: Basic Books, 1972.

Mitchell, Arnold. *The Nine American Lifestyles: Who We Are and Where We Are Going*. New York: Macmillan, 1983.

Swanson, David L., and Jesse G. Delia. *The Nature of Human Communication*. Chicago: Science Research Associates, 1976.

3

Knowledge as Power

Success in every aspect of public relations practice requires practitioners to develop and maintain extensive bodies of knowledge. Programming and production are no exception. They demand considerable insight into the dynamics of individual and organizational behavior under varying environmental conditions.

Foundations for requisite bodies of knowledge are established in educational programs. Baccalaureate degrees, however, are little more than "licenses to learn." The "half-life" of knowledge, to apply a term from nuclear physics, today is estimated at five years. Virtually all knowledge acquired in the college or university thus requires renewal within a decade of graduation.

Renewal is accomplished through one or more of several techniques: graduate education, formal continuing education, and individually designed self-study programs. The most successful among them are based on an understanding of systems theory on the one hand and communication theory on the other. These constructs suggest that individuals and organizations are interactive entities; that they are influenced by and in turn influence their environments. Their behaviors can be best understood in this context.

SYSTEMS THEORY

Systems theory views organizations as components of larger systems and as composed of smaller systems. They alternatively may be viewed as external and internal environments. The latter term may be more meaningful in public relations practice in that it more strongly implies individual/organizational interaction.

In systems theory, external systems or environments are termed suprasystems; internal are referred to as subsystems. Both of them influence and are influenced by the organization and thus should be of primary concern to public relations practitioners.

Suprasystems

The external environments or suprasystems with which organizations are involved include the natural, human, political, socioeconomic, market, and technological structures. Change in any of these areas will produce organizational consequences of varying degree.

Natural: The natural environment encompasses those elements man once considered limitless. They include the human beings who populate the organization, the air they breathe, the water they drink, and the raw materials they use. Change in supply or demand for any of these elements inevitably impacts the organization.

Human: The human environment is equally diverse. It includes humans and all of the skills, abilities, and organizational levels with which they may be equipped. The human environment is especially significant to public relations practitioners in that it is the source of attitude and opinion.

Political: The political environment includes special interest groups of every hue as well as elected and appointed members of the several political systems. Special interest groups are the most volatile component of the political system in that they include informal as well as formal groups that form around emerging issues.

Social: The socioeconomic or social environment is equally dynamic. It defines individual and organizational obligations to society and each other. The relative ambiguity that attaches to these definitions tends to be troublesome to organizations and the individuals who manage them.

Market: The market environment or marketplace is one of the more volatile of organizational suprasystems. Competition, consumer behavior, and changing consumer values originate in this sector. They are compounded by change in the technological environment.

Technological: The technological environment includes a number of technologies. While those applicable in consumer products are most noticeable, robotics and other technologies of primary interest to organizations are equally important.

Although considered individually above, the suprasystems are interrelated. An advance in technology, for example, may concurrently yield new consumer products for the market environment while reducing organizational need for human resources. Resulting layoffs may produce change in the social environment, which in turn can lead to new pressures on and from the political environment.

Subsystems

Organizational subsystems are fewer in number but no less complex. They include the psychological, social, political and technological. Their individual complexity is compounded by their interrelationships with one another and with the six suprasystems.

Psychological: Of the four internal subsystems, the psychological is most complex. The individual motivations, needs, values, attitudes, perceptions, beliefs, emotions, and personalities of every member of the organization are involved. These elements collectively constitute the environment from which the social subsystem originates.

Social: The social subsystem tends to be more dynamic than the psychological but is no less complex. It consists of the collective behaviors of all groups within the organization, formal and informal. The social subsystem thus is more than the aggregate of individual behaviors. It spawns what has been called an "organizational culture," which has been described as a collective consciousness or intelligence, as well as informal power structures and political subsystems.

Political: The power and influence wielded by natural rather than formal leaderships arise in the political subsystem. Both the individuals involved and the roles they occupy are created here. Formal leaderships may or may not originate in the political subsystem. Their power, however, in most cases is enhanced or diminished through the subsystem's influence.

Technological: The technological subsystem is no less complex. It includes the collective attributes of machines and the individuals and systems that support them. The potential influence of the technological system is perhaps best seen today in the influence of computer programmers and operators in the typical organization. Computerization, mechanization, automation, and robotization originate in the technological system.

The collective interplay of suprasystems and subsystems molds the organization. Any change in any of them thus is significant to the public relations practitioner. Change occurs as suprasystems and subsystems influence organizations and the individuals of which they are constituted. Influence is exercised through communication in any of several forms.

CONCEPTS OF COMMUNICATION

Communication once was considered a relatively simple process. Humans were perceived as logical, rational beings who would respond accordingly when exposed to information. Continuing research over the past several decades has demonstrated, however, that neither of these concepts is valid. Communication is a complex process subject to distortion by a host of intervening variables. Humans are equally complex and only partly susceptible to logic and reason in assimilating information.

Individual Perception

Each individual functions within a self-constructed set of perceptions that constitute his or her reality. Individual worlds, in other words, consist of constructed realities or beliefs. They may be modified from time to time in keeping with messages originating in individual environments, but the process at best is beset with uncertainty. Information is as apt to be rejected as accepted. Individuals constantly are interpreting their worlds, processing messages, rejecting some while accepting others, and modifying their interpretations of reality in the process.

Individuals' worlds thus consist of constructed realities or beliefs that may be modified from time to time in keeping with some of the messages received from their environments. Messages and events are ordered and understood through application of personal interpretive constructs or beliefs.

Nature of Beliefs

Individuals' beliefs can be ordered in much the same manner in which psychologist Abraham Maslow constructed his hierarchy of needs. They range from fundamental to superficial.

Primitive beliefs, those dealing with the nature of reality and which enjoy social support, are central to humans. They are comparable to Maslow's fundamental needs for food, clothing, and shelter. Superimposed over primitive beliefs are self-beliefs, including sensitive concepts of self-worth.

Authority beliefs adopted through the influence of others considered trustworthy or otherwise constitute a third layer. Negative beliefs tend to be implanted by those considered suspect.

Derived and inconsequential beliefs form the final layers. Derived beliefs originate with trusted individuals. Inconsequential beliefs deal with product quality and similar minor matters.

The several levels of belief are described in descending order of strength, a significant factor in the work of public relations professionals and other communicators. Primitive and self-beliefs are least amenable to change while derived and inconsequential beliefs can be modified with relative ease.

Self-belief or self-concept is central to individual perception. Personal perceptual categories, self-concept and individual goals, needs, and situational requirements create frameworks by which individual perceptions are organized, as Swanson and Delia (1976) have pointed out:

Each person, within an individual system of perceptual categories, makes sense of the world. The sense that is made of the world is, hence, ultimately individual and personal.

Each person lives only his own life; he knows the world only through his own personal system of interpretive schemes. Subjective experience, thus, in a very genuine way is private. It is the possession of only the single individual.

Compounding Factors

These elements are not alone in influencing individuals' perceptions of messages. Demographic elements, reference groups, personality variables, and salience or importance of content all influence message acceptance or rejection. Selectivity in exposure, perception, and retention also play a part.

Demographic variables: Characteristics by which groups and subgroups are categorized are known as demographic variables. They include age, race, sex, education, and occupation, among others. They help shape perceptions of messages to which individuals are exposed. Recipient age, for example, influences reaction to messages concerning such matters as legal drinking age, mandatory retirement age, and so on.

Reference groups: To a greater or lesser extent, groups demand conformity. Membership exacts a price in behavior and belief. Members embrace group norms and identify with group interests. This concept applies to formal and informal groups. The former category includes professional and trade associations while the latter involves antique collectors, hobbyists, and the like. In either case, group membership tends to produce shared beliefs that may be barriers to or facilitators of message acceptance.

Personality variables: Humans vary in intelligence, authoritarianism, susceptibility to persuasion, and other factors that influence response to messages. Intelligence is a governor of understanding of complex messages. Authoritarianism influences willingness to accept new ideas. Strong self-esteem tends to slow change in position on any issue.

These are but a few of the many factors that influence individual perception of, and reaction to, messages. They are among the strongest governors of the process, however, and thus of critical importance in public relations practice.

Saliency: Messages are screened by individuals in terms of relative importance. Usefulness of information governs the extent to which messages will be assimilated. The result is most readily seen in terms of advertising. Acceptance of messages concerning automobile tires becomes increasingly likely as need for tires grows. After tires are purchased, subsequent messages seldom are heeded.

Selective exposure: Receipt and processing of information is strongly influenced by individual beliefs. That which conforms to beliefs is readily accepted and may even be sought after. The converse also is true. Information inconsistent with beliefs is rejected and may be avoided. The selection process is most readily seen in the manner in which individuals choose the books or magazines they read and the television programs they watch.

Selective perception: Need, experience, mood, and memory are primary determinants of the manner in which individuals organize their perceptions. These elements serve as "filters" through which only information of interest to the individual can pass. The result is striking variation in recollection, as best evidenced in connection with events such as political speeches. Listeners retain information most significant to them. Senior citizens tend to remember comments concerning Social Security, for example, while young people recall information about student loan and scholarship programs.

Selective retention. Variation in individual recall of message content is called selective retention. Utility of information involved and individual beliefs or interests influence retention. The latter elements may be negative or positive. Ideas may be remembered for their repulsiveness as well as their attractiveness.

Public relations professionals' ability to communicate thus is influenced by multiple intervening variables. Facts can not be simply poured into the heads of audience members. The fabric of individual beliefs and experiences is resistant to modification by information alone. Performance and communication consistently applied over time are essential in changing attitude and opinion in individuals and in organizations.

A New Concept

Need for consistency in communication in a fast-changing environment in the 1980s led to a new dimension in public relations practice: issues management. What has been called issues management pragmatically varies from traditional public relations practice in only two respects. The process focuses on those problems or issues with which government ultimately may become involved and seeks to identify them earlier than otherwise might be the case. More broadly applied and called environmental assessment, the identification process long has been an integral part of public relations practice.

ENVIRONMENTAL ASSESSMENT

Environmental assessment fulfills multiple roles in public relations practice. As an ongoing process, it provides practitioners with continuing insights into individuals, organizations, and the environments in which they function. This information is central to the strategic planning process on which public relations programming is based. It guides ongoing research efforts essential to programmatic success (see Chapter 4). It also provides direction for professional development programs, formal or informal, necessary to practitioner career development.

The environmental assessment process is designed to identify and monitor emerging issues or trends that ultimately may create problems or opportunities. They are identified through scanning and tracked through monitoring. The process thus serves as an early warning system for practitioners and their clients or employees.

Scanning involves periodic examination of every organizational horizon. It has been described as "a 360° process" to identify specific events which may signal the onset of trends. Monitoring techniques then are used to determine if trends are developing and, if so, to assess their strengths and directions.

Primary environmental assessment techniques in public relations practice include media monitoring, organizational monitoring, participation in professional organizations, and continuing education. Each of these processes is oriented to professional practice generally; to the commercial, industrial, or institutional sectors in which practitioners' employers or clients operate; and to the individual organizations with which they deal.

Bodies of knowledge necessary to successful public relations practice largely can be assigned to one of three categories: environmental, client or employer, and professional. The professional component is most readily identified. It includes contemporary knowledge of every aspect of public relations practice and the disciplines with which public relations inevitably is involved. Although varying from one occupational setting to another, they most often include marketing, advertising, sales promotion, law, and accounting. The client/ employer component can be relatively narrow or quite broad. Organizational practitioners need monitor only the commercial, industrial, or institutional sector in which their employers are involved. Counselors must be conversant with the fields in which all of their clients are involved. Environmental knowledge is the most complex of the three components. It encompasses the internal and external environments with which all organizations are involved.

Media Monitoring

As implied above, media monitoring requires practitioners to scan several sets of publications. Mass media, professional media, and commercial/industrial/institutional media all must be read on regular bases. Most practitioners over time develop media monitoring lists that meet their specific needs. They often vary with organizational size, where responsibility for the process in part can be successfully delegated. Some publications nevertheless are virtually "must" reading.

Mass media. The mass medium that most frequently appears on public relations professionals' list is the *New York Times.* Several factors are involved. First, the *Times* is an opinion leader among many influential individuals. Arguably to a greater extent than any other publication, the *Times* influences national agendas.

Other mass media read on regular bases include the "hometown" press. The term here encompasses newspapers published in every city in which the organization maintains facilities of any kind. Other mass media on the list may include the *Washington Post* for those whose clients or employers are vitally concerned with national government, as well as so-called city magazines in larger communities.

Professional Media. In public relations, as in most disciplines, professional media can be subdivided into two groups: the practitioner-oriented and the academic-oriented. In public relations, they are so few in each group that all should be on practitioners' required reading lists.

Practitioner-oriented media include *Public Relations Quarterly; Public Relations Journal,* a monthly publication of the Public Relations Society of America; *IPRA Review,* a quarterly publication of the International Public Relations Association; and *Communication World,* a monthly issued by the

International Association of Business Communicators. Multiple newsletters also serve the industry. Arguably most valuable among them is *pr reporter*.

Academic- or research-oriented publications that should be regularly read by practitioners include *Public Relations Review*, and *Public Relations Research and Education*. Their content often is academically oriented to a point at which reading is difficult for laymen but they nevertheless should be read. Editors of the *Review* regularly review all new books of interest to the field and publish an annual index of articles and academic papers that otherwise might escape practitioner attention.

Other Media. As is the case with the professional media, those dealing with the commercial/industrial/institutional sectors in which practitioners' clients or employers are involved fall into two categories. Some might be termed "general business" publications while others are sector-specific.

A few of the nation's general business publications readily can be categorized as "must" reading for public relations professionals regardless of their employers' or clients' interest. Most prominent among the are the *Wall Street Journal*, *Business Week*, and *Industry Week*. These publications are especially significant for their in-depth analysis of business and industry problems and opportunities. They frequently focus on change in one or more of the suprasystems or subsystems with which every organization must deal.

Industry-specific publications are equally important to public relations practitioners. They must be selected with care from among those specializing in client or employer industries. Practitioners must be especially sensitive to the scope of the publications they select in relation to the industry in question.

Those involved in the trucking industry, for example, will find multiple magazines dealing with trucks and trucking. They would be derelict, however, to ignore publications dealing with distribution generally and with other forms of transportation specifically. A significant portion of the problems that the nation's railroads have experienced in recent years arose out of their failure to recognize that they were in the transportation industry as well as the railroad business.

Given necessary breadth, the media monitoring process can become complex and burdensome, especially where practitioners have little or no staff support. Potential difficulties in some cases can be avoided by using one of several commercial services. The better known among them are offered by the Naisbitt Organization and SRI International.

Organizational Monitoring

Media monitoring in part may be delegated where public relations practitioners are burdened with multiple environmental processes. This usually occurs where complex organizations are involved and practitioners are managing multiple communication programs. These circumstances make two internal assessment systems advisable.

Walking around. One consists of "management by walking around." It requires public relations practitioners to delegate a sufficient volume of work to permit them to maintain an extensive network of organizational contacts. These are individuals in all walks of organizational life with whom the practitioner maintains regular contact.

Peers, their subordinates, practitioner subordinates, and superiors all should be involved in a "networking" process. Contacts from their perspective may appear casual. Network maintenance requires, however, that they be carefully developed and regularly maintained.

The objective of the process is twofold. First, it keeps the public relations practitioner aware of impending changes within the organization, which those involved may fail to recognize as significant. More important, it permits practitioners to "keep a finger on the organizational pulse."

The former information at times may prove worthy of dissemination through internal and, occasionally, external channels. The latter is more significant in fulfilling public relations practitioners' roles as counsel to management. Senior organizational executives frequently find themselves isolated by the press of day-to-day duties. Where this is the case, they depend on subordinates to maintain a "feel" for the organization. Their confidence often is misplaced. Many middle managers avoid transmitting "bad news" at all cost, in the process permitting small difficulties to become major problems.

Varying roles. "Walking around" is as readily practiced by counselors as organizational practitioners. The best of them develop extensive formal and informal networks within clients' organizations as well as their own. Those developed in client organizations are essential to maintaining strong counselor-client relationships. Concurrently, however, they yield information that can be applied in service to the client. This especially is the case where the counselor's assignment involves internal as well as external stakeholder groups.

Types of information. Most of the information gained through informal organizational monitoring is more significant as to general tone than in content. Experienced public relations practitioners, for example, claim to be able to "sense" the relative strengths of employee-employer relationships. In reality, they appear unconsciously to measure collective attitudes through such relatively intangible factors as employees' demeanors, the appearance of their work places, and similar indicators. A lobby floor polished to a high gloss, for example, is not merely a clean floor. It also is evidence that the worker responsible takes pride in his or her work as well as the organization. Contrary conditions, of course, imply the reverse.

Existing data. The second internal assessment system requires use of more measurable information also available to those who take the time to find it. The advent of the computer has led most organizations to amass data on almost every factor that contributes to operating cost. While developed primarily to provide greater insight into organizational productivity, much of it also is indicative of employees' attitude toward and opinion of the organization.

Absenteeism and tardiness rates, for example, generally are considered highly sensitive indicators of morale. No less sensitive are such elements as product rejection rates in the quality control area, volume of material wasted, customer complaints, and the like. All tend to vary with the strength of employees' commitments to organizations.

These data are most meaningful when viewed over an extended period of time. Absenteeism and tardiness rates necessarily are inconsistent from month to month. They tend to be higher during bad weather. They also may peak in special circumstances, such as on the first day of the duck-hunting season. Viewed historically with special attention to trends, however, such data are sensitive indicators of employee attitudes.

Applying information. Data obtained through environmental assessment techniques are applicable in multiple situations. The level of effectiveness at which they will be applied, however, is a function of practitioner rather than organizational variables. Critical in this context are the extent and efficacy of individual professional development programs. These programs necessarily overlap the earlier-described media monitoring program. The latter play concurrent roles in environmental assessment and professional development. They are necessary but not sufficient, however, to professional development.

PROFESSIONAL DEVELOPMENT

The depth, breadth, and currency of knowledge and skills that public relations practitioners bring to their work are among the more critical governors of their success. Environmental assessment processes dealing with the profession play a significant role in professional development. They assure that practitioners are conversant with the state of the public relations art. Unfortunately, the nature of public relations practice continues to change and, with it, the scope of the body of knowledge practitioners require.

Until relatively recent times, public relations practice dealt primarily with communication; with disseminating information in efforts to change the perceptions of organizations' constituent groups. Only in recent years have public relations professionals become involved in issues identification and policy making. The transition involved a change in roles from technician to consultant.

Public relations practitioners presumably come into practice armed with a basic body of knowledge in multiple areas. In addition to the technical aspects of public relations practice, they should include such diverse subjects as economics, psychology, sociology, anthropology, management, marketing, sales promotion, interpersonal and mediated communication, and research methodologies.

Their entry-level baccalaureate or master's degrees, however, are beginning rather than ending points in acquiring knowledge. They are little more than "licenses to learn," attesting to the presence of a core of knowledge on which must be built and maintained a superstructure necessary to professional success. This can be created only through acquisition and maintenance of contemporary knowledge throughout the individual's career. Since no individual can maintain conversancy with all human events, practicing professionals find it necessary to establish a systematic approach to the process.

New Requirements

The consultant role requires greater depth and breadth of knowledge. While maintaining their proficiency in communication, consultants must master social and managerial sciences.

Only a minority of practitioners have dedicated sufficient time and effort to professional development to establish and maintain this broadened professional perspective. The minority includes some of the least experienced and some of the most experienced members of the profession.

Recent graduates of accredited college and university programs in public relations constitute the former group. Their curricula were far different than those of their predecessors. They have included substantial background in both the social sciences and business-related disciplines, especially management and marketing.

Most of their more experienced colleagues who have gained comparable knowledge and skill levels are members of larger counseling firms. Burson-Marsteller, Hill and Knowlton, and a few others have installed internal educational and/or professional development programs for their personnel.

Some few other practitioners have pursued supplemental educational programs in one of several forms of their own volition. These programs are increasing in number and accessibility but remain woefully "underenrolled" in terms of the numbers of practitioners in the United States. They have been estimated in recent years to be in excess of 200,000.

Educational Programs

Formal and informal programs in public relations and related disciplines abound in the United States and are increasing in quantity and quality at an accelerating pace. They include degree programs offered by postsecondary educational institutions, individual courses offered by those institutions for academic credit, and a host of continuing education programs.

Degree programs. Public relations practitioners continue to come from diverse academic backgrounds. While increasing numbers are the product of undergraduate degree programs in public relations, graduates from other programs continue to find their way into the profession in significant numbers.

For members of the latter group, especially where employed by organi-

zations lacking in professional development programs, supplemental undergraduate study is appropriate. Many colleges and universities offer diploma
"endorsements" in additional disciplines and almost all will admit degree
holders as "special undergraduate" students.

Individual public relations courses also are being developed for mediated
delivery through television and computer-based systems. The Electronic University Network, a California-based subsidiary of Telelearning, Inc., has pioneered in this area and was offering undergraduate public relations course
work as early as 1986.

Graduate-level programs in public relations and other disciplines also offer
considerable potential for practitioners. Research conducted at Memphis State
University indicates that employers of public relations practitioners increasingly are predisposed toward those with master's degrees, especially where
degrees in business administration are superimposed over undergraduate
public relations degrees.

"External degree" programs at the graduate level have been proliferating
in recent years. Requiring little or no on-campus work, these programs have
been offered by highly reputable institutions as well as so-called diploma mills.
Among leaders in the former group are components of the state university
system of California.

Continuing education. Professional organizations in the communication
disciplines have been a primary source for continuing education programs.
The Public Relations Society of America (PRSA) long has sponsored such
programs at New York University. PRSA and the International Association
of Business Communicators (IABC) have conducted extensive programs in
conjunction with their annual conferences.

Other groups, both more specialized and more generalized in their scope,
also have been active in this area. The International Communication Association's annual conference includes multiple educational programs. So does
that of the American Society for Hospital Marketing and Public Relations
(ASHMPR).

PRSA, IABC, and ASHMPR sponsor internal professional development
programs as well. PRSA and IABC offer accreditation for members and
ASHMPR sponsors a fellowship program. Each requires acquisition of experience and knowledge beyond practice entry level.

Individual study. The journals of the organizations specified above and a
host of other publications are available to practitioners seeking to maintain
professional proficiency. They include academic publications, professional
magazines, and a proliferating number of newsletters.

Specifically applicable in public relations are *Public Relations Quarterly*, a
professional journal, and *Public Relations Review*, an academic publication.
Public Relations Review also publishes an extensive annual bibliography in
public relations. PRSA publishes an annual bibliography as well while Sage

Publications of Beverly Hills, California, publishes *Communication Abstracts*, covering public relations and other disciplines.

The 1980s also have seen an explosion in books on public relations deserving of practitioner attention. Arguably among the most significant of them are Grunig and Hunt's *Managing Public Relations*, Nager and Allen's *Public Relations Management by Objectives*, Wilcox, Ault, and Agee's *Public Relations: Strategies and Tactics*, and Brody's *The Business of Public Relations*. They have been accompanied by a host of new editions of virtually every significant public relations text published since the 1950s as well as several other newcomers.

The extent to which any of these approaches to enhancing knowledge and skill levels is applied varies with individual practitioners and the environments in which they function. Some find it appropriate to focus their professional development activities on public relations practice generally. Others narrow the scope of their efforts to specific commercial, industrial, or institutional sectors such as health care or high technology. Still others approach more broadly from a social science perspective. No universally applicable formula exists but the need for professional development among public relations practitioners apparently will continue for the foreseeable future.

IN SUMMARY

The power of knowledge long has been recognized in public relations as well as other disciplines. Nowhere does mastery of contemporary knowledge so directly influence practitioner results, however, than in public relations.

Successful practice requires contemporary knowledge of public relations and much more. Client or employer endeavors and the industries within which they function must be known as well. So must the nature of individuals and organizations in general.

Systems theory offers the most successful approach to identifying, mastering, and maintaining the required bodies of knowledge in a fast-changing world. Organizations in this context are viewed as open systems, as components of suprasystems, and as composed of subsystems.

Suprasystems are organizations' external environments, the natural, human, political, social, market, and technological systems within which they must function. Subsystems are the mechanisms that influence organizational personnel, the psychological, social, political, and technological.

Organizations and individuals under the influence of these subsystems and suprasystems seek to communicate effectively in the face of numerous significant barriers. Among the most difficult to breach are individuals' perceptions. These literally are the worlds within which they function; worlds fashioned by the nature of their beliefs. Beliefs are influenced by demographic variables, reference groups, personality variables, and message-related factors. The latter include significance of content, and selectivity in exposure, perception, and retention.

Maintaining conversancy with these and other variables in the several environments with which public relations practitioners deal requires applying a process known as environmental assessment. It examines events in subsystems and suprasystems through a scanning process to identify those of significance to organizations and their public relations consultants. Significant events then are monitored over extended periods to assess the strength of trends involved and enable organizational planners to anticipate their impact.

Scanning and monitoring involve oversight of multiple media as well as the organization itself. The processes also require state-of-the-art knowledge and skill on the part of public relations practitioners. This is developed and maintained through group or individual professional development planning, which may include formal education, continuing education, and individual study programs.

ADDITIONAL READING

Aronoff, Craig E., and Otis W. Baskin. *Public Relations: The Profession and the Practice*. St. Paul: West, 1983.

Brody, E. W. *The Business of Public Relations*. New York: Praeger, 1987.

Cantor, Bill. *Inside Public Relations: Experts in Action*. Chester Burger, ed. New York: Longman, 1984.

Crable, Richard E., and Steven L. Vibbert. *Public Relations as Communication Management*. Edina, Minn.: Bellwether, 1986.

Cutlip, Scott M., Allen H. Center, and Glen M. Broom. *Effective Public Relations*, 6th ed. Englewood Cliffs, N.J.: Prentice-Hall, 1985.

Dunn, S. Watson. *Public Relations: A Contemporary Approach*. Homewood, Ill: Irwin, 1986.

Goldman, Jordan. *Public Relations in the Marketing Mix: Introducing Vulnerability Relations*. Chicago: Crain, 1984.

Grunig, James E., and Todd Hunt. *Managing Public Relations*. New York: Holt, Rinehart and Winston, 1984.

Nager, Norman R., and T. Harrell Allen. *Public Relations Management by Objectives*. New York: Longman, 1984.

Newsom, Doug, and Alan Scott. *This Is PR: The Realities of Public Relations*, 3rd ed. Belmont, Calif.: Wadsworth, 1985.

Nolte, Lawrence W. *Fundamentals of Public Relations: Professional Guidelines, Concepts and Integrations*, 2nd ed. New York: Pergamon, 1979.

Nolte, Lawrence W., and Dennis L. Wilcox. *Effective Publicity: How to Reach the Public*. New York: John Wiley, 1984.

Phillips, Charles S. *Secrets of Successful Public Relations*. Englewood Cliffs, N.J.: Prentice-Hall, 1985.

Reilly, Robert T. *Public Relations in Action*. Englewood Cliffs, N.J.: Prentice-Hall, 1981.

Simon, Raymond. *Public Relations: Concepts and Practices*, 3rd. ed. New York: John Wiley, 1984.

Swanson, David L., and Jesse G. Delia. *The Nature of Human Communication*. Chicago: Science Research Associates, 1976.

Wilcox, Dennis L., Phillip H. Ault, and Warren K. Agee. *Public Relations: Strategies and Tactics*. New York: Harper & Row, 1986.

4

Creating Knowledge

Professional development and environmental assessment create foundations on which practitioners build information systems to solve client and employer public relations problems. They are the first of a set of ongoing data-gathering and knowledge-building processes that enhance potential for programmatic success.

From professional development and environmental assessment, practitioners proceed to communication audits, statistical reviews, and surveys. Although each is ongoing, the processes are undertaken and applied sequentially to specific problems. Scope of inquiry narrows at each level.

DUAL SYSTEMS

Professional development deals with the fundamentals of human and organizational behavior and development. Environmental assessment examines the universe in which practitioners and their clients or employers function. Informal research expands on the assessment process by assembling all available information concerning problems at hand. Communication audits, which fall between "informal" and "formal" processes, assess the effectiveness of organizational strategies and practices. Statistical reviews examine published data relative to the organization and surveys generate new data.

Nature of Research

Reviews and surveys are more formally categorized as secondary and primary research, terms that tend to be intimidating. They conjure up images of complex mathematical formulae, sophisticated statistical tests, endless columns of figures, and the like. Reality is less forbidding. Most primary research in public relations involves relatively simple designs and produces data amenable to analysis by microcomputer. Professional research organizations usually are retained where more sophisticated efforts are required. Those engaged in public relations practice, however, must be sufficiently conversant with research to direct the process and analyze results.

Data gathering and knowledge building processes are directed toward two goals. The first is success in achieving public relations objectives. The second is measurable results. Both require information that can be obtained only through research, formal or informal.

Programmatic Objectives

The information-gathering processes involved are designed to meet specific management needs. They include:

1. Data to serve as a basis for planning. Objective information concerning audiences, messages, and channels of communication is essential.
2. An early warning system that will point to potential trouble spots inside or outside the organization. Research is applied here as an extension of environmental assessment processes.
3. Consensus on organizational strategies. Public relations frequently is in competition with other organizational functions for resources. Research data are more credible than practitioners' opinions or intuition in such circumstances.
4. Evidence of programmatic progress and data by which program components can be evaluated on continuing bases.
5. Baseline or benchmark data applicable in charting organizational progress.

Access to baseline data is of inestimable value in timing public relations programs in keeping with the ebb and flow of attitude and opinion among stakeholder groups. It enhances ability to synthesize messages precisely and select communication channels. It enables programmers to focus their efforts on primary objectives and key audiences. Research also can be used to pretest messages and channels and generate continuing audience feedback. The process thus is invaluable in enhancing program design and measuring results.

Measuring Results

Attitudinal and behavioral change are the primary objectives of public relations, but they are not readily accomplished. Months or years of effort may be required in inducing acceptance of new ideas or concepts. These circumstances require continuing flows of valid data indicating the extent to which acceptance has been achieved and the relative efficacy of public relations program components.

Such data provide answers to multiple critical questions. Which messages are most successful in producing desired audience responses? What channels of communication are most efficient in reaching those audiences? To what extent are objectives being achieved? Answers are essential for two reasons. First, they enable practitioners to "fine tune" public relations programs; to reallocate resources to most productive program components or make appropriate changes in those that have been less productive. Second, they demonstrate results. They justify organizational investment in public relations programming.

ORIGINS OF RESEARCH

Information gathering, research, and knowledge building are related terms. They deal with related processes, which are individually necessary and collectively sufficient for successful public relations practice. They enable practitioners to attack client or employer problems by collectively applying intuition, facts, and knowledge. The latter is a synthesis of the former.

This has not always been the case. Practitioners in earlier years obtained information by intuition, observation, and questioning. More often than not, they were successful. Their successes occurred, however, in a society considerably less complex than today's. Life-styles were less diverse. Individual behavioral patterns were more strongly controlled by social mores and folkways. Individual media were more pervasive. Their audiences were less fragmented than now is the case and practitioners were without the information-gathering tools of the new technologies.

A Unified Process

Research, in a narrow sense, came late to public relations. It was far earlier used, first episodically and later continuously, in marketing and advertising. The same progression occurred in public relations. The product of practitioner intuition, observation, and questioning first was supplemented by isolated research studies. Serial studies conducted at regular intervals then came into vogue. By the mid–1980s these elements had been combined to create a new and more complex process.

The process begins for contemporary professionals during postsecondary education. Here they begin their educational-professional development and learn the environmental assessment processes that constitute the foundations of research.

In practice settings, they become involved in observation and questioning processes and start to develop an instinctive or intuitive "feel" for organizations with which they deal. Up this point, they are dealing more with facts and feelings than knowledge.

Beginnings of Research

Levels of knowledge beyond the purely academic begin growing in public relations as practitioners apply environmental assessment techniques to organizations and their needs (see Chapter 3). Observation, questioning, and informal information-gathering processes expand their information bases. Communication audits constitute a logical next step in the information-gathering process and arguably can be considered a form of research.

Informal information gathering, or informal research, encompasses a multiplicity of techniques applied to gain information concerning individuals, organizations, and issues. None are universally applicable but all can be productively applied in specific situations.

Informal Research

The informal research process involves exploring all available sources of information concerning any specific problem. Many generate valuable information. Among the more popular of them are:

1. Organizational materials, including published financial reports of publicly owned organizations, sales materials, newsletters, product literature, and the like.
2. Information published or broadcast by the mass media. In this category are copies of newspaper and magazine articles, transcripts of broadcasts, and audio- and videotapes.
3. Commercial, industrial, and institutional data available through a host of business and professional associations at national, regional, state, and local levels. These organizations often maintain extensive libraries and conduct considerable research in their areas of interest.
4. Advisory panels or boards formed by organizations to serve as channels of communication with specific stakeholder groups.
5. Analyses of information contained in mail and telephone contacts initiated by stakeholders. Content of employee suggestion systems also falls in this category.
6. Information generated by focus groups formed to provide feedback from specific stakeholders on selected issues.
7. Statistics available from within the organization and ranging from sales data to manufacturing defect rates and employee absenteeism and tardiness records.

Some would categorize information available from public libraries and communication audits as "informal" information sources. Libraries yield not only trade and professional publications but academic journals and statistical summaries. Reviews of the latter documents is better viewed as secondary research, a subset of formal research. Communication audits logically constitute a category of their own. Techniques applied vary in level of formality.

Communication Audits

Pragmatically, audits are hybrids. They provide considerable ...
to supplant or supplement that gained in observation and questioning. They
may or may not meet criteria for formal research imposed in the social or
physical sciences.

Audits provide insight into the effectiveness of organizational strategies and
practices. They first were applied in public relations practice to assess strengths
and weaknesses of existing communication programs. They later came to be
used to gain knowledge of specific stakeholder groups. Audits in contemporary public relations practice are applied to any area in which more information is required.

Audit objectives. Audits may deal with internal or external stakeholders
and can be designed to generate information necessary to achieve an almost
limitless range of objectives. Improvement in communication programs, diagnosis of problems or opportunities, and evaluation of relative strengths and
weaknesses often are among internal objectives.

External audit objectives are even more diverse. Audits may examine attitude and opinion in any group in context with any issue, problem, or opportunity in which the organization is interested. They can be used to assess
stakeholder understanding, determine program effectiveness, measure prospective impact of a new plant or a plant closing on a community, and examine
the reputation of organizations and/or their products or services.

Methodology. Audits can be combined with formal research but this seldom
is the case. Demographic data and statistical analyses only infrequently are
significant in audit data analyses. Interviewers generally are sufficiently familiar
with audiences to elicit accurate information without benefit of more sophisticated techniques.

Audits usually are conducted by administering printed questionnaires or
through series of structured interviews. Each approach has advantages and
disadvantages. Printed questionnaires tend to produce suspicion as to confidentiality, especially where used on employer premises. They also can be
administered by mail, but at greater cost and often with lower response rates.
On-site administration by consultants encourages greater participation, especially where completed questionnaires are placed in locked receptacles and
removed from the premises for tabulation.

Individual interviews. Personal interviews are preferable to the telephone
variety in that they permit interviewers to better evaluate responses. Structured lists of questions always are used although respondents are permitted
to digress in their responses. Subjects often are made known to respondents
in advance, enabling them to give the matter some thought and to preclude
any need for time-consuming explanations of purpose.

Skilled interviewers should talk with cross sections of the groups or organizations involved. They should be representative of the whole and their

anonymity should be assured. Questions should deal with both negative and positive aspects of the subjects at hand.

Organizations involved. Respondent anonymity requires audits be conducted by firms or individuals external to the organization. Most are handled by public relations or management consulting firms. They differ in approach and product.

Management consultants deal primarily in compensation and benefit programming. Communication programs are added in clients' discretion to assure that information about other services are adequately disseminated. Data usually are presented to management in statistical or graphic form.

Public relations firms, in contrast, are concerned primarily with communication and use audits to provide information essential to productive program development. Their results usually are presented in prose and statistical form for ease in management comprehension.

FORMAL TECHNIQUES

Audits may differ from formal research in two primary areas. First, they may involve interviews with individuals who are not chosen by chance. They may be representative of groups in which auditors are interested but may not be chosen through random sampling processes. Second, validity in their responses is assumed to be created in part through exercise of interviewer judgment rather than scientific objectivity. Audit questions often are subjective rather than objective and those who prefer formal research often question the validity of the process.

Primary and Secondary Research

Formal research conforms to the more rigorous standards of science. They are applied directly in primary research and indirectly in secondary research. Secondary research tends to predominate in public relations for economic and temporal reasons. It almost always is less costly and less time consuming. The secondary research process involves gathering, evaluating, and, occasionally, reanalyzing data gathered previously by applying accepted scientific methods.

The volume of existing data applicable to public relations practice and readily available to practitioners has been growing at an accelerating rate since the advent of the computer. Development of computer-accessible data bases in recent years has made this information almost instantaneously available to practitioners in their offices.

Public and Private Data

Volume and accessibility have been enhanced in recent years by proliferating for-profit research services. Many offer sophisticated demographic and market data generated by applying proprietary computer programs to information gathered and sold by the Bureau of the Census and other governmental agencies.

Information obtained in this manner infrequently is applicable to the carefully circumscribed audiences with which public relations programs are concerned. It is available in such detail, however, as to be of considerable assistance to practitioners in the design and implementation of their own primary research.

Typologies and matrixes developed by the Bureau of the Census, for example, can be adapted to public relations research. Where appropriate, they are highly attractive in that bureau figures can be applied as baseline data in analyzing survey results. Where respondent groups conform to published demographic data, practitioners can safely assume that respondents are reasonably representative of populations under study. For all of these reasons, contemporary formal research in public relations practice almost invariably includes a disproportionately large secondary research component.

SECONDARY RESEARCH

Secondary research in public relations almost inevitably begins with data generated by the U.S. Commerce Department's Bureau of the Census. Data gathered through the bureau's decennial surveys of the nation's population are readily available through many libraries as well as a variety of other agencies that engage in economic research.

Demographic data from the Census Bureau deal with age, sex, family status, household income, educational level, and a host of other factors significant in public relations. They are especially enlightening in two contexts. First, they are available not only for states and cities but are subdivided by U.S. Postal Service ZIP codes. Correlated with employee or customer residence data, they yield geographically oriented profiles. Second, these data can be examined together with life-style and other patterns to create still further insights into the population of interest.

Other Cost-Free Data

Information generated by the Bureau of the Census can be obtained at negligible cost from the bureau or the U.S. Government Printing Office. Computer tapes from the bureau are more expensive but may be worthwhile in some circumstances. Further information available without significant expense comes from the Bureau of Labor Statistics, the United States Chamber of Commerce, and several other governmental and quasi-governmental agencies at state and local as well as federal levels.

Most states and many localities monitor and compile data through several types of departments and agencies. Commerce and agriculture departments tend to be especially helpful. Their data often follow formats modeled after their federal counterparts, which makes interpretation easier for users.

State and local business and economic research and development agencies often maintain extensive statistical files as well. Some are located on college and university campuses, often in schools or departments of business or economics. These schools and their libraries also can be valuable resources. Individual faculty members frequently have data pertinent to their research interests that they are willing to share with professionals. Academic library privileges often are available to nonstudents as well.

Many public relations practitioners also use several major university research facilities. More popular among these are the University of Michigan Survey Research Center, Ohio State University's Center for Human Resource Research, and the University of New Mexico's Technology Application Center.

The University of Michigan unit maintains a valuable Survey of Consumer Expectations. National Longitudinal Surveys conducted at Ohio State generate information concerning the nation's labor market, while the University of New Mexico maintains industrial and energy information programs.

Low-Cost Information Sources

College and university libraries can be especially valuable resources to public relations practitioners who lack computer communication facilities. Their resources almost invariably include computer terminals, subscriptions to data-base services, and personnel skilled in their use. The skills of library personnel accustomed to working with data bases are especially valuable. Search strategies and computer command schemes vary from one data base to another. The uninitiated can spend considerable expensive on-line time obtaining data that can be quickly retrieved by experienced computer researchers.

Library computer users usually are highly skilled by virtue of their necessarily extensive experience. They spend significant amounts of time doing searches, especially for faculty and graduate students.

The data bases at their disposal in most cases are more numerous and less expensively accessed than would be the case in practitioners' offices. Two factors are involved. First, extensive use minimizes on-line cost since basic subscription charges are amortized over a larger user group. In many cases, subscription charges are so high as to render occasional use of individual data bases impractical in public relations practice. Second, colleges and university libraries invariably have access to data bases used almost exclusively for academic research such as that of the Educational Research Information Center (ERIC). These data bases include master's theses, doctoral dissertations, academic papers, and other documents otherwise inaccessible to practitioners.

Academic research is something of a mixed blessing for public relations practitioners. Turgid writing styles used by faculty and graduate students make these materials difficult to read and assimilate. The information they contain often is the latest available, however, and worthy of close examination.

Direct Computer Access

Where appropriate library facilities are not available, public relations practitioners without direct access to data bases are at a distinct disadvantage. So important have these resources become, however, that practitioners arguably cannot afford to be without them.

Access then is gained through microcomputers equipped with modulator-demodulators (modems) for telecommunication. The hardware involved comes in a broad range of configurations and capabilities. Virtually any computer will suffice. Data base owners and resellers have configured their hardware to gain as many subscribers as possible.

Ease of access. With appropriate equipment in hand, data bases can be accessed directly or through so-called gateway services. The latter are resellers of data-base services. They buy on-line time wholesale and sell at retail. Their charges are no higher than those of individual data-base operators and often are lower. More important from an economic standpoint, those who use gateway services usually are not required to pay initial subscription fees or minimum monthly charges generally required for access to individual data bases. They thus can more economically access relatively expensive data bases at minimum cost.

Gateway services are available in two forms. Some are components of computer utilities such as CompuServe and The Source. They provide user services beyond data-base access. On-line conferencing, electronic bulletin boards, libraries of games, and shopping services are among them. These services are provided at relatively low rates. Charges may be as low as $6 per on-line hour during evenings and weekends. Where users elect to access data bases, additional charges are levied approximating those that would be made by the data-base operator. In combination, the two may exceed data-base operators' hourly rates. Seldom, however, will they produce user costs equivalent to operator hourly rates and/or monthly minimums plus basic subscription fees.

Other services. Other gateway services, such as those operated by Western Union and General Electric, offer only data-base access. Dozens of data bases are accessible through some gateway services. Some are accessible through more than one service but each service usually has exclusive contracts with one or more.

Users of gateway services face several challenges. The first of them arises in selection of services. Rarely do users find gateways providing access to all services they may ever want to use. Comparing gateways alone can be a problem. The National Federation of Abstracting and Information Services, for example, incorporates some 800 data bases in its Searchlink service. In addition, services vary in ease of use. Some gateways come equipped with uniform search protocols. These are standardized sets of terms and commands through which all of the service's data bases can be searched. In other cases, terms and commands vary from one data base to another.

The latter circumstances make data-base usage more difficult but nevertheless worthwhile. Many larger public relations firms and departments are training individual staff members, usually research department personnel, in search procedures. Others endure necessarily higher unit costs by letting individual staffers handle their own on-line searches. Still others, in increasing numbers, turn to commercial or consultant sources for data.

Direct Services

Some of the more popular direct services among public relations practitioners are Mead Data Central's NEXIS, Lockheed Information Systems' DIALOG, and some of the 57 services of the A.C. Nielsen Company.

NEXIS is perhaps most used in public relations. The service includes the former *New York Times* Information Bank, acquired by Mead some years ago. NEXIS also contains the editorial content of most major domestic publications. Magazines available include *Fortune, Time, Newsweek, Business Week, U.S. News & World Report, Barron's,* and *Dun's Review.* Also accessible through NEXIS are other newspapers, such as the *Los Angeles Times* and news services such as *Associated Press* and *United Press International.*

DIALOG contains more than 70 international data bases with information on human development, science, and business. The Nielsen company's Media Research Services, Retail Index Services, and Customer Research Services also can be helpful. Media Research Services measure television audiences. Retail Index Services measure product sales rates in the United States and more than 20 other nations. Customer Research Services evaluate marketing problems and strategies.

The nature and extent of available services is in a state of flux. PR Newswire, for example, provides a research service called Newsnet as well as distribution services (see Chapter 10). Newsnet incorporates the news releases of PR Newswire's distribution clients and the texts of some 150 newsletters offered by more than 80 publishers.

The so-called data-base field concurrently in this manner is becoming increasingly complex and progressively more important to those who seek to maintain state-of-the-art knowledge in specialized areas. Among their more valuable tools is *Online Access,* a bimonthly magazine published by Chicago's Online Access Publishing Group and designed to keep readers abreast of developments in the field.

Some Consultant Services

An almost limitless array of consultant services also are available to those who prefer to subcontract research functions or who require more sophisticated services. Many of the latter are enhanced versions of data that originated with the Bureau of the Census.

Enhancements for the most part involve superimposing additional economic, geographic, or other files over the basic census data to provide information not otherwise available. The products of Urban Decision Systems, Inc., of Los Angeles and Westport, Connecticut, are representative of the types of information available through commercial vendors. They include:

1. Census reports taken from 1980 Census Summary Tapes and enhanced with medians, averages, and percentages calculated by Urban Decision Systems (UDS).

2. Population Benchmark reports based on UDS estimates extrapolated from state and federal data. Benchmark reports provide data on population, households, race, age, household income, family size, motor vehicles, the labor force, educational levels, and housing for virtually any geographic area.

3. Retail Potential reports for individual retailers and shopping centers. They cover virtually every type of business, from apparel to variety stores.

4. COLORSITE Grid Images, computer-generated colored maps showing distribution of almost any variable.

5. Income and Demographic Trend reports, which project census data for the current year and five years hence.

In addition to the reports, UDS offers access to data by telephone on pay-as-you-go or contract bases and by microcomputer on license or time sharing bases. The company also sells machine-readable data for processing through clients' own computer systems on tapes, diskettes, and other media.

Woods & Poole Economics, Inc., of Washington, D.C., offers a set of products more strongly oriented to economic forecasting. The firm maintains a comprehensive county-level data base encompassing 300 economic and demographic variables for 4,100 geographic areas. Primary variable categories are population, employment, personal income, total earnings, and net earnings.

Woods & Poole updates county data bases and makes new 20-year forecasts each year. The forecasts are based on more than 3,000 individual computer-generated county models that capture specific local conditions and are interlinked regionally and nationally to reflect broader trends as well. Reports are available in printed and computer readable form for virtually any geographic area.

Other data and other formats are available from Donnelly Marketing Information Services, a subsidiary of Dun & Bradstreet. The Donnelly reports fall into two basic categories: American Profile Reports and Market Potential

Reports. The latter are designed primarily for those interested in selected business sectors and are of relatively little value to public relations practitioners. The former are another matter.

Donnelly's American Profile consists of a set of reports through which readers gain insight into the population of any geographic area. The reports include:

1. Census Reports containing 1970 and 1980 data as well as Donnelly projections for the current year and and the fifth subsequent year, e.g., 1986 and 1991. Data include population breakdowns by race, households, age, sex, and household income.

2. Census Change Reports comparing data from the two most recent census reports. Data are shown numerically and in percentages and percentage change is reported as well for race, population age, male population age, female population age, numbers and size of households, household income, per capita income, home value, rental rates, and occupancy data (owner occupied, renter occupied, or vacant). The reports also cover occupational, educational, and employment levels.

3. Census Population Details reports covering race, age, education, income, and marital status by sex. Also provided are industry, occupational, employment status, and worker travel data plus numbers of working mothers with children and private school enrollment figures.

4. Census Household Details reports providing raw and percentile data for race, marital status, and a broad set of household characteristics. The latter include householder age and sex, numbers of children, numbers of persons, income levels, home values, rental rates, types and age of housing units, numbers of vehicles and air conditioners per household, mortgage age, and telephone and utility services.

5. Update Reports covering change between the most recent census and the current year in population, households, household population, and income. They also provide population counts, population by age and sex, neighborhood mobility in the form of moving data, numbers of passenger vehicles, and age of vehicles.

6. Economic Reports categorizing area firms by primary Standard Industrial Code number, indicating numbers of firms, numbers of employees, and estimated sales volume. Financial institution deposit data for the area also are summarized.

7. Profile Reports providing comparative data across three geographic sectors, such as a city, a county, and a state or three municipalities. They cover employment, population projections and percentage change, race, age, educational level, and household/household population projections. Also provided are household income, family income, and housing data as well as labor force characteristics.

8. Summary Reports comparing Profile Report communities with the nation as a whole in terms of race, population age, worker characteristics, educational levels, households, household income, and housing data.

Another frequently helpful service in public relations is Claritas Corporation's PRIZM or Potential Rating Index by ZIP Markets. PRIZM is used primarily for consumer marketing but data available can provide considerable assistance in public relations as well.

PRIZM examines the more than 35,000 ZIP code zones in the United States in 40 regional clusters. Some 1,000 characteristics including age, education, income, and such are examined on the premise that humans are attracted to those of similar socioeconomic status, which leads to development of homogenous neighborhoods.

Claritas has assigned a set of colorful descriptors to similar ZIP clusters: Money & Brains, Shotguns & Pickups, Back-Country Folks, Bunker's Neighbors, Blue Blood Estates, and the like. Most important in public relations practice, however, is the fact that motivational and life-style characteristics are similar within the homogenous clusters. Public relations activities thus can be planned in keeping with socioeconomic and related audience characteristics.

Claritas, Urban Decision Systems, Woods & Poole, and Donnelly are but a few of the many research organizations whose products may be valuable to public relations practitioners. Their prices are not low, but where data available include information that practitioners need, costs may be significantly lower than those involved in primary research.

Shared-Cost Research

An alternative sometimes appropriate in reducing expenses is shared-cost research. Shared-cost studies are designed by a number of research companies for multiple participants. They usually are conducted on repetitive bases—daily, weekly, monthly, or quarterly—and are considerably less expensive than specialized studies. At the same time, however, individual participants sacrifice the ability to examine issues of specific interest in considerable depth.

Shared-cost research studies are available from several relatively well-known firms such as The Gallup Organization and Opinion Research Corporation and from a number of other organizations as well. Public relations practitioners considering such research often find periodic surveys conducted by business, professional, and trade organizations in behalf of all members to be equally beneficial and available at little or no cost.

PRIMARY RESEARCH

Where existing and available data are inadequate to meet specific needs, primary research is necessary. Adequacy in most cases is a function of reliability. Considerable information often is available, much of it obtained through one or more of the informal techniques itemized earlier. More often than not, however, information is not equivalent to valid data.

Advisory panels, trade associations, and published materials express opinions that may or may not mirror those of the groups with which public relations practitioners are concerned. They may be of value, however, in preparation for the formal research process.

Advisory panels and focus group interviews deal primarily with qualitative rather than quantitative matters. They are designed to generate sufficient information concerning the research topic to enable researchers to specify objectives, develop questionnaires, and plan a successful quantitative study.

Quantitative studies follow generally accepted procedures to create statistically valid data to enhance the productivity of specific public relations programs. Such studies are not inexpensive and can be exceptionally wasteful when based on information that may or may not be reliable. Formal research therefore follows rigorous procedures designed to assure that resultant data are accurate. Sampling technique, questionnaire design, and survey method are the most critical components of the process.

Most research in public relations deals with attitude and opinion among organizations' constituent groups. It also may involve emerging issues, marketing problems, the relative efficiency of channels of communication, and other factors. An eight-step process usually is involved:

1. Problem identification
2. Developing research objectives
3. Identifying groups involved and survey respondents
4. Qualitative, often informal research to define problems
5. Questionnaire development
6. Information gathering
7. Data analysis
8. Report preparation

Problems, Objectives, and Audiences

The first two steps in the process usually are undertaken almost concurrently. Problems in organizations usually are first evidenced by symptoms. Where employees are involved, for example, morale problems often are first seen in absenteeism, tardiness, and deterioration in qualitative or quantitative performance. The primary research objective almost automatically becomes identifying underlying causes.

The audience in this case is self-evident: the employee population. The nature of the organization and the population may have a significant influence, however, on selecting survey respondents.

Sampling Technique

Surveys are designed to measure attitude and opinion in specific groups or populations. Since most groups are of a size that would make population surveys prohibitively costly or time consuming, sample surveys are used. Their validity is governed by the mathematics of probability, which have demonstrated that samples taken at random will be statistically representative of populations involved.

Random sampling. Selection of a random sample, or probability sample as it sometimes is called, requires that every member of the population have an equal chance to be selected. A random sample of television watchers in a community, for example, could not be taken from the subscription list of a television magazine. Nonsubscribers would not have an equal chance to be selected.

Quota sampling. Researchers who are interested in subgroups within populations often employ a technique called quota or stratified sampling. Survey respondents then are selected at random but with proportional numbers selected from each subgroup. Where the population is all the students at a college, for example, proportionate numbers of respondents could be selected at random by age, sex, race, or class standing.

Sample size. Accuracy of survey results is a function of sample size. Put another way, the greater the accuracy the researcher requires, the larger must be the sample. Roper, Gallup, and other national opinion research firms may use samples of fewer than 2,000 to obtain accurate data. The average poll will cover some 1,500 respondents and generate a 3 percent margin of error at a confidence level of 95 percent. If the same questions were asked 20 times, in other words, response levels would be within three percentage points on 19 of the 20 occasions.

This level of accuracy is necessary where, as in the case of national polls, researchers seek to predict future events such as election results with relative precision. Survey data in public relations research for the most part need not achieve that level of precision. They are sought as indicators of attitude and opinion rather than as predictors of events. Samples of 100 to 500, producing margins of error between 5 and 10 percent, usually are considered sufficient.

Such margins are most acceptable where periodic surveys are undertaken to monitor change in attitude and opinion over time. Researchers then are in a position to evaluate the extent of change as well as abstract data.

Purposive sampling. Nonprobability or purposive sampling often is applied in public relations where researchers are most concerned with a small component of the population, such as economic or opinion leaders. The volume of resistance that a health care organization might encounter in attempting to establish a birth control clinic, for example, probably would be more a function of the attitudes of community clergymen than the population as a whole. The success of a community fund raising effort similarly would be more strongly governed by the thinking of business or foundation executives.

In the first instance, clergymen are acknowledged leaders where moral or ethical issues are involved. Their pronouncements from their pulpits will exert a disproportionately strong influence over community response. In the second case, presence or absence of support from prospective major donors is critical. They often provide as much as 90 percent of all monies collected in a communitywide campaign.

Questionnaire Design

The sampling process thus is a critical factor in generating valid survey results. Questionnaires are of equal if not greater importance, however, in that respondents are highly sensitive to wording. Ineptitude in preparing questions readily can produce distorted results. As managers frequently are cautioned in supervisory training programs, there is a world of difference between "that was a dumb mistake," and "that was a mistake, dummy." The words are not far different but the meanings are worlds apart.

Bias in questions. Questions may appear to be asking the same thing when in actuality addressing very different issues. Wilcox, Ault and Agee (1986) illustrated this principle with these questions:

"Is it a good idea to limit handguns?"
"Do you think registration of handguns will curtail crime?"
"Do you think laws curtailing the use of handguns would work?"

The questions are very different. "The first stresses the value of an idea, the second explores a possible effect, and the third examines the practicality of a proposed solution."

The nature of questions thus can bias results. Bias can be introduced inadvertently through carelessness or deliberately by individuals or groups seeking "research data" to support their points of view. Public relations practitioners thus must exercise care in developing their own survey questionnaires and carefully examine "survey data" displayed by others in support of their own positions.

Other distortants. A number of other factors can interfere with efforts to generate accurate research data. Compound questions, distorted response categories, and what is called "courtesy bias" are encountered most frequently.

Compound questions defy accuracy in response. "Should dirt bikes and all-terrain vehicles be more stringently regulated" is such a question. They are two distinct categories of vehicle that vary in use.

"Strongly agree," "agree" and "disagree" would constitute a distorted set of responses to any statement. They necessarily would produce results skewed toward the affirmative. At least one and perhaps two other responses would be necessary. Addition of "strongly disagree" would create a balanced set of response categories but would force some level of either agreement or disagreement. This could be eliminated by adding "uncertain."

"Courtesy bias" most often occurs where questionnaire respondents believe their individual answers will be known to researchers or others. They tend, in these circumstances, to respond in keeping with what they believe to be the questioner's perspective. Respondent anonymity usually eliminates such bias, especially where questionnaires are administered appropriately.

Survey Techniques

Care in sampling and question design will not necessarily eliminate all potential research problems. Bias can be reintroduced through survey technique, especially where in-person interviews are to be applied. Alternatively, interviews can be conducted by telephone or questionnaires can be circulated by mail or otherwise and anonymously returned. Each technique creates advantages and disadvantages.

Mail questionnaires. Delivery and return of questionnaires by mail permits researchers to control samples and geographic factors while limiting cost. Their greatest weakness arises out of low response rates. These range from as little as 1 to 2 percent where surveys are sponsored by business firms to 70 percent or more for membership organizations.

Where response rates are important, a number of devices can be used to improve them, although not without cost. Monetary rewards ranging from 25 cents to $1 and mailed with the questionnaire have produced the most salutory results. Follow-up mailings also stimulate response, as do reminder postcards although at a reduced rate. Including a return envelope with postage prepaid and an individually signed cover letter also are helpful. Research has shown that even the manner in which senders handle postage can influence returns. Metered postage usually brings a better response than bulk rate indicia, and stamps—especially issue-oriented commemorative stamps—produce still better response rates.

Telephone surveys. Use of telephones in survey research arguably is steadily declining in effectiveness with increasing use of telemarketing techniques. The latter appear to be engendering increasing resentment among individuals called upon ever more frequently by telephone solicitors. A number of states are considering legislation to limit telephone solicitation. The technique nevertheless can be the most productive available.

Telephone surveys are especially applicable where time is of the essence, as in the course of a political campaign. Weeks may be involved in the return of significant numbers of mailed questionnaires.

The telephone also can produce relatively high response rates and is less expensive than in-person interviews. Samples often are not as representative of the population as researchers prefer, however, since substantial numbers of household telephones are unlisted in many cities.

In-person interviews. Staff training and travel make in-person interviewing the most expensive of survey techniques. Necessary interview appointments often are difficult to arrange and strangers are unwelcome in many homes.

Some researchers have attempted to reduce costs by interviewing during business and professional meetings but this technique assumes those in attendance are representative of the group involved.

Unless the assumption is valid, as seldom is the case, data will be unreliable. Those who attend such meetings, as Wilcox and his colleagues (1986) pointed out, usually are the more successful and affluent in any given business or profession.

Data Analysis and Reporting

Most survey data today are analyzed by computer. Capabilities of microcomputers and the extensive range of software available permit an increasing number of analyses to be handled using these tools. They are especially helpful in public relations practice in that resulting tabular material can be combined with report texts and illustrations written or prepared on the same computer.

Where repetitive studies are involved, as often is the case in measuring the results of public relations programs, the value of computer applications compounds. Comparable data from each of a set of surveys can be examined for trend analysis, compounding the value of individual research efforts.

An Alternative Technique

A relative newcomer to the research component of public relations is the so-called public issue study. It involves organizational sponsorship of formal research by an independent agency in an area of interest to the organization in which a public issue is emerging. The effort thus is in part research and in part a component of the public relations programs.

Public issue studies, as Finn and Harrity (1984) have pointed out, can be used as a basis for comprehensive public relations programs or to meet single problem situations. The Miller Brewing Company's *Miller Lite Report on American Attitudes Toward Sports, 1983* is exemplary of the public issue study. A study of economic progress and environmental protection sponsored by The Continental Group, Inc., is another example of the genre. The organization is active in packaging, energy, and forest products as well as insurance.

IN SUMMARY

Research and knowledge-building processes applicable in public relations practice focus first on environments and individual practitioners. Professional knowledge and skill coupled with environmental overviews create the foundation for a knowledge structure necessary to successful practice.

Informal and formal research then are applied to generate data necessary for planning, create organizational early warning systems, build consensus on strategies, and develop benchmark data for program evaluation and organizational progress.

Informal research involves exploring all available sources of information applicable to specific problems. Sources range from organizational materials and published reports to advisory panels, focus groups, and statistics originating in the organization and its industry.

Information gathered through such sources often leads to internal or external audits of stakeholder groups. They are used to provide information to improve communication programs, elaborate problems or opportunities, or evaluate organizational strengths and weaknesses. They may be combined with formal research but more often lead to subsequent research efforts. They differ from formal research in that participants are not selected by chance and results are more subjective than objective.

Formal research can be categorized as primary or secondary. The former "breaks new ground" to obtain previously unknown information or data. The latter involves reexamining existing bodies of knowledge applicable to the problem or issue at hand.

Information used in secondary research comes from a variety of sources. Published information obtained from the Bureau of the Census is perhaps most frequently used. Multiple state, regional, and national governmental and quasi-governmental agencies compile and make available extensive data as well. University research centers and libraries also are extensively used. In more recent years, computer utilities and data bases have grown in number and quality as well as accessibility and are used with increasing frequency.

Consultant organizations also can be called upon for information from their private data bases. Some also offer shared-cost research; studies are conducted for multiple clients at costs lower than those that would be involved in individual efforts.

Completing the spectrum of research methodologies is primary research, an eight-part process involving problem identification, developing research objectives, identifying constituent groups and survey respondents, qualitative research to define problems, questionnaire development, information-gathering, data analysis, and report preparation.

Sampling technique and questionnaire content are the two most sensitive components in the process. Samples must be representative of populations involved and questions must be designed to induce objective responses. Surveys then can be undertaken by mail, telephone, or in person.

ADDITIONAL READING

Finn, Peter, and Mary-Kay Harrity. "Research." In Bill Cantor, *Inside Public Relations: Experts in Action*, Chester Burger, ed. New York: Longman, 1984.

Phillips, Charles S. *Secrets of Successful Public Relations*. Englewood Cliffs, N.J.:
    Prentice-Hall, 1985.
Wilcox, Dennis L., Phillip H. Ault, and Warren K. Agee. *Public Relations: Strategies
    and Tactics*. New York: Harper & Row, 1986.

5

Missions, Goals, and Objectives

Programming in public relations is an exercise in logic. It follows a well-charted path that begins with organizational philosophies and mission statements. Every component of the public relations process must be consonant with these statements of organizational values.

From philosophies and mission statements, the process proceeds to goals and objectives in three areas. First are organizational goals and objectives the public relations program must support. Second are the goals and objectives of organizational subunits, primarily divisions and departments. These enhance practitioner insight into the short- and long-range aims of the organization and permit development of an effective and optimally productive public relations program. Finally, programmers turn to the public relations unit to establish its goals and objectives.

PROCESS PERSPECTIVES

The process in one sense applies, in another parallels, and in still another extends a decades-old concept advanced by management theorist Peter F. Drucker: management by objective (MBO). Drucker conceived and George F. Odiorne popularized refocusing management from process to outcome or objective. Norman R. Nager and T. Harrell Allen (1984) more recently applied the MBO concept to the public relations process.

The concept is merely a systematic approach to managing an organization, a program, or a project. It applies in public relations programming in two contexts. It defines the role of the public relations department or consultancy in meeting employer or client objectives and it provides a logical framework for public relations programs and processes.

MBO casts public relations as a vehicle through which organizations accomplish predetermined objectives. The department and/or consultancy and its several activities are organized and developed to achieve specific outcomes that in turn will be supportive of the organization in achieving its objectives. The objectives of the public relations effort thus are derived from those of the organization.

They create a cohesive program through which all effort is directed toward producing predetermined results that will contribute to achieving organizational goals. They concurrently involve management in the public relations process, create an active rather than a reactive approach to public relations programming, and induce greater efficiency through improved programming.

DEFINING OBJECTIVES

Effective application of management by objectives, or management by objectives and results, to public relations programming assumes compliance with two prerequisites. First, organizational mission statements, goals, and objectives must be in place. No public relations program can be optimally productive in the absence of clear organizational direction. Second, public relations practitioners must have "done their homework." A solid informational base created through information gathering and research is essential.

Most organizations have written statements of purpose, goals, and objectives. Purposes are specified in mission statements, which are usually freely distributed. Goals and objectives are another matter. They often contain information that must be kept confidential for competitive or other reasons, but they must be available to public relations practitioners.

Where goals and objectives have not previously been defined, public relations professionals should assume responsibility for creating them—at least to the extent necessary to permit developing an effective public relations program. Planning necessary to success in public relations requires no less. Efforts launched in the absence of careful planning are predestined to be wasteful. In the long term, they threaten the personal and professional welfare of public relations practitioners as well as the economic health of organizations.

Mission Statements

Organizations usually address several subjects in their statements of mission or purpose. Organizational values usually are clearly stated. Attitudes toward stakeholder groups frequently are expressed. The organization's definition of public or social responsibility increasingly is included and some specific issues may be addressed as well. The latter most frequently entail organizational attitudes toward government, environmental matters, and the like.

Statements of social or public responsibility and any others that focus on obligations to stakeholder groups are especially important to public relations practitioners. Several factors are involved.

First, organizations are expected to conduct themselves in keeping with the spirit and letter of such statements. Failure to follow through can can create inestimable damage. Performance must follow organizational commitment. Performance or commitment must be changed where these conditions do not exist.

Second, performance must be communicated to stakeholder groups involved. The public relations organization inevitably will be responsible for the communication function. Public relations objectives, goals, programming, and funding thus relate to any communication need implied or implicit in mission statements.

Third, philosophies and attitudes expressed in mission statements should be reflected in organizational behavior and messages. Consistency is vital to credibility, an increasingly scarce and highly valued organizational attribute in contemporary society. Public relations practitioners have an obligation to clients or employers and to themselves to preserve organizational integrity by avoiding any real or perceived conflict between philosophy and performance. The organization's principles must be accurately reflected in programs they devise and messages they transmit.

Statements of mission or philosophy should not be confused with organizational purposes. The latter are general statements of the role of the organization in society. They reflect the expectations of society rather than the intentions of managers. The mission statement, in contrast, differentiates between an organization and others that serve the same purposes.

MBO Plans

More valuable to public relations practitioners than organizational mission or philosophical statements are copies of management by objectives plans. Statements of goals and objectives are especially helpful. Well-designed, they provide specific information as to what the organization seeks to accomplish for the ensuing year and in the longer term.

In larger organizations, these documents often are prepared on divisional and departmental as well as organizational levels. All should be obtained and carefully reviewed by public relations practitioners. Even relatively insignificant statements can signal substantive public relations needs.

A goal calling for reduction of an organizational work force to a predetermined level by attrition, for example, should result in a plan to exploit the affirmative aspects and negate potential problems. Since such plans imply increased profitability, they are of considerable interest in the financial community, where they influence perceived market value of corporate securities. They also create potential difficulties, however, in terms of employee morale and community relations. Early detailed disclosure to all involved is preferable to rumors and media leakages that otherwise almost inevitably result.

Absence of divisional or departmental mission statements, goals, and objectives should be met in the same manner prescribed for the organization as a whole. Public relations practitioners should assist managers involved in developing them. Offers of assistance seldom are refused or ignored since they benefit managers involved as well as organizations and their public relations programs.

Goals and Objectives

Complete sets of organizational, divisional, and departmental goals and objectives constitute points of beginning for public relations programming. The process starts with an analysis of documents involved to produce detailed responses to a series of questions.

1. What actions or activities will be necessary on the part of those involved in implementing plans to achieve stated objectives?
2. What perceptions, negative or positive, might the actions or activities engender on the part of stakeholder groups?
3. What will be the real impact of organizational actions or activities on those groups?
4. What further organizational action may be necessary or appropriate to protect the interests of stakeholders in light of existing plans?
5. What communication efforts will be necessary to guard against misunderstandings and/or gain optimum salutary response to anticipated actions/activities?

Multiple benefits flow from such analyses for organizations, managers, public relations practitioners, and stakeholders. Perhaps most important among them is expansion of the knowledge base vital to public relations programming. Information as to what is happening and what is going to happen within the organization is essential to successful public relations practice. It equips practitioners to design comprehensive programs, minimizes potential for unpleasant surprises, and enables those involved to more easily deal with the day-to-day problems that inevitably arise.

Equally important, ability to develop and maintain comprehensive overviews of organizations better equips practitioners for their counselor roles. It permits them to best serve as organizational consciences; to speak as ombudsmen for diverse constituent groups; and to alert senior managers preoccupied with "more important matters" to unanticipated consequences that may arise from seemingly logical and rational management decisions.

The value of the comprehensive overview can be readily seen, for example, in the case suggested above: a reduction in manpower by attrition. Planned reductions in one division or department can produce adverse reactions unless properly communicated. If communicators also are aware that they will be more than offset by the sum of planned work force increases in other divisions, what might have been difficult circumstances can be turned to organizational advantage. Early announcements can address the sum of the year's anticipated work force changes, generating media exposure focused on net increases rather than isolated declines in numbers of jobs.

Total access to organizational information in these and other ways enhances the efficiency of the public relations operation and equips practitioners to best serve their organizations and stakeholder groups. It inevitably produces a superior public relations program.

Public Relations Objectives

Many if not most public relations objectives are derived from the mission statements, goals, and objectives of the organization or its operating components. The remaining few, however, may be the more significant among them.

Public relations objectives can and do extend beyond operational objectives, especially where public issues are involved and the organization needs political understanding and support. These conditions can best be illustrated through the case of a hospital in a large Southern medical center confronted by highly competitive circumstances as well as the endemic health care cost problems of the mid–1980s.

A hospital problem. The hospital ranked second in size among four not-for-profit general acute-care institutions in a city that also maintained a large governmentally funded hospital. Medicare cost controls had reduced patient flows and competition had compounded. In addition, government was seeking to avoid tax increases to fund needed indigent care. Politicians were calling on the not-for-profit hospitals to assume a greater portion of the indigent care burden.

The situation was rendered doubly complex by other factors. Neither community residents nor physicians perceived one hospital as superior to another in virtually any context. All of them already were bearing relatively heavy economic burdens as a result of Medicare compensation shortfalls, bad debts, and indigent care. Each was being forced into more "cost shifting," a process by which rates for paying patients were raised to compensate for losses in other areas. Since the elderly are the largest consumers of health care services, the cost shifting was creating the equivalent of a tax on old age.

An effective solution. All of the hospitals involved were absorbing considerable public abuse at the hands of politicians until one heeded the advice of an experienced public relations counselor:

Stop reacting and start acting. Challenge the politicians to come to grips with the underlying health care issues rather than levy a tax on old age. Demand that they address the indigent care entitlement issue first as a matter of policy and then through an equitable funding mechanism.

Then, to attack the competitive problem, start issuing "honest" bills to your patients. Don't charge $1.50 for two aspirin when everyone knows they're for sale at drugstores for pennies. Charge what you have to for rooms and nursing service and price everything else on the basis of cost. Add a markup for overhead. Then add further markups for Medicare funding shortfalls, bad debts, and indigent care. Let your patients and their families see the problem for themselves.

You'll have the first honest hospital billing system in the country, a windfall of media exposure, and a separate identity in the community in short order.

General versus Specific

The approach defined above is exemplary of the manner in which public relations can respond to general rather than specific organizational needs. Practitioners often are far better positioned than senior managers to develop such initiatives in that they tend to be "in the organization" rather than "of the organization." They are better able to view client and employer problems and needs from nontraditional perspectives.

Their development of public relations goals and objectives as a result should proceed from three bases. One consists of organizational, divisional, and departmental goals and objectives as discussed above. The second involves prevailing community and industry problems with which the organization is involved. The third consists of responsibilities and role definitions assigned by the organization.

DEVELOPING GOALS AND OBJECTIVES

Public relations roles and responsibilities vary from one organization to another. In some, the function is housed in a unified communication unit that may deal with advertising and marketing as well as public relations. In others, these are separate operating entities. In still others, employee communication is housed in a separate unit. Coordination between and among the several functions is necessary in any event and should extend to their several planning processes. In most organizations, public relations responsibilities include:

1. Collecting and analyzing information concerning the organization and its stakeholder groups and making recommendations to management in this context.

2. Coordinating organizational activities involving those groups.

3. Serving as a central information source and distribution point; disseminating information on request and in keeping with organizational goals and objectives.

4. Planning and implementing informational programs to fulfill these responsibilities.

Developing Goals

The general statements contained in definitions of roles and responsibilities serve to define the broad areas in which public relations programs are to function. They necessarily are general and nonspecific. They constitute general guidelines, however, within which goals and objectives can be constructed.

The developmental process progresses from broad to narrow. Goals are more specific than responsibilities; less specific than objectives. Goals provide general direction for the public relations program. In the hospital case described above they might have included:

1. Moving from a defensive to an offensive posture in the governmental relations area.
2. Establishing a clear identity for the hospital in the community.
3. Gaining the support of senior citizen groups, patients, prospective patients, and other constituencies.
4. Encouraging a rational community response to indigents' need for adequate health care.

Listing goals and objectives is necessary but not sufficient to the public relations programmer. They also must be examined in context with their importance and with resources available in order that priorities can be established and difficult budget decisions made.

Priority/resource reviews are advisable at every step in the programming process. Without them, programmers tend to drift away from a time-honored guideline: Do only as much as you can do well with the resources at hand. Spreading available resources over every program component that might in any way benefit the organization often deprives all of them, regardless of priority, of the means to produce tangible results. Resources that might have engendered significant benefits if concentrated in fewer areas thus may be wasted.

Specifying Objectives

While goals provide general direction, objectives specify outcomes that programs then must be designed to accomplish. Appropriately stated, they meet several criteria:

1. Community of interest between the organization and one or more stakeholder groups must be implicit.
2. Outcomes must be tangible and measurable.
3. Target dates must be established.

4. Results must be achievable within limitations imposed by resources or other practical constraints.
5. Anticipated benefits and costs must be clearly stated.

Public relations objectives may be exclusive to the public relations department or counselor, as in the hospital case discussed above, or shared
with other organizational units. Given public relations' concern with multiple
constituencies, the latter circumstance is more often the case. In almost any
organization they might include:

1. Reducing employee absenteeism, tardiness, and turnover 5 percent by improving
   employee morale, thus engendering lower labor costs and higher profits.
2. Increasing consumption of the organization's products or services 2 percent by
   educating consumers concerning the benefits involved, thus improving profitability.
3. Encouraging personnel to prepare for promotion through increased use of educational benefit programs, thus reducing turnover and lowering costs.

Among publicly owned corporations, improved perception in the financial
community and among shareholders would be equally likely objectives. Reduced per capita consumption in the interests of conservation would be an
appropriate objective for public utilities. In each case, all of the basic conditions
and operational criteria for public relations objectives would have been met.

STAKEHOLDER GROUPS

Before proceeding to develop programs and plans based on goals and
objectives, practitioners must pause to attack what has become one of the
most difficult of public relations problems: defining stakeholder groups. Two
primary strategies are used in this process. One, a relatively simplistic approach, involves sorting groups into three categories: primary, intervening,
and special. Those most significant in terms of the public relations problem
at hand then are selected as priority groups. The second requires examination
of demographic and psychographic characteristics as well and produces enhanced insight into group composition. The two approaches are best applied
sequentially for optimum results.

Types of Stakeholders

Stakeholders involved in any issue can be sorted into three basic categories
from which those most important to the organization then can be selected.
The categories are primary, intervening, and special interest.

Primary groups are those directly impacted by organizational action or
activities. Intervening groups are those that can influence primary groups but
are not directly involved in the problem at hand. Special interest groups for

the most part are membership organizations dedicated to self-interest or some public interest.

Were a manufacturing plant experiencing difficulties in meeting emission control requirements established by the Environmental Protection Agency, for example, and thus in danger of being closed, groups involved might be defined briefly as follows:

- Primary: Owners, employees, customers, vendors, legislators and regulators, and those proximate to the plant and potentially impacted by emissions.
- Intervening: Media, other opinion leaders such as clergymen and educators, and health-related organizations.
- Special: Environmentalist groups such as the Sierra Club as well as labor unions active in the plant, neighborhood associations proximate to the plant, and so on.

Stakeholder Analysis

Listing these groups is readily accomplished. Defining them in terms sufficiently precise to permit productive programming and planning is another matter. Stakeholders are those groups of individuals whose interests coincide in one or more ways with the organization with which the public relations practitioner is dealing. Exhaustive stakeholder lists can be compiled, as indicated above, only in context with specific organizations and individual public relations problems. Lists will vary in composition to an extent that otherwise precludes complete listings.

Most organizational stakeholder lists would include owners or shareholders, employees, prospective employees, managers, consumers, prospective consumers, vendors, and communities. In individual circumstances, members of the financial, governmental, media, and other communities are added.

These and other groups can best be enumerated through a relatively simple technique involving listing groups and then subgroups (excluding the general or "nonpublic"). After completing a gross listing along the lines described above, primary groups should be broken down into subgroups.

Employee subgroups. Employees, for example, can be sorted by race, sex, age, location, occupation, shift, department, and a host of other criteria. Members of the financial community can be subdivided into current stockholders, potential stockholders, institutions, brokers, and security analysts. They can be further sorted by size, location, influence, and still other factors.

The next step in the stakeholder definition process is crucial: relisting in order of importance. Resources are limited and virtually no public relations budget will permit programs of a magnitude adequate to address every group regardless of importance. Most practitioners concentrate resources on the relatively few key audiences involved in any situation.

Two further steps are necessary after key audiences have been defined.

leaders must be identified. Key audiences then must be reex-
final time to determine the extent to which overlap may exist.
f *influence.* Opinion leaders or gatekeepers can make the differ-
en success and failure in any public relations effort. Their implied
endorsements can influence the inclinations or decisions of limitless
others. a minor extent, the media often play a gatekeeper role. They
seldom influence audience decisions but play a major part in establishing
issue agendas.

Audience overlap is an important element in public relations planning due
to potential message conflict, real or perceived. Organizations necessarily take
a "best foot forward" approach to communication, which often leads to
apparent conflict. Statements to employees concerning limitations on wage
increases due to financial problems, for example, can conflict with more
optimistic annual report statements to shareholders. Neither need be untruth-
ful, although this appearance well may arise among employees who also are
shareholders and thus are exposed to both messages.

Only when primary stakeholder groups have been selected, overlaps identified, and demographic characteristics established can public relations practitioners safely proceed to programming and planning. Public relations
activities, the components of plans, must conform to limitations imposed by
all of these factors.

PROGRAMS AND PLANS

Goals and objectives are not an end in themselves. They are but another
step in a series that progressively defines public relations practices in narrower
and more detailed terms. Following goals and objectives in that progression
are programs and plans. Programs are sets of plans designed to achieve one
or more objectives.

The term "program" has become distorted over time. It has been attached
to the overall public relations effort as well as to audience-specific programming. Employee relations programs, customer relations programs, and financial relations programs, for example, are common terms and usually are
appropriately applied. They deal with sets of plans, each of which may involve
multiple public relations activities.

Programs in essence are designed to achieve objectives. Plans are components of programs. Each consists of a set of activities. An organization's
employee relations program, for example, logically would address objectives
dealing with recruitment and retention.

Defining Terms

Employee relations objectives might involve attracting better-qualified ap-
plicants, improving employee retention rates, and reducing absenteeism and

tardiness. The recruiting program then might include plans for displays at professional meetings and on-campus recruiting efforts. Recruiting activities then would would encompass developing displays, audiovisuals and literature, scheduling meeting appearances and campus trips, and the like.

Financial public relations objectives, in similar manner, might include attracting new shareholders, inducing enlarged holdings on the part of existing shareholders, and achieving greater recognition in the financial community. Plans then would be established to influence each constituent group. Activities amenable to inclusion in a financial community recognition plan then might encompass presentations to financial analysts, calls on financial media editors, preparation and distribution of news releases and other informational materials, and the like.

Objectives thus are addressed through programs that may consist of any number of plans, each involving one or more public relations activities.

Types of Plans

Public relations plans and activities fall into three general categories: single-use, standing, and ongoing. Programs, in contrast, almost invariably are ongoing other than where change occurs in basic organizational goals and objectives.

Financial public relations programs may be instituted or terminated as companies "go public" or "go private." Vendor relations programs may begin and end where organizations turn from manufacturing to services or the reverse.

Single-use plans are applied in most organizations in celebrating an anniversary, introducing a new product or service, or opening a new plant. Organizations may open multiple plants or introduce several products or services over time but plans usually are specific to the events involved.

Standing plans, in contrast, are standardized for application in situations that occur infrequently if ever. Disaster, proxy fight plans, and similar contingency plans of all kinds fall into this category. They are detailed descriptions of sets of activities designed to provide organizational guidance in circumstances that can create sudden and imperative demands on the public relations organizations.

Ongoing plans, as the name implies, cover sets of activities that are continuing in nature. Staffing plans, distribution plans, and production plans are examples of this category. In public relations, most components of employee relations, vendor relations, and financial public relations programs would qualify. In the former area, for example, ongoing plans would govern newsletter production schedules, service awards systems, and the like.

PITFALLS AND CONSTRAINTS

Several dangers exist in public relations programming; they arise in two areas. One is the program itself, which may be overly rigid or overly flexible. The other involves multiple social constraints and intervening factors that can require programmatic adjustments.

Flexibility and Rigidity

Where public relations programs are overly rigid, practitioners are denied the ability to take advantage of opportunity; to capitalize on external intervening events that offer significant benefits.

Unexpected availability of a celebrity to speak at a testimonial dinner, for example, should not be ignored because the circumstances were not anticipated in the plan. Neither should a planned attack on a political candidate be executed after he or she has had the misfortune to make a damaging misstatement during a major speech. The attack would merely detract from preexisting embarrassment and perhaps breathe new life into the candidate's supporters.

At the other extreme, overly flexible programs may become so burdened with externally suggested "bells and whistles" they resemble and function with the flair of ocean-going tugboats rather than 12-meter yachts. Programs that produce optimum results concentrate resources in optimally exploiting the few plans and activities that promise greatest potential return. A few well-placed rifle shots usually are more effective than an awkwardly managed machine gun.

Programmatic Constraints

Organizational policy, ethical and legal limitations, sociocultural norms, and other factors all can limit programming decisions in public relations. In practice, these elements frequently combine to constrain practitioners.

Most senior managers follow codes of business conduct. They range from self-imposed requirements for gentlemanly conduct to such ethical constraints as prohibitions against profiting from the misfortunes of competitors. More often than not, those who observe such codes also bar colleagues' entry into so-called gray areas in which ethics bar what laws may allow.

Sociocultural norms also may intervene in programming. Most often, they induce organizations to eschew conduct in conflict with the mores and folkways of any group. In some cases, such standards have been incorporated into organizational cultures or policies.

A Persistent Problem

One other contingent problem occurs frequently in programming and other components of the public relations process: a tendency on the part of practitioners to become "caught up" in individual process components to the neglect of primary goals and objectives.

Goals, objectives, programs, plans, and activities are not ends unto themselves. Each is a component of a process organized to produce optimum results. The ultimate objective is the behavior or attitudinal change toward which the effort is directed.

Practitioners nevertheless tend to become enthralled by the components. Those of a creative bent come to value writing and design more than outcomes. The more mechanistic as readily can become preoccupied with programming or planning for their own sakes.

A broader perspective is necessary, especially on the part of those charged with producing programmatic results. Every aspect of the process is important but practitioners' overriding concerns must be with message recipients and the extent to which they receive, assimilate, and act upon content.

IN SUMMARY

Programming in public relations is most readily accomplished through application of management by objective techniques. They were originated by Peter F. Drucker, popularized by George F. Odiorne, and first applied to public relations practice by Norman R. Nager and T. Harrell Allen.

Management by objectives or by results, as some prefer, takes the public relations programmer through a logical series of steps based on the purposes, goals, and objectives of organizations they represent. Organizational purposes usually are elaborated in mission or philosophical statements, which in most cases define what the organization "stands for."

Such statements often define the organization's concept of social responsibility. Stakeholder groups and obligations that the organization accepts as to each of them may be spelled out in considerable detail. Public relations programming necessarily must be consonant with such statements. Conflict or dissonance will undermine organizational credibility.

Having assimilated available mission or philosophy statements, public relations practitioners then must turn to goals and objectives in three areas. The first of them deal with the organization, the second with its divisions and departments, and the third with the public relations program.

The first two provide considerable guidance in public relations programming. They specify not only the longer-term (goals) but the short-term (objectives) aims of the organization and its several significant subdivisions. By examining these collectively, public relations practitioners gain insight into organizational priorities. These provide the basis for public relations programming.

Analysis of organizational goals and objectives and those of their operational units enables practitioners to develop supporting goals and objectives for the public relations unit. Some, especially where aggressive strategies are adopted, will be independent of organizational goals and strategies. Others are shared with the organization as a whole or with specific operating units, usually marketing, advertising, sales promotion, and human resources departments.

When goals and objectives have been established, lists of stakeholder groups should be associated with each. Special attention should be paid to opinion leader or "gatekeeper" groups within each set of stakeholders. Seldom, if ever, do adequate resources exist to target all stakeholders in a proposed public relations program.

Programs then are developed based on goals and objectives. Typically, there are employee relations, financial relations, media relations, and similar programs. Each consists of a set of plans that in turn consists of a set of activities. Plans specify the nature of the messages and channels of communication to be used in the program. Activities specify details as to implementation.

Plans may be categorized as ongoing, standing, and single-use. Publication of an employee newsletter is ongoing. Most disaster and emergency plans are in the standing category. Those covering open houses and plant dedications would fall in the latter category.

All activities must be structured in keeping with a lengthy set of constraints ranging from legal and ethical to those imposed as a matter of business practice or otherwise by organizational executives.

ADDITIONAL READING

Aronoff, Craig E., and Otis W. Baskin. *Public Relations: The Profession and the Practice.* St. Paul: West, 1983.

Cantor, Bill. *Inside Public Relations: Experts in Action.* Chester Burger, ed. New York: Longman, 1984.

Crable, Richard E., and Steven L. Vibbert. *Public Relations as Communication Management.* Edina, Minn.: Bellwether, 1986.

Cutlip, Scott M., Allen H. Center, and Glen M. Broom. *Effective Public Relations,* 6th ed. Englewood Cliffs, N.J.: Prentice-Hall, 1985.

Dunn, S. Watson. *Public Relations: A Contemporary Approach.* Homewood, Ill.: Irwin, 1986.

Nager, Norman R., and T. Harrell Allen. *Public Relations Management by Objectives.* New York: Longman, 1984.

Newsom, Doug, and Alan Scott. *This Is PR: The Realities of Public Relations,* 3rd ed. Belmont, Calif.: Wadsworth, 1985.

Nolte, Lawrence W. *Fundamentals of Public Relations: Professional Guidelines, Concepts and Integrations*, 2nd ed. New York: Pergamon, 1979.
Simon, Raymond. *Public Relations: Concepts and Practices*, 3rd ed. New York: John Wiley, 1984.

6

Plans and Activities

Developing goals and objectives in public relations is a straightforward process. Planning and developing public relations activities is more complex. Stakeholder groups identified and preliminarily characterized during earlier phases of the programming process must be delineated with excruciating detail to insure success. The process also requires that commmunication channels be specified, another demanding process that relates directly to stakeholder specifications.

DEMASSIFICATION AND FRAGMENTATION

Criticality in both sectors arises from a process identified by Alvin Toffler. He called it "demassification," the process through which a relatively homogenous national population was and is fragmenting into a host of special interest groups. A more appropriate term especially applicable to communication channels is "fragmentation." It applies particularly to audience fragmentation among the media.

Demassification

The process Toffler called "demassification" has been progressing in the United States for several decades. Many historians trace its origins to the early days of the Vietnam conflict, which produced several chasms in the body politic. Division of the national population into pro and anti-Vietnam factions was the more obvious split. A parallel generational fracture developed as well, separating those who followed "my country, right or wrong," from a younger generation demanding political and governmental change.

Divisive issues. Foundations for other divisive issues also took shape during this period and multiple special interest groups formed around them. The civil rights, gay liberation, women's, antinuclear, gray power, and other "movements" took form and gained momentum. There soon followed abortion and right-to-life groups and many others. Allegiances changed in each case. Individuals became committed primarily to specific issues rather than to the nation's basic tenets.

Political change. The process was paralleled in the Congress of the United States, where party allegiance became secondary to several "caucuses" that formed around narrow issues. Here, as in the nation as a whole, primary commitments shifted from a set of national values to narrow viewpoints on specific issues.

Values and life-styles. "God, motherhood, and the flag" in essence became secondary in the minds of many to school prayer, abortion, and nuclear weapons. The national consensus on values was changing and individuals increasingly were attracted to militant groups that aggressively expressed their positions on single issues. Unanimity as to life-style also rapidly was being replaced by diversity. So-called nuclear households consisting of male wage earner, nonworking spouse, and children were becoming anachronistic. By the mid–1980s they no longer constituted a majority in the United States.

The typical "middle class" family instead consisted of a single mother and two children, or an unmarried couple who didn't want children. Children being born in the United States had a 60 percent chance of being reared through at least one separation. The family was earning a smaller income and, most importantly, was suffering from a vanishing sense of community.

Sociologists call this process "desocialization," suggesting that society no longer imposes a common mold; that values and life-styles are continuing to fragment. Some suggest the fragmentation process will continue, perhaps accelerating as a result of proliferation among the media—especially cable television and magazines.

Mass communication helped create many of the commonalties that held the middle class together, they contend. Stereotypical situations portrayed by network television broadcasts in the 1960s and 1970s played a major role in the process. These and other media now portray a diversity of life-styles and values and audience fragmentation is further diminishing the cohesiveness to which they once contributed.

Media Audience Fragmentation

The very words "mass media" threaten to become an oxymoron, a term composed of conflicting words. They less and less can be considered channels of mass communication reaching large percentages of any specific audience.

The fragmentation process began immediately after World War II and has progressed at an accelerating pace. The starting point was the introduction of television, which at the outset captured significant portions of radio and newspaper audiences. Radio recovered but newspaper readership continued to decline, especially with the introduction of cable television and the video-cassette recorder.

Further change. A parallel change occurred in magazine publishing. The leading mass magazines of earlier years, from *Life, Look,* and the *Saturday Evening Post* to *Colliers, Pageant,* and a host of others disappeared. They were replaced by burgeoning numbers of narrowly focused publications serving the several special interest groups listed above and many others.

Most recently, there appeared the computer and the electronic data bases. They increasingly are becoming major sources of information, especially among professionals and students. They also are starting to play a role in mass merchandising, banking, and many other areas involving information exchange.

Fragmented audiences. The result necessarily is a highly fragmented public in terms of media. Economic logic and casual observation both demonstrate this outcome. Given that every individual is limited by time and economic resources in the pursuit of information, every new medium that succeeds essentially chips away at the total number of minutes and dollars devoted to others.

Observers of the media scene in most major metropolitan areas have seen local newspapers decline. They doubtless have been supplanted in part by electronic media catering to a population less oriented to reading. There also have appeared, however, "national newspapers" that have captured portions of local newspaper readerships. The *Wall Street Journal,* the *New York Times,* and *USA Today* are predominant among them.

Practice implications. Public relations practitioners thus are faced more with special interests than mass audiences. Specific groups, other than in terms of issues of truly national interest, seldom can be reached with any semblance of efficiency through mass media. Channels of communication therefore must be selected with greater care than earlier was the case. Mass media generally are less appropriate. Special interest media usually are more efficient. And specialized channels are taking positions of increasing importance in public relations practice. They often prove far superior in producing desired results.

PLANS AND GROUPS

Plans in public relations encompass sets of activities designed to convey information to specific groups to produce predetermined results. Activities contained in plans must be appropriate to groups involved. Appropriateness is a function of several factors. Preeminent among them are types of objective(s) involved, relationships of groups to objectives, and the nature of the groups.

Achieving objectives in public relations may involve changing realities, perceptions, or both. Relationships between objectives and groups vary with strength or level of interest or involvement. The nature of groups is determined in large part by demographic and sociographic factors.

Public Relations Objectives

Several perspectives of public relations objectives are essential to the planning process. The first involves the source of the problem at hand. Is it perceptual or substantive? In other words, does it arise out of perception or reality? Must the organization act to improve performance before communicating, or will communication suffice to resolve a misunderstanding? If action must precede communication, management commitment is necessary before planning can proceed.

Second is the nature of the problem at hand. Organizational managers frequently confuse problems with symptoms. Excessive absenteeism and tardiness, for example, are symptoms of morale problems. Underlying causes most often involve middle managers and supervisors in the department or other operational unit involved. Morale problems also can be triggered, however, by working conditions, rumors of organizational disaster, and the like.

Practitioners have an obligation to employers and clients to examine all problem sources and recommend appropriate research and analysis to assure that public relations programs focus on problems rather than symptoms. Practitioner reputations are at stake as well.

Third is the nature of the public relations objective(s). Is the plan to be designed merely to inform or to produce behavioral change? What levels of belief must be modified to clear the way for the desired response? Inducing change in superficial beliefs, such as those involving the best brand of deodorant, is accomplished with relative ease. Change in basic beliefs is quite another matter.

Groups and Objectives

Relative level of group interest in issues also is a determinant of problem complexity. Those with the most to gain or lose in given situations tend to be more receptive to communication than those only marginally involved. Extent or magnitude of self-interest, in other words, may facilitate or discourage communication.

Another concept that may be helpful in evaluating potential group responsiveness is "proximity." Those closest to a problem are most responsive. In a rezoning dispute, for example, owners of nearest properties are inclined to be most involved. Where rewards are involved, those who would receive them most rapidly or in greatest amounts are disposed accordingly.

Nature of Groups

Perhaps most important in the planning process are the demographic and psychographic characteristics of groups. These factors should guide public relations practitioners in developing a community of interest and in message synthesis as well as in planning.

Age, sex, race, educational level, and economic level are among demographic factors of primary interest to public relations practitioners. They serve as predictors of individual and group reaction to specific issues. They also are indicators of individual and group responsiveness to specific public relations activities of which plans are constituted.

Psychographics. Psychographic factors are more complex. The PRIZM System developed by Claritas, for example, goes beyond Arnold Mitchell's *The Nine American Lifestyles: Who We Are and Where We Are Going* (1983). It encompasses 12 social groups composed of 40 clusters. "Educated, Affluent Executives and Professionals in Elite Metro Suburbs," for example, are subdivided into "Blue Blood Estates," "Money & Brains," and "Furs & Station Wagons." "Educated, Young, Mobile Families in Exurban Satellites & Boom Towns" similarly are composed of "God's Country," "New Homesteaders" and "Towns & Gowns."

Where significant numbers of stakeholder group members fall into such categories, their levels of concern over specific issues and their responses to organizational initiatives can be predicted with considerable accuracy. As a National Geographic Society (NGS) study demonstrated in 1987, however, attributing characteristics to relatively broad groups can be risky.

Categories and subcategories. The NGS study dealt with Americans interested in outdoor recreation, a descriptive but still broad category. The research showed significant differences among five subgroups: Get Away Actives, Excitement-Seeking Competitives, Health Conscious Sociables, Fitness-Drivens, and the Unstressed and Unmotivated.

Their responses to a municipal proposal to develop recreational facilities would vary with group members. So would their response to organizational efforts to install what have come to be called "wellness" programs.

Availability of psychographic data as to specific public relations problems is limited. Demographic data usually are more readily obtainable from organizational or Bureau of the Census records. In general, the greater the knowledge public relations practitioners have of the stakeholder groups with which they deal, the more likely they are to develop plans and activities most appropriate to organizational goals and objectives.

COMPONENTS OF PLANS

Public relations activities of which plans are constituted occur in several types. The more traditional among them consist largely of communication in one of several forms. A second group can be described as events. They range from traditional open houses and plant tours to fund-raising galas and telethons.

A third category consists of moral and ethical acts undertaken by organizations in the interests of others. Pregnant employees may be banned from one area of a plant, for example, when statistical data suggest that a portion of the manufacturing process may be hazardous to their unborn infants. New emission control devices may be quickly and voluntarily installed when wastes are identified as toxic.

Social responsibility. Yet another category includes activities undertaken by organizations in the discharge of social responsibilities. These range from donations to educational institutions to funding neighborhood rehabilitation projects in areas adjacent to organizations' plants or offices. This listing necessarily is incomplete; however, it demonstrates that public relations activities extend far beyond communication. Action followed by communication often is most effective among public relations activities. It is not, however, without risk.

The risks are not overly great but nevertheless they exist. They have been demonstrated by those who claim corporate philanthropy is potentially or directly self-serving. Most organizational activity necessarily involves self-interest. No organization can fulfill social responsibilities without creating an element of benefit for itself either coincidentally or by design.

Mutual interest. There was indeed an element of truth in former General Motors executive Charles Wilson's much maligned statement that "what's good for General Motors is good for the country." The same holds in organizational activities. Critics miss a key point. The mutual interests that encourage social responsibility and form the basis for success in public relations necessarily run in two directions.

TYPES OF ACTIVITIES

The nature of activities selected for inclusion in public relations programs is generated by several factors. Most important are the nature of audiences involved and the type(s) of problem(s) or need(s) the activities are expected to address. With these elements established, a more complex set of criteria comes into play. Time, cost, level of control, and speed of feedback usually are critical but other elements also must be considered. These include historical patterns of communication between organizations and stakeholder groups, past successes and failures in communication, and prevailing levels of credibility.

Most communication activities can be readily categorized. They first divide into interpersonal and mediated communication. The interpersonal range from conversations between individuals to speeches delivered to large audiences. They also include what might be termed a specialized category:

communication by education. Mediated communications generally fall into print or electronic categories although some hybrids and "nonmedia" activities do exist. Within mediated categories, communication can be further subdivided as controlled or uncontrolled.

Controlled print media include brochures, pamphlets, and leaflets of all kinds; direct mail; annual and quarterly reports; newsletters and similar publications; statement stuffers and catalogs; letters and memoranda; manuals and handbooks; and the content of bulletin boards, billboards, and trade shows and print advertising.

Uncontrolled print media include news releases and fact sheets distributed to the mass media; feature releases to trade publications, and the like.

Controlled electronic media include audiovisual presentations of all kinds; telecommunications via telephone, satellite, and computer; organizationally produced television programming for closed circuit, cable, or public access channels; and electronic advertising.

The so-called hybrids involve two categories. In one are combinations of print and electronic activities. In the other are presentations to civic clubs or similar organizations that often include highly controlled audiovisual presentations and difficult-to-control question and answer sessions. "Nonmedia" activities range from special events, including open houses, plant tours, and anniversary celebrations, to sponsorship of athletic events, concerts, and other functions.

INTERPERSONAL ACTIVITIES

Virtually every practitioner long involved in public relations can recall hearing a client or employer remark: "If only I could sit down and talk with them individually, . . . " These words attest to a principle often neglected: Virtually every activity undertaken in public relations is a substitute for interpersonal communication.

Mediated communication, the transfer of thoughts and ideas through impersonal media, necessarily is less efficient and more prone to breakdown. Only in interpersonal communication are messages accompanied by gestures, facial expressions, and other "body language." They provide immediate "feedback," permit instant clarification and elaboration, and otherwise benefit both parties.

Enhanced relationships. Enhanced personal relationships are perhaps the greatest of the intangible benefits. Personal contact is increasingly valued by most individuals in an ever more computerized, automated, and otherwise mechanized world. A greater sense of organizational caring and humanity is perceived by those who are party to interpersonal communication. This is the very essence of "managing by walking around."

Interpersonal activities include meetings of all kinds with all types of individuals. They are designed to create opportunities for interchange of information. Within organizations, they also are intended to reduce hierarchical separation and traditional compartmentalization among component groups.

Many organizations today maintain multiple advisory groups to enhance communication between management and organizational constituencies. The degree to which such arrangements have proliferated is most readily seen in the employee relations sector. Abolition of private dining rooms for upper echelons most often is cited as evidence of the trend involved but many organizations go considerably further. Meetings between employees and senior managers are becoming scheduled with increasing frequency and for almost any reason.

Techniques applied. A financial services organization, for example, until recently brought rank-and-file personnel together with executives only on an annual basis for awards luncheons. The organization now conducts two awards luncheons annually. They are supplemented by monthly meetings of senior executives with small groups of employees selected at random from throughout the organization. Several annual picnics have been added. So have regular luncheons among those at all levels who participate in the firm's quality circle program.

Organizational executives acknowledge that these programs have been developed to enhance communication but deny that they have reached the "overkill" stage. "We continue to grow," one of them pointed out, "and the numbers of employees with whom our executives are regularly in contact is proportionately no greater than before."

An even more aggressive posture in employee communication has been adopted by the Federal Express Corporation. The organization's managers' manual prescribes at least monthly meetings with all subordinates. Results, including all questions raised, must be summarized for senior managers. Their responses subsequently must be conveyed to those who raised questions. Federal also mandates managerial assistance for employees in performance improvement and establishes employee communication as a primary responsibility for every manager.

COMMUNICATION BY EDUCATION

The same principles are being applied by increasing numbers of organizations in communicating with external groups, especially in the financial and sales areas. Traveling "dog and pony shows" for financial analysts long have been a feature of public relations practice. These efforts of late have been expanded to include news media "briefings" following analyst presentations.

Of more recent vintage are educational programs designed to expose organizational products, services, and personnel to prospective customers in a "helping" atmosphere. Manufacturers of Armstrong steam traps, for example, offer one- and two-day "schools" for trap users through their distributors. The programs have proven productive for users, who learn how best to apply these devices. The manufacturer and distributors concurrently spend considerable time selling while educating.

Even more organizations work with trade and professional groups by providing educational or professional development programs to their mutual benefit. Instructors and educational materials are provided at little or no cost. Associations generate revenue by charging nominal fees to members, and organizations reap benefits in the form of goodwill and sales contacts.

These circumstances create significant implications for public relations practice, especially in light of audience fragmentation among uncontrolled media. Mediated communication historically has been a cost-efficient substitute for interpersonal communication. As fragmentation erodes cost-efficiency factors, interpersonal communication becomes relatively less costly. For as long as the process continues, it also will be increasingly worthy of consideration in public relations programming.

PRINT ACTIVITIES

"Print activities" encompass a wide range of communication vehicles, controlled and uncontrolled. The controlled include publications of all kinds, brochures and leaflets, books and monographs, letters and memoranda, statement stuffers and coupons, and a host of miscellaneous items ranging from table tents to door hangers. The uncontrolled include traditional news releases as well as magazine and trade journal feature articles. All vary in effectiveness with the circumstances in which they are applied. Major concerns in their selection and development include cost and time factors, both of which vary with complexity.

Uncontrolled Print

While traditional mass media news releases continue to be used extensively in public relations practice, they arguably are less prevalent than earlier was the case. Two factors appear to be contributing to the decline. First, relatively few organizational issues or problems are national in scope and impact. Second, the efficacy of mass media in reaching national audiences has been declining.

Use of news and feature releases to reach narrower audiences, on the other hand, appears to be increasing. Numbers of audience-specific publications, especially trade, professional, and special interest magazines, have been proliferating. Most are receptive to material generated by public relations practitioners that meets editorial criteria.

Magazine content, to a greater extent than newspaper articles, also is amenable to reuse in reprint form. Many magazines make reprints available at nominal cost. They make inexpensive and authoritative substitutes for traditional merchandising literature.

Newspapers and, to a lesser degree, magazines occasionally will make use of fact sheets, biographical sketches, organizational histories, and similar material. These often are provided in media kits in conjunction with news releases. Larger organizations typically maintain up-to-date biographical sketches, complete with photos, concerning officers, directors, and key personnel.

Both magazines and newspapers make extensive use of "product" news releases of interest to their readers. They may deal with services as well as products and are most commonly used by newspapers in food, fashion, and travel pages as well as special sections. The latter focus on such subjects as gardening, do-it-yourself, and other seasonal activities of interest to advertisers. Business, professional, and special interest publications also use material appropriate to the interests of their readers.

Controlled Print

Organizational publications arguably are the single most popular controlled activity in the print sector. Most organizations of any size publish periodicals to convey information to employees, customers or clients, and others. They vary in size, frequency, sophistication, and cost.

At the "glossier" end of the scale are customer publications distributed by Mercedes-Benz of North America, private aircraft manufacturers, and other producers and distributors of "high ticket" merchandise. At the other extreme are mimeographed and spirit-duplicated newsletters distributed to organizational employees.

Process color and other costly production techniques are routine at one extreme and seldom seen at the other. More sophisticated production techniques tend to become more common as circulation increases. Additional costs involved are concentrated in preprinting stages and decline rapidly on a "per copy" basis as press runs increase. Many if not most publications are issued from 4 to 12 times annually in 4 to 12 pages ranging in size from 8 ½ × 11 to 11 × 17.

Brochures and booklets. Virtually no limits can rationally be applied to the range of sizes and levels of sophistication commonly used in what are termed brochures and booklets. They range from leaflets consisting of a single 8 ½ × 11 sheet to full-blown catalogs. Catalogs have become increasingly popular in recent years with the growth of mail-order organizations offering products ranging from clothing to hardware. Quarterly and monthly catalogs are common.

Other material used in direct mail solicitations—the financial reports of publicly owned companies and the "statement stuffers" used extensively by retailers in their statements to customers—also are part of the "brochure and leaflet" category.

Books and monographs. While often unrecognized as such, books and monographs have been increasingly popular in public relations. Books developed in large part for public relations purposes are most frequently seen in two contexts. Many are "written" by aspirants to public office, usually appearing during the early stages of political campaigns. Others often are published in conjunction with the "major" anniversaries of large corporations, detailing their development over 50, 75, or 100 years.

Monographs or "minibooks" often contain speeches of public figures or, occasionally, convey expanded versions of a particularly successful speech or presentation. Some also have been published by organizations in tribute to retiring founders or others. The latter often appear to be the corporation's equivalent of a gold watch.

Other items. A near limitless number of other printed materials often are used in public relations. They range from simple business announcements and invitations to letters and memoranda. They include table tents in restaurants and cafeterias, door hangers, personnel manuals and handbooks, calendars, and virtually any other item that conveys a message. As in the case of other controlled and uncontrolled channels of communication, each is appropriate in specific circumstances.

ELECTRONIC ACTIVITIES

Other than in educational applications, electronic-based activities in public relations follow the print pattern. They fall for the most part into uncontrolled and controlled categories although some worthwhile hybrid applications exist. "Hybrid" here refers to activities in which essentially identical material is used in multiple communication applications, as subsequently will be discussed.

Uncontrolled Electronic

The content of uncontrolled electronic media parallels that of uncontrolled print media. It includes electronic news releases and feature material prepared for radio or television and disseminated in recorded form. "Feature" material in this category, however, also may include live or taped appearances on radio or television. In recent years this category also has included "print" material stored in computers and made accessible to the media and others.

Use of electronic news and feature releases, especially for television, has increased in recent years with the advent of videotape and satellite technology. Unlike film, which remains in use to a limited extent, videotape is readily prepared and edited, reducing costs as well as delays in distribution.

Recent development of multiple electronic distribution services further accelerated the trend toward increased use of electronic material. The services in question use satellites as well as conventional distribution systems to deliver broadcast-quality material to multiple outlets.

Opportunities for in-person appearances on radio and television, especially the latter, have increased with the advent of cable systems. With two Cable New Network channels as well as local access programming, these systems have become insatiable consumers of information. Multiple programs cater to the interests of businessmen, home owners, cooks, gardeners, and the like.

Controlled Electronic

The technological advances that produced increase use of uncontrolled electronic media are creating varying but more dramatic changes in the controlled sector. The variation arises out of differences in application. "In-house" applications in organizational communication and employee training have increased explosively. External use of videotape technology has been limited to some extent due to availability of playback equipment.

Organizations can insure availability of necessary equipment for on-premises use. Where videotape is intended for off-premises application, users often find appropriate playback equipment unavailable. Rental or "bring your own" become the only alternatives. The former is expensive, the latter cumbersome.

These circumstances, which are changing relatively slowly, encourage continued use of slide/tape presentations where transportable equipment is required. Presentations to civic clubs and similar organizations that often meet in hotels and motels generally fall in this category.

Use of motion pictures in public relations has declined as a percentage of the audiovisual mix in percentage if not absolute terms. The medium remains applicable in some situations, especially in the educational sector, where motion picture projectors have not been wholly replaced with videocassette player/recorders. Almost total replacement eventually can be expected, however, which may render the motion picture obsolete other than in traditional theaters.

"HYBRID" ACTIVITIES

Many contemporary public relations activities involve producing material amenable to multiple applications. Productivity of practitioner efforts often is compounded in the process. This is the case whether communication originates in interpersonal, electronic, or print form. Multiple use of original material is the key to enhanced productivity. Results inevitably improve where this principle is applied.

Print-Based Hybrids

Perhaps most often used among hybrids in contemporary practice is the direct mail or promotional literature item that originated as a magazine article.

Newspaper material is used occasionally but magazine articles are favored by practitioners.

Two factors contribute to their preferences. First, magazine material usually is more complete and better illustrated. Second, magazines, unlike newspapers, often provide reprints at low cost. Most involve reproduction of the magazine's front page on the face of a four-page leaflet with the article reproduced on the remaining pages. Publisher charges for these reprints often are as low as $50 to $100 per thousand copies since they are assumed to benefit the magazine as well as the user.

Benefits from the user standpoint extend beyond cost, although reprints are much less expensive than comparable promotional literature. Users benefit from magazine editors' implied endorsement. Reprints also are amenable to multiple applications. Many are used as direct mail literature. Others are distributed by sales personnel. Still more are distributed as "hand-outs" at trade and professional meetings and conventions.

Electronic-Based Hybrids

Several techniques are used in developing hybrid electronic activities. Many if not most involve repetitive use of audiovisual presentation components.

These applications are common in organizations equipped with videotape equipment used in employee communication, training, and other applications. Segments of tapes produced for such purposes, for example, often appear in electronic versions of annual reports. Electronic annual reports similarly are often modified for internal consumption.

The same process applies in developing material for sales meetings, trade and business show applications, financial analysts' meetings, and the like. Once on videotape, visual and aural components can be reused separately or together.

Videotape sound tracks occasionally are transcribed onto audio tape for extended distribution. This device is used more frequently, however, to gain enhanced exposure for executives' verbal presentations in a variety of forums. Speeches may be taped "live" or given for recording purposes before or after principal presentations.

The same approach often is used in sales training and professional development programs, especially where organizations function at geographically diverse locations. High travel costs for such meetings then are eliminated. Teleconferencing or videoconferencing may be used where information must be conveyed to all recipients simultaneously. Taping otherwise is usually adequate. Teleconferences and videoconferences may be preserved on tape for reuse as well.

More and more organizations are maintaining videotape libraries to permit repetitive use of taped material and maintain more extensive historical records than was earlier possible. Audio segments often must be rewritten and re-

recorded but costs of resulting products are significantly lower than those that would be involved in developing new material.

Interpersonal-Based Hybrids

Small group meetings with rank and file employees have joined "management by walking around" as a favored communication technique among senior managers. These and other meetings are recorded with increasing frequency where groups involved do not find recording equipment obtrusive. Their content joins officers' speeches and other events as content for distribution through print or electronic channels.

Where speeches are involved, hybrids can originate in print, interpersonal, or electronic form. The beginning point for the distribution process, in other words, may be executives' typewritten, verbal, or audiovisual presentations. Each can be readily transformed into the other formats.

This approach has become especially favored where executive speeches are concerned. They often are distributed to the news media shortly in advance of or immediately after presentation in either printed or electronic form. Where content is deemed appropriate, they also may be printed in booklet or brochure format for further distribution over an extended period of time.

Distribution lists increasingly include leading academics who write the bulk of the textbooks in use in any discipline. Organizations find exposure in texts desirable for recruiting and marketing purposes. Where speeches and other materials are reproduced for media or other purposes, college and university faculty members often are added to mailing lists.

OTHER HYBRIDS

Many other public relations activities once were categorized as special events. They have become so diverse, however, as to make the term obsolete. Trade shows, open houses, anniversary celebrations, and demonstrations all conform to the earlier definition. In recent years banks have sponsored Neighborhood Watch and child safety programs; hospitals have sponsored communitywide health fairs; and business firms have combined their efforts to further commercial and industrial development.

Self-interest continues to motivate such activities but linkages between organizational objectives and individual projects have become less and less direct. Typical hospital-sponsored health fairs, for example, involve virtually every health-related organization in a community other than competing hospitals. Volunteer agencies such as disease-oriented charities, health departments, and blood banks almost invariably participate. So do groups dedicated to stamping out illicit drugs, preventing teenage suicides, and helping runaways.

The breadth and communitywide appeal of such events also encourages applying other communication tools. Advertising specialties ranging from balloons to wearing apparel—especially tee shirts, sweat bands, and the like—are used extensively. This general category also includes planning kits and similar material designed to be helpful to recipients in their businesses. The Weyerhaeuser Company, for example, long has provided paper samples printed in multiple colors to those in advertising and public relations to demonstrate the use of their products. Billboards and bus cards are used to announce events and honor winners. Media attention frequently is engaged by recruiting a major newspaper or television station as cosponsor, compounding exposure before, during, and after events.

Old devices are being dusted off and refurbished and new technologies are being applied to produce further support. Speakers' bureaus, telephone networks, and employee "hot lines" spread news of special events. Computer bulletin boards and business marquees add to the din of messages. Collectively, they add considerably to what once was a minor component of public relations activity.

IN SUMMARY

Developing plans and activities in public relations practice is a more complex process than that used in establishing goals and objectives. It requires that stakeholder groups be precisely delineated and appropriate communication channels be specified.

These processes are complicated by what Alvin Toffler called demassification. Fragmentation or desocialization might be even better terms. They refer to a progressive deterioration in social cohesiveness in the United States, which arguably has been in progress since the Vietnam War years.

This process has been accompanied by continuing fragmentation in media audiences, which began with the introduction of television subsequent to World War II. Television viewing options and magazines have steadily increased in number since then. Increasing numbers of channels and publications cater to special interest groups. Daily newspapers have declined in number and market penetration although some more or less national newspapers have come into being.

These circumstances make practitioners' tasks more difficult. The public relations plans they develop must assure delivery of predetermined messages through selected media to precisely delineated audiences. Each plan consists of a set of activities, all of them aimed at influencing a specific group or groups.

Plan development is guided by goals and objectives. The process requires attention to the nature of the problem at hand, real or perceptual; the level of involvement of the group(s) involved; and the nature of those groups. Demographic and psychographic characteristics are especially helpful in providing insight into the nature of groups and guiding development of messages and selection of activities.

Activities traditionally have involved communication. In contemporary practice, they increasingly involve organizational action prior to communication. Perceptual problems may be solved by communication. Where reality must be changed, action must precede communication. In either event, community of interest must be established.

Communication activities can be classified as controlled and uncontrolled within several basic categories. These include interpersonal, print, electronic, and "hybrid," the latter involving either a combination of categories or alternative techniques.

Uncontrolled activities include print and electronic news releases, feature material, and similar devices through which senders lack complete control over the form and shape of messages ultimately delivered. Controlled activities include brochures and other literature in the print area and audiovisual presentations in the electronic sector. Content control is wholly in practitioners' hands in both cases.

Interpersonal activities include individual and small group communication in any of several forms. They include "management by walking around," small group meetings, and individual counseling. Communication by education falls largely in the interpersonal category. It involves providing information in which constituent groups are interested in order to attract them to interpersonal communication settings.

"Hybrid" activities largely consist of those in which messages are reprocessed or repackaged for multiple uses. They include reprints of published magazine releases used in seminar or sales settings as well as speeches recirculated in printed or taped form. They also include more elaborate versions of what once were considered "special events." These include community health fairs and similar "multimedia" extravaganzas that have outgrown the historical special event category.

Hybrid activities frequently include use of "specialties," ranging from tee shirts and product samples to complex devices such as the production planning kits prepared for use among public relations and advertising practitioners.

ADDITIONAL READING

Bryant, Barbara Everitt. "Built for Excitement." *American Demographics*, March 1987.
Mitchell, Arnold. *The Nine American Lifestyles: Who We Are and Where We Are Going.* New York: Macmillan, 1983.

7

Messages and Media

The word "activity" in public relations is used in two senses. It can refer to actions taken by organizations in meeting obligations to and engendering support from stakeholder groups. In a narrower sense, activities are components of the public relations process, especially message synthesis and delivery. Earlier discussions employed the word all-inclusively. Here it refers to message synthesis and delivery.

To be received and acted upon, messages must appeal to recipients' interests and be delivered through media to which they are exposed. The concepts are simple and straightforward. Their incorporation into public relations activities is more complex.

Successful communication activities traditionally have been based on practitioner instinct and experience. More systematic contemporary approaches to the process tend to produce greater consistency and quality in results. They are based on knowledge of several concepts. These include the processes through which individuals communicate and accept ideas, the nature of persuasion, and the principle of self-interest. While necessarily functioning concurrently, they are most readily understood when examined individually.

ESSENTIAL INSIGHTS

The concepts specified above are best applied in light of two simple principles. First, communication is controlled by the receiver. Decisions to turn a television set on or off, to buy or not buy a newspaper, to read or discard a piece of sales literature all illustrate this point. Second, patterns of self-interest are in a constant state of change. The ebb and flow of multiple needs govern level of interest and the mental "filters" with which individuals control the deluge of messages directed toward them.

Consider, for example, as simple a product as automobile tires. Individuals' interest in tires varies with their condition. As one's tires show wear and need for replacement mounts, interest in tires and receptivity to messages about tires increases. Both continue to mount until a purchase decision is made and then decline precipitously. If the new tires function satisfactorily, interest in tires and receptivity to tire messages remain low until the wear again prompts concern over replacement.

Self-Interest

Self-interest and receptiveness thus are a function of need, real or perceived. In the case of the tires just mentioned, perceived lack of reliability could induce a sense of need before wear progresses to a point at which replacements are needed. More important, interest and receptiveness are functions of relative need. Individual behavior is governed by the sum of multiple needs of varying intensity. The strongest at any given moment are granted highest priorities and produce greatest receptivity to pertinent messages. Human needs, in order of strength, were categorized by Abraham Maslow as follows.

1. Physiological: food, air, water, shelter, sleep, sex
2. Safety: freedom from danger and fear
3. Social: interpersonal relationships and group activity
4. Ego: status and respect
5. Self-actualization: being the best that one can be

Maslow's concept is more complex than it appears. All of the needs he specified exist at all times. They vary only in relative strength. Social and ego needs tend to become dominant as physiological and safety needs are satisfied but the latter never are wholly absent. In addition, individuals do not necessarily progress logically from one need level to another. Physical or social deterioration in once stable neighborhoods, for example, can produce intensifying levels of concern over safety. Loss of a job inevitably produces greater concern over physiological needs.

Attitude, Opinion, and Belief

Operating in concert with varying needs as filters of incoming messages are individual opinion, attitude, and belief. They also vary in nature and intensity among individuals but fluctuate little over time. Self-concept and individually imposed barriers to communication (see Chapter 2) significantly limit potential for change, especially as to attitude and belief.

Belief is the strongest of the three elements. Individual beliefs arise out of environments and experience and are most resistant to change. Attitudes, or predispositions to think in certain ways, most often reflect group norms and thus are more flexible. Opinion, at the opposite extreme, is fleeting and subject to sudden change.

Opinion is readily influenced by events. Acceptability of Tylenol as a headache remedy, for example, fluctuated radically during the early 1980s. The product was quite acceptable prior to a cyanide poisoning scare, which caused it to be equally unacceptable. Acceptability returned virtually to the original level when the manufacturer intervened with tamper-resistant packaging.

Attitude toward work in the United States, in comparison, required decades to change perceptibly. The Protestant ethic that governed when colonists settled the new world prevailed through much of the ensuing century. Only in recent years has it been recognized as no longer prevalent in domestic society.

Beliefs are still more intransigent. Centuries were required to convince the bulk of the world's population that the earth's surface was spherical rather than flat. Similarly, significant numbers of individuals today remain to be convinced that man actually reached the moon in the twentieth century.

The Adoption Process

Changing human needs and beliefs thus underlie the manner in which individuals handle new concepts or ideas: the adoption process. It consists of five steps or phases during which information sources vary in credibility and the messages they convey vary in receptivity. Stages in the process and pertinent information sources are shown in Figure 7.1.

The Persuasion Process

Public relations practitioners must determine how best to induce desired responses among organizations' stakeholder groups in light of the nature of humans and the adoption process. Multiple alternatives are available, all of which have succeeded in some circumstances.

Persuasion alternatively has been viewed as a learning process, a power process, and an emotional process. Each concept has been and continues to be used in salesmanship. Computers largely are sold through teaching/learning processes. Aluminum-siding salespersons tend to employ the power process while those who sell insurance often seek to engage the emotions of their prospects.

Pragmatically, these techniques tend to be used in combination rather than separately. Those involved are apt to apply one or more of five designs for

Figure 7.1. Adapted from Herbert F. Lionberger, *Adoption of New Ideas and Practices* (Ames: Iowa University Press, 1960), and E. A. Wilkening, "The Communication of Ideas on Innovation in Agriculture," in *Studies in Innovation and Communication to the Public* (Stanford, Calif.: Institute for Communications Research, 1962).

```
                    Variation in Message Source Credibility
                         During the Adoption Process

        Process Stage                          Ranking of Sources
                                                   by Credibility

                               Awareness

Individual learns of                    1. Mass media
existence of idea or                    2. Friends and neighbors
practice but has                        3. Professional/business
little knowledge of                        agencies/organizations
it.                                     4. Dealers/salespeople

                                Interest

Interest in idea                        1. Mass media
develops; more                          2. Friends and neighbors
information sought;                     3. Professional/business
idea considered on                         agencies/organizations
merit.                                  4. Dealers/salespeople
The Adoption Process

                               Evaluation

Idea mentally applied;                  1. Friends and neighbors
weighed on merits                       2. Professional/business
for use in individual                      agencies/organizations
situation.  More                        3. Dealers/salespeople
information obtained                    4. Mass media
and trial planned.

                                 Trial

Idea or practice                        1. Friends and neighbors
applied, usually on                     2. Professional/business
small scale.  Interest                     agencies/organizations
focuses on techniques,                  3. Dealers/salespeople
application conditions                  4. Mass media

                               Adoption

Idea adopted if                         1. Friends/neighbors
proven acceptable.                      2. Professional/business
Experience most                            agencies/organizations
important factor                        3. Mass media
in continued use.                       4. Dealers/salespeople
------------------------------------------------------------------
```

persuasion delineated by Otto Lerbinger in 1972: stimulus-response, cognitive, motivational, social, and personality.

Stimulus-response: The mechanism involved in the stimulus-response technique is readily grasped through two examples: efforts by eating places to induce greater consumption and budget-conscious food shoppers' efforts to resist. Restaurants use "color psychology" to enhance sales, decorating in warm shades which psychologists believe encourage appetite. They also decorate tables with bottles of wine and menus with photos of desserts. The stimulus-response approach may function reasonably well in such circumstances. Photos of cold beer in ice-filled containers similarly may help sell the product in hot weather. The stimulus-response concept is unlikely, however, to produce desired reactions where complex issues are involved.

Cognitive: Logic and reason are assumed to govern individual behavior by those who use the cognitive approach. They expect audience members to assimilate information and come to appropriate conclusions. Desired results on occasion are attained but universally desirable outcomes will not necessarily be achieved. Those interested in faster automobiles, for example, can be convinced by data as to horsepower and gear ratios only if they already are equipped with sufficient knowledge to cope with relatively technical information. Mechanics probably would respond affirmatively but the information might fail to impress housewives, even where speed was their objective.

Motivational: The motivational approach arguably is most frequently used in public relations and relates directly to Maslow's hierarchy of needs. It also embodies the "community of needs" approach, which suggests ideas are most readily accepted and acted upon where desired actions satisfy perceived needs of message recipients as well as those of senders. Successful use of motivational appeals requires practitioner understanding of groups with which they are concerned. Only through careful examination of demographic and psychographic variables can primary or dominant needs be identified and appropriate motivational elements be introduced into messages.

Social: Group membership rather than individual need is the focal point of the social approach to motivation. Practitioners look to group backgrounds, social classes, and behavioral norms for motivational elements to be incorporated into messages. This approach is most readily seen in television commercials, where products are displayed in environments in which viewers presumably would like to see themselves. Cadillacs are shown being operated by the affluent in front of country clubs, while Jeeps are driven by outdoorsmen in rugged terrain. Desire among audience members to emulate either actors or individuals they portray is expected to produce desired motivation.

Personality: Individual personalities necessarily govern response to messages and media of all kinds. Arguments that tend to produce desired results among emotional individuals, for example, probably would be less successful among the unemotional. Unfortunately, such personality characteristics virtually never are uniform across large groups. Since public relations practice deals primarily with groups, appeals that address personality characteristics infrequently prove productive.

Steps in Persuasion

With all of these perspectives in mind, practitioners are relatively well-equipped to address message development and media selection. These steps must be undertaken, however, in keeping with the nature of the process through which information is assimilated. Most who have studied the process suggest five steps are involved: reception, consideration, comprehension, assimilation, and response. The concepts involved are readily understood.

Reception: Ideas must be received in order to be considered. Those who fail to read newspapers, watch television news, or otherwise "tune in" the media or channels through which messages are delivered are unlikely to receive them. The public relations practitioner's first concern thus must be messa ge delivery.

Consideration: The fact that the radio or television set is on can not be taken as evidence that information transmitted is received and considered. Many television commercials never are received. The mayor of New York expressed concern before the 1987 Superbowl football game, for example, over a possible sudden decline in city water pressure during half time. He assumed a large portion of the television audience at that time would head for their bathrooms and flush toilets. They also would be missing commercials then being broadcast. Those who remained at their television sets also may have been otherwise occupied. Messages thus would have been denied the attention and consideration they require for assimilation.

Comprehension: Language becomes the predominant factor in determining comprehension where message delivery is achieved. Too technical language, verbiage oriented to high educational levels, and similar barriers prevent comprehension even where messages are received and recipient interest is preliminarily engaged. The problem probably is best characterized by a very old joke concerning a plumber who had developed a new way to clean pipes. He attempted repeatedly to communicate his "invention" to a federal agency that, only after several long letters in "governmentalese," responded in comprehensible fashion: "don't use hydrochloric acid. It eats h—l out of the pipes."

Assimilation: The assimilation factor involves a simple question: will the individual who receives and comprehends a message retain it long enough to act on it? Human tendency to forget, in fact, is at the root of repetitive advertising. Advertisers require more than message acceptance. Content must be retained until the time of purchase arrives. The process fails where housewives forget brand names and package designs before arriving at the detergent shelves in the grocery store.

Response: Even where efforts to persuade succeed, unforeseen results may thwart the persuader. Consider, for example, the football fan who sees a commercial about a new imported sports car. The message well may induce him to go shopping for cars but his wife and four children may cause him to buy a domestic station wagon rather than the two seater that infected him with "new car fever."

THE COMMUNICATION PROCESS

Each of the factors described above is a potential obstacle to completion of the communication process. All must be overcome if the communicator is to succeed. The process involves a sender, a message, a channel, a receiver, and an effect. All must function in keeping with communicator intent to produce desired results. And all are at least equally prone to malfunction.

Sources

Sources exert considerable influence over the extent to which message content is accepted and acted upon. Variables among sources include credibility, identity, and power.

Credibility: Credibility involves two factors: believability and objectivity. The former includes receiver perceptions of sender knowledge levels as well as truthfulness. The latter involves the extent to which senders' motivations are perceived as potentially influencing their statements. Those perceived as honest but lacking adequate knowledge tend not to be believed; nor are those who have an economic or other interest in seeing that messages are accepted.

Identity: Individuals are susceptible to influence by peers and/or those who are liked or respected. This principle is exemplified in advertisers' selection of television or motion picture personalities as spokespersons for their products. It also is seen in the extent to which entertainers have been identified with national political campaigns in recent years. Identity also plays a role as public relations practitioners seek out "centers of influence" to espouse their points of view. The ideological positions of officeholders and members of the clergy, for example, may add to message acceptance on the part of those who share their views.

Power: In some instances, as in superior-subordinate relationships within an organization, power may lead to message acceptance and subsequent action. It is equally likely, however, to lead to action without conviction, or to results contrary to those desired. A superior may successfully influence an employee's purchase of a domestic rather than an imported auto in the face of contrary preferences. This result would be especially likely where the organization involved was in competition with imported products. A recommendation from a boss might produce exactly the opposite result, however, were he to seek to convince an employee to vote for a political candidate.

All three of these factors require attention as public relations practitioners approach the necessarily complex process of message design.

Messages

Several variables beyond the audience characteristics discussed above must be addressed in message design and synthesis. Scope of content, sequence, and conclusions are predominant among them.

Scope of content. Messages may be balanced or unbalanced in content. They may address one side of an issue or both. Other than in rare circumstances, some balance is essential. It may involve merely touching on and responding to significant points that might be made by opponents. It is necessary, however, to avoid the appearance of total bias.

On occasion, practitioners encounter situations in which friendly audiences are disposed to accept "one side of the story." Neglect of "the other side" even in these circumstances is inadvisable. Audience members later may be

Public Relations Programming & Production

faced with contrary views, prompting them to question original senders' credibility.

Where issues are dormant, questions also arise as to whether they should be addressed or "triggered" on the one hand or ignored on the other. The latter approach may be tempting but often is inadvisable. Those who first raise issues gain a significant advantage from a public opinion standpoint.

Experienced practitioners suggest that the "early advantage" coupled with presentation of a weak "other side" creates optimum results.

Sequence. The case for "affirmative first" versus "negative first" or "good news first" versus "bad news first" is another matter. The sequence-of-presentation issue has been argued and researched at length without clear resolution.

Many successful practitioners suggest what might be described as a "sandwich approach" in which clients' or employers' positions are first presented in brief but strong terms. Opposing viewpoints then are advanced even more briefly with each followed by strong rebuttal. In some cases, rebuttal need be nothing more than a sentence raising a question as to the validity of the opposing point. The sequence then becomes positive-negative-positive.

Conclusions. Individuals who draw their own conclusions from a set of facts have been found to cling to them more tenaciously than otherwise is the case. Not everyone, however, will come to the same conclusion. Most public relations practitioners take these circumstances as an adequate basis for building explicit rather than implied conclusions into issue-related messages.

Exceptions arise, as in the case of hostile, defensive, or exceptionally intelligent audiences. Implicit conclusions in the first instances may produce nothing but resentment. In the latter they may be considered insulting. Where these conditions prevail, the best approach may involve no conclusions at all. Instead, a series of questions, each addressing one of the key points on the other side of the issue, may be most effective. "Given A, B and C, can D be valid?"

The extent to which emotional appeals should be used also is open to question. Fear, hate, and love are intense emotions that, once unleashed, are difficult if not impossible to control. When employed as motivators in group rather than individual situations, they also may trigger diverse responses. Patriotism and other emotions may be employed more effectively. Most practitioners seek to blend emotion and logic but exercise caution to avoid unanticipated consequences.

Many other factors enter into message synthesis. Clarity of verbiage, brevity of expression, and good use of language are but a few of them. Writing methods, however, are beyond the scope of this text. More significant here are techniques necessary to selection of communication channels.

MEDIA SELECTION

Other than message synthesis, no public relations process today is more complex than media selection. Fragmentation in society and media audiences primarily is responsible, and both processes continue. They demand that practitioners avoid any tendency to permit habit or personal preference to become involved in selection processes. They must be focused in their entirety on audience(s) involved and media through which they best can be reached.

"Best" in these circumstances is a somewhat difficult term to define. Multiple variables among media as well as audiences and messages must be considered in determining what is "best" in any situation. Variation in audiences and messages were addressed earlier. Primary among media variables are degree of personalization, audience penetration levels, costs involved, and time required. Prospective gatekeeper perception of proposed messages also is a significant factor in dealing with uncontrolled media.

Degree of Personalization

Interpersonal media are most effective in terms of personalization. There is no substitute for face-to-face communication between senders and receivers of messages. Variation nevertheless exists even in this category. One-on-one encounters create the greatest potential for effective communication. They often are impractical, however, due to the size and geographic distribution of the stakeholder group involved.

Meetings. Where relatively small groups are involved, group meetings may be substituted for one-on-one communication. A degree of personalization often can be maintained even where larger groups are involved, but cost then becomes a concern as well.

Many publicly held corporations periodically fly groups of senior executives to major financial centers to make presentations to financial analysts and others. Such meetings and the interpersonal contacts they create are superior to distribution of information in other forms. They also are extremely expensive in executive time and travel costs.

The time of managers and supervisors also is expensive in organizations such as the Federal Express Corporation, which makes employee communication a primary managerial/supervisory responsibility at all levels. The value of personal interchanges in these organizations is deemed worthy of the costs involved.

Other barriers. Other limitations exist as well. Financial analysts may be willing to attend meetings reasonably proximate to their offices. Employees have little choice but to participate during working hours. Other groups are not as accessible.

Small groups of employees at far-flung sites can create difficulties. Some others, such as prospective customers or prospective employees, cannot be identified. Still others, such as existing customers or vendors, in most cases would be disinclined to grant the time or accept the expense involved. In these and other situations, substitutes must be used.

Other techniques. Some degree of personalization can be perpetuated with substitute techniques. Live teleconferences and videoconferences permit verbal or verbal and visual interchanges across great distances but, in the latter case, at tremendous costs. Federal Express spends millions annually in preparing and staging a virtually worldwide employee videoconference.

An element of personal attention also is provided in individual telephone calls, letters, and cards. Beyond this point, however, alternatives involve mediated communication; delivery of messages through impersonal means.

Audience Penetration

By audience penetration is meant the "reach" of a particular channel of communication; the percentage of the total stakeholder group that reasonably can be expected to receive a message transmitted through the medium at hand. Other than in small organizations where handfuls of employees readily can be gathered together, virtually no channel will reach 100 percent of a stakeholder group.

In larger organizations, some inevitably will be ill, on vacation, out of town, or otherwise inaccessible. Where organizations operate around the clock, seven days a week, as in the case of hospitals, the problem is even more complex. On-site communication audits in such organizations frequently are carried out around the clock over three days to obtain maximum participation. They nevertheless fall short of 100 percent.

Problems compound. The problem is compounded, as in interpersonal communication, where multiple sites are involved. Communication audits usually have the longest "reach," delivering messages to larger percentages of stakeholder groups involved than any other. Virtually all other channels deliver messages to significantly smaller percentages of target audiences.

This principle applies to virtually every medium other than personal telephone calls. Memoranda and letters often are lost in the mail or go unread. Organizational newsletters are less thoroughly examined than personal mail. Bulletin boards frequently are ignored.

Efficiency deteriorates. The efficiency of communication channels deteriorates rapidly where objectives require that messages be delivered to groups less readily contacted than employees. Customers and clients may or may not read first class mail and other mail material is even less well read. They may or may not read business or professional journals regularly. Only a small percentage attends trade or professional meetings and significant numbers of those fail to visit displays and exhibits.

Extensive exposure through multiple mass media might create superior response, but most public relations problems are not of a magnitude to engender such exposure. Johnson & Johnson's Tylenol problem and the Coca Cola Bottling Company's "new Coke" difficulties are atypical. The products involved are used so extensively as to be of interest to most of the population and, therefore, to the media. Lesser usage levels necessarily create lower levels of media interest.

While no data are available, logic suggests that programs dealing with relatively narrow audiences outnumber those of national or even regional interest. Most employee relations, investor relations, and customer relations programs are in the former category. Total expenditures on such programs also may well exceed those involved in the relatively few that command or require national media attention.

These conditions collectively require that repetitive messages be delivered through channels of lesser reach. In public relations, unlike advertising, repetition is accomplished more through multiple channels than repetitive use of one or two channels. These conditions also lead to increasing use of the hybrid media discussed earlier.

Message Delivery Costs

Hybrid applications and multiple use of materials also are encouraged by developmental costs. These must be defined as including all expenses incurred in operating the public relations department as well as the consultancy. Cost, in other words, includes all labor, vendor charges, and overhead. The latter should include approximate charges for space the department uses, utilities, telephones, and all other items. As will be discussed later, these elements must be taken into account in budgeting and in determining whether use of vendors at any time may be more economical than in-house production.

Calculation techniques. Cost analyses also require careful handling in another sense. They must be calculated for individual communication efforts on the basis of stakeholder group members reached rather than total audience. Exposure on a network station's television newscast, for example, may reach hundreds of thousands of individuals. The audience is unlikely, however, to include substantial percentages of any organization's employees, shareholders, customers, or other groups. In almost any community, those whose television sets are on at any given time will be fragmented. The three network stations, at least one educational station, and dozens of channels accessible by cable or satellite dish each will attract some viewers. While cost per thousand viewers may be low, cost per thousand members of target stakeholder groups can be excessively high.

Caution necessary. This caution necessarily applies to all uncontrolled media, print and electronic. Costs per stakeholder are more readily calculated where interpersonal or controlled channels are used. Production and distribution expenses for print and electronic media are known or readily determined by combining vendor charges with in-house cost. Interpersonal communication costs also are easily determined. In most cases, they involve little more than the sum of the wages and benefits of individuals involved. Significant exceptions occur only where travel or other expenses are involved. These can be considerable, however, where organizations undertake to ferry multiple executives to major cities for meetings with financial analysts or in similar circumstances.

Time Factors

Costs in public relations must be examined in context with time factors because efforts to compress the latter almost inevitably expand the former. Production time requirements usually compound with increasing sophistication in production techniques. They can be reduced to some extent through careful planning. Beyond that point, however, they tend to increase precipitously as practitioners press for earlier-than-normal deliveries.

Printers, photographers, photoengravers, sound studio personnel, and others can be persuaded to work evenings and weekends, but only at a price. As time charges increase to time and one-half or double time, costs escalate. Perhaps more important, pressure compounds potential for errors, which require even more costly correction.

"Normal" production costs vary from one market to another and within markets. They respond to market pressures and produce more competitive bids and estimates when work is slow than otherwise is the case. Public relations practitioners thus are well advised to maintain working relationships with several vendors in each production area.

Production time requirements in any situation can best be calculated in terms of that component of the project at hand that requires the greatest volume of time. Time required to complete a project, in other words, is a function of the most time-consuming process involved. This principle applies regardless of the nature of the project, with one possible exception. Since most public relations writing is done within the organization, that process usually can be expedited by shifting organizational priorities. Other elements of production that organizations are equipped to handle internally can be expedited in like manner.

Interpersonal activities. Time requirements in preparation for interpersonal public relations activities vary with the formality of the activity. Brief small group meetings or "management by walking around" usually require little preparation and can be activated almost instantaneously. More formal presentations, especially to organizations' external stakeholder groups, are another matter.

While senior managers usually are sufficiently at ease with small, internal audiences and messages that require no preparation, they generally take an opposite approach with external and larger groups. A speech often must be written, which can require days or weeks. If audiovisual aids are to be employed, production can be even more time-consuming, especially where work involved must be performed by vendors.

Electronic activities. With one significant exception, time requirements in preparation of audiovisual materials have been reduced by the new technologies. The exception is the motion picture, which requires considerable equipment in filming as well as a great deal of time for processing, editing, and addition of sound tracks. The total process can consume a year for films that will run less than 30 minutes.

Production requirements for other audiovisual activities are considerably less demanding. Given an appropriate script, sound studios can produce audiotapes in almost any quantity in a matter of hours. Accompanying slides can be produced in little more time once film has been exposed. Photography thus becomes the primary governor of time requirements in slide-tape production with perhaps one exception: Where graphs are required, they can be generated by computer and converted to slides through the Polaroid process in a matter of minutes.

Studio videotaping and editing can be little more demanding from a time standpoint. Where equipment must be transported to other locations, time requirements increase. Time required in creating the finished product otherwise is a function of the level of sophistication required. Extensive editing and addition of special effects such as background music, titles, and fades can add considerably to total time needs.

Print activities. The term "print" today covers a multitude of techniques. They range from the time-worn mimeograph process to four-color printing with supplemental embossing, engraving, die cutting, and foil stamping. Each of the latter elements adds to time requirements.

Until recently, most printed products required a relatively rigid set of processes subsequent to copywriting. They included layout, typesetting, composition, photography, preparation of lithographic negatives, and printing. The advent of computer-based "desktop publishing" permits shortening the process in some circumstances.

In desktop publishing, the writer's original "manuscript" can be used as computer input for typesetting. Page layout then can be completed on a computer screen. Camera-ready line copy is produced by laser printer. In more sophisticated systems, negatives are produced from computer input.

Finished product quality is perceptibly reduced where less sophisticated systems are used. Results often are nevertheless acceptable for employee newsletters and printed material of similar quality levels. Total production time often can be reduced to a week or less.

Time and cost factors compound where more polished products are required. Design and layout by graphic artists can add days or weeks to the production process. The same is true where type is set from hard copy rather than electronically, and where composition is handled by mechanical artists.

Inclusion of full-color photographs requires more demanding photography as well as color separations. Where color fidelity in photo reproduction is critical, as in the case of food products, days or weeks of studio work may be required. If engraving, foil stamping, die cutting, or other sophisticated processes are used, time requirements again increase.

Total elapsed time can be collapsed to some extent through precise production scheduling. Text and photos can be prepared concurrently, although both must be available to graphic designers in preparation of layouts. Thereafter, color separations can be completed while type is being set and mechanical artwork is prepared. The total process seldom can be completed under the best of conditions, however, in much less than 60 days.

IN SUMMARY

Message design and media selection require insight into the nature of human communication. Individual receptiveness to messages is a variable function of self-interest coupled with preexisting attitudes, opinions, and beliefs.

Message acceptance and subsequent reaction are a function of the adoption process. As individuals move through awareness, interest, evaluation, trial, and adoption, they are subject to influence from several sources in varying degrees.

These concepts form a backdrop against which practitioners employ the persuasion process to gain behavioral response. Persuasion may involve one or more of several techniques. These include stimulus-response, cognition, and motivation as well as social and personality factors.

Steps involved in the process include reception, consideration, comprehension, assimilation, and response. Individuals move through them at varying speeds under the stimulus of communication. The components of communication are source, message, channel, receiver, and effect.

Public relations practitioners identify receivers and desired effects and then concentrate their efforts on the three remaining factors. Source variables include credibility, identity, and power. Messages vary with scope of content, sequencing, and nature of conclusions. They can be delivered through a multiplicity of channels.

Media are selected in keeping with several criteria. They include degree of personalization, audience penetration, message delivery costs, and time factors. These elements are interrelated and thus require concurrent attention.

Cost generally increases under time pressure. Personalization tends to reduce cost in some respects and increase it in others. The primary focus of cost is expenditure per stakeholder group member. This concept requires that practitioners avoid calculating costs on the basis of total audience.

Overall program effectiveness thus is a matter of control through media selection, budgeting, and scheduling, as will be discussed in detail in Chapter 8.

ADDITIONAL READING

Lerbinger, Otto. *Designs for Persuasive Communication*. Englewood Cliffs, N.J.: Prentice-Hall, 1972.

Newsom, Doug, and Bob Carrell. *Public Relations Writing: Form and Style*, 2nd ed. Belmont, Calif.: Wadsworth, 1986.

Pesman, Sandra. *Writing for the Media: Public Relations and the Press*. Chicago: Crain, 1983.

Walsh, Frank. *Public Relations Writer in a Computer Age*. Englewood Cliffs, N.J.: Prentice-Hall, 1986.

8

Audiences and Gatekeepers

Two factors unique to uncontrolled media require careful practitioner scrutiny during the design of public relations programs and selection of activities of which they are constituted: the nature and predispositions of media gatekeepers. Considerable time, effort, and money may be wasted unless news releases and feature material are published and broadcast.

The extent to which these products of practitioner effort will be used and induce desired audience responses is always uncertain. Levels of uncertainty can be controlled, however, where practitioners are sensitive to the nature of the media, their audiences, and their gatekeepers.

MEDIA ANALYSIS

Publication or broadcast of information by the uncontrolled media is a function of several factors. Client and employer desires and preferences are not among them. They include, instead, economic factors that control publishing and broadcasting, the nature of the gatekeepers involved, and the interests of media audiences. Each element requires attention by those who would succeed in inducing publication or broadcast of material they prepare.

Media Economics

With few exceptions, such as the Public Broadcasting System, the mass media of the United States are for-profit organizations. They exist to produce profits for their owners. Public service is a secondary or tertiary concern of their owners.

Owners' economic orientation arguably has become increasingly dominant in recent decades with the spread of broadcasting and publishing chains. More and more media once individually or family-owned by residents of communities they served have been acquired by broadcasting and publishing corporations. Their profits have grown apace. Community commitment, however, has not developed in keeping with profits.

The numbers game. Success in publishing and broadcasting is a "numbers game." The most important number, from owners' standpoints, is "the bottom line," the number of dollars of profit generated each year. The bottom line, in turn, is governed primarily by advertising revenues and expenses, especially the former.

Advertising revenues are audience-driven. The greater the newspaper's readership or the brodcast outlet's audience, the higher are the advertising rates the owners can charge. The primary function of news content in these circumstances is to attract as large a readership or audience as possible.

The latter factor is critical to a public relations practitioner in assessing media receptivity to news or feature release content. The value of such material from the standpoints of newspaper editors or broadcast news directors is proportional to their assessment of the extent to which it will attract readers, listeners, or viewers.

Media criticism. Critics often have argued that media ill-serve their communities; that news reports are too superficial, sensationalized, and otherwise inappropriate to the higher purposes of journalism. They believe the primary responsibility of the media is to inform readers, listeners, or viewers; to encourage development of the informed electorate that the Constitution of the United States assumes to exist.

This concept fails to meet the tests of history and economics. The media have catered to the interests of their audiences since the days of Joseph Pulitzer and William Randolph Hearst. They continue to do so today. Pragmatically, they reflect the interests of those they serve. Their readerships, audiences, and revenues vary with the extent to which those interests are served. Editors and news directors who digress from that clearly marked path risk finding themselves jobless. Publishers and broadcasters who neglect these basic business principles rapidly can become ex-publishers or ex-broadcasters.

Understanding essential. Complete understanding of these points is vital to success in public relations practice. That which is published or broadcast by the mass media is not a matter of editorial caprice but a function of economic survival. A news release occasionally may be "sold" through carping or cajolery. Practitioners can make such nuisances of themselves as to induce editors or news directors to use material merely to get rid of them. These practices inevitably are destructive. They are costly to practitioners and those with whom they deal. Editors and news directors lose audience interest. Practitioners lose credibility and respect. Their clients and employers are ill-served as well.

Those who press public relations practitioners to gain media exposure inappropriate to the information they seek to convey inevitably gain little and may lose much. Information in which media audiences are not interested. seldom will be heeded even if published or broadcast. Editors and news directors will resent the pressure exerted on them and their resentment often will extend to subsequent informational offerings that may be of greater interest to the audiences they serve.

An Affirmative Approach

These conditions should not be taken as implying that news releases are inappropriate in contemporary public relations practice. They should instead encourage practitioners to seek out media that, by the nature of their audiences, will be interested in the information involved. That which is inappropriate to the daily newspaper may be well-received by weekly or business newspaper editors and their readers. Where these media are disinterested, a business, trade, or academic publication may be appropriate.

Public relations practitioners must seek out media where gatekeepers necessarily share the interests of their clients or employers. This does not mean settling for "second best." Levels of interest expressed by editors and news directors are valid indicators of potential news release productivity. Gatekeepers essentially express what they believe to be the opinions of prospective readers or viewers. They are saying, in essence, "my audience will be interested. This information is apt to be assimilated and acted upon."

Exposure versus success. Clients and employers may not be similarly disposed. Where this is the case, fault may rest with public relations practitioners rather than editors or news directors. Unsophisticated clients and employers often demonstrate a strong tendency to equate mass media exposure to success. This may or may not be the case. Where it is not, the practitioner's first responsibility is to educate the client or employer to the realities of media life. The process can be time consuming but nevertheless is worthwhile.

Clients and employers must be made to understand that exposing an organization, its products, or its services in any medium will not necessarily induce greater acceptance or sales. These results develop only to the extent that the audience involved is interested or may become interested in the product or service. Absence of results ultimately can become a problem for practitioners as well as clients or employers. This especially is the case where programmatic objectives have been clearly delineated in quantitative and/or qualitative terms. The glow induced by media exposure is transient and quickly forgotten when programmatic objectives are not achieved.

Intervening problems. Hidden agendas nevertheless occasionally intervene in what appear to be straightforward public relations programs. Product sales and enhanced corporate identities are not always the primary objectives of clients or employers. They occasionally may seek personal aggrandizement, for example, under the guise of organizational achievement. Where this is the case, they attach more importance to daily newspaper or local television exposure than rationally would be the case.

These circumtances are not unusual but constitute a different problem than may originally have been identified—a problem that requires different techniques and different measures of success. It can be successfully attacked only where practitioners induce mutual understanding of objectives. Clients and employers understandably may be reluctant to discuss hidden agendas but open communication is essential. No public relations program can be successfully completed and evaluated where objectives and measures of performance are not precisely established and mutually understood at the outset.

AUDIENCE ANALYSIS

The objectives of public relations programs are expressed in terms of specific audiences. They may be shareholders, financial analysts, employees, customers, prospective customers, or others. These audiences must be characterized demographically and sociographically before communication channels can be selected with the precision necessary to produce optimum results.

Public relations deals with neither the general public nor the mass media in the general meaning of those terms. Literally none of the organizations that employ public relations techniques are concerned with every member of any population. There are virtually no products, services, or institutions of universal interest. While every individual necessarily must consume food, for example, food product purchases are not uniformly spread across the population. Neither is the ability to influence such purchases. Some groups are more influential than others. Homemakers and institutional buyers control disproportionate amounts of food purchases. Mothers purchase the bulk of all baby food sold. Young people purchase considerably more "fast" food than others.

At least equally important from public relations as well as marketing standpoints is variation in factors that motivate purchases. Price and reliable delivery are among institutional buyers' greatest concerns. Speed and convenience are paramount for fast food buyers. Successful communication with these groups requires divergent media and varying messages.

Most members of mass media audiences can be viewed as prospective purchasers of fast foods or influencers of fast food product sales. The public relations practitioner's challenge in these circumstances is to create news that keeps company or product names before prospective buyers through the mass media. McDonald's uses two primary vehicles to achieve this objective. One is the company's All American Band, which appears in major parades around the country. Members are drawn from the ranks of the nation's high school bands to the accompaniment of considerable publicity fanfare. The other is the Ronald McDonald House, motel-like facilities built adjacent to major medical centers for use by the families of young children under treatment. They generate considerable media attention, especially during planning and construction phases, and thereafter serve as a constant reminder of McDonald's to local residents through the media and otherwise.

Institutional food buyers constitute a quite different public or stakeholder group. There are relatively few of them in any single community. They are a small component of any newspaper's readership or broadcaster's audience. They can be effectively and efficiently reached only through trade publications, trade shows, and similar activities oriented specifically to them.

They are interested in anything that might make their jobs easier or enhance the results of what they do in the eyes of their superiors. New products or services, new applications of old products or services, and similar information of benefit to them in performing their duties are among their major needs. These elements thus are of primary interest to the trade publications that serve them. All media are not created equal, however, and public relations planning requires detailed examination of all that may be pertinent to the problem at hand.

COMPARING MEDIA

Comparison processes apply to almost all media. They are universally used because similarities between media often are more apparent than real. Significant differences in content and/or audience exist even among the mass media. Some are a function of media characteristics. Others are developed by the media to attract audiences that managers perceive to be most attractive to advertisers.

Newspaper Differences

Variation in newspapers occurs primarily in geographic coverage, frequency of publication, and audiences served. Most can be classified as dailies or weeklies although some publish at other intervals. Some dailies, such as the *New York Times* and the *Wall Street Journal*, are distributed nationally. Others are more regional or local in character. Their audiences vary accordingly.

Public relations practitioners attempt to match client or employer needs with newspaper circulation patterns. The manufacturer of a product produced and consumed locally or regionally thus would be better served by a local or regional newspaper than one that circulates nationally. In like manner, the owner of a single retail store in a suburban shopping center would benefit more from exposure in a community weekly than a metropolitan daily.

Variation in newspaper content also requires practitioner attention. Morning newspapers usually carry stock market quotations and tend to be better read in the financial community. They therefore better serve the interests of publicly owned companies than their afternoon counterparts. Afternoon newspaper readerships tend to be concentrated in more limited geographic areas. Their sales are influenced by their ability to reach newsstands before afternoon "rush hours" begin, which limits publisher ability to have them trucked to remote locations. Where circulations are approximately equal, afternoon newspapers usually are of greater benefit to organizations that serve limited geographic areas.

Dailies may or may not be superior vehicles for other organizations, especially where the communities in which they operate support legal or business newspapers. These tend to be better read than daily newspapers by members of audiences to which they cater. Their circulations usually are smaller than those of the dailies. Numbers of prospective users of specific products or services nevertheless may be greater among their readers than among those who read daily newspapers. The content mix to which their editors are committed also may be more appropriate to the information that practitioners seek to convey.

Radio Differences

Variation among radio stations of interest to public relations practitioners occurs in three areas: signal pattern coverage—a function of transmitter power, targeted audience characteristics, and the extent of informational programming.

"Informational" rather than "news" is applicable in radio since many markets include "news-talk" stations that confine their operations to news broadcasts and talk or discussion shows. At the other end of the spectrum are stations that broadcast nothing but music and commercials.

Stations in the latter group are of little value to public relations practitioners. The former offer the greatest potential since representatives of clients or employers often can gain individual exposure by appearing on appropriate programs. "News-talk" stations "consume" a tremendous volume of information and tend to be far more "open" to news releases than other outlets.

Between the extremes are two types of stations that can be useful in public relations programming. One uses a "rip and read" approach to news coverage and devotes little time to news as opposed to entertainment. The other maintains a staff of one or more news personnel and aggressively seeks information-oriented listeners.

"Rip and read" refers to a practice in which announcers or disc jockeys tear news reports from teletype printers and read them on the air. "Rip and read" stations usually use little locally oriented information of any kind, although some are not averse to "pirating" a bit of information from local newspapers. Stations that maintain their own news staffs are more ready to entertain public relations practitioners' submissions, especially where they are intensely time-oriented, giving radio stations a time advantage in relation to television.

Like newspaper readerships, radio audiences vary in composition. "News-talk" and music formats attract different listeners. So do specific types of music. The major point of variation among stations by type of music is age of listeners. Youngsters are attracted to contemporary "sounds" while vintage and classical music appeal to older groups.

Television Differences

A somewhat similar set of differences exists among television broadcasters. Most major markets include educational stations, which usually offer a greater volume of community-interest programming. They tend to appeal especially to members of upper socioeconomic groups of a more intellectual bent. Public television stations are especially open to "public service" programming. Contributions from nonprofit and public service organizations often are welcome, even to the extent of panel shows and special programs.

The remainder of most communities' television stations at this writing fall into one of two categories. The first consists of affiliates of the major networks. The second involves independent broadcasters. A third "tier" of low power or neighborhood stations is being licensed by the Federal Communications Commission.

Network outlets. Network affiliates more closely approximate mass media than any other television outlets. They seek to attract homogenous audiences and present programming more heavily entertainment-oriented than is the case with public broadcasting. A relatively few public service programs, usually in the form of panel discussions, are broadcast primarily during early mornings and weekends. Most broadcast local and network news at noon and in early and late evenings.

Network television newscasts are oriented to mass audiences. Action-related items are preferred due to the visual characteristics of the medium. A spectacular accident that commands little interest on the part of the print media, for example, often will draw television attention, while a more durably significant event such as passage of a piece of municipal legislation may be mentioned only in passing.

Independent stations. News directors' criteria vary considerably where independent broadcasters are involved. Some in major metropolitan areas specialize in news and information. They are exceptionally open to material generated by public relations practitioners. Independents in smaller markets tend to specialize in motion pictures and syndicated features. They often broadcast something akin to occasional "rip and read" radio newscasts but may offer no news at all.

Cable systems. Cable system programming usually is more diverse than local although not necessarily more open as public relations channels. Most cable systems offer public access channels but audiences tend to be exceptionally small. Most systems carry one or more of Cable News Network's channels with content oriented to national audiences. They can be important media for practitioners dealing with national audiences and information of mass appeal but otherwise are of negligible potential value. Cable systems in most markets penetrate little more than half of all homes.

New stations. A set of low-power television stations is in process of being licensed by the Federal Communications Commission, which ultimately may prove of value in public relations practice. Their signal patterns seldom will extend beyond five miles from their transmitters but they may broadcast considerable volumes of neighborhood and community news, becoming electronic replicas of weekly newspapers.

In all cases, public relations practitioners must examine these media in terms of their "reach": their ability to deliver messages to significant numbers of specific audiences. They usually are less efficient in this context than other media.

Magazine Differences

No set of media in the United States is more diverse than the nation's magazines. Over the past several decades, they have grown in number and become increasingly specialized. One or more have been created to serve virtually every conceivable special interest group.

They include a few general interest magazines such as *People* and *Reader's Digest* but far greater numbers of more specialized publications. The latter include the news magazines such as *Time* and *Newsweek*, women's magazines including *Cosmopolitan*, avocational or special interest magazines such as *Popular Photography* and *Car and Driver*, and business publications including *Fortune, Business Week,* and *Industry Week.*

There also are a host of business-specific magazines. They include *Public Relations Quarterly, Editor & Publisher*, and *Modern Healthcare.* Many industrial, business, and professional associations also publish magazines or newsletters. In the areas touched upon above, such publications are issued by the Public Relations Society of America, the American Newspaper Publishers Association, and the American Hospital Association. Other magazines or newsletters are published by organizations for members, shareholders, customers, employees, and retirees. Finally there are an equally plentiful number of academic publications. They serve educators and researchers in fields ranging from public relations to each of the medical specialties.

So numerous are magazines that public relations practitioners seldom find themselves at a loss when seeking media to reach specific audiences. More often, they find several that superficially appear virtually ideal to their purposes. Close examination then is required to select the medium that best meets specific needs. The same process, essentially a research strategy, is applicable in targeting any mass medium.

Other Media

The channels of communication that fall neatly within the categories discussed above are not all-inclusive. Print and broadcast sectors are served by multiple news services. Associated Press and United Press International supply them for radio, television, and newspapers. Both agencies also provide news film services for television. The major broadcast networks also maintain news services for client stations. Other providers are active in serving the media as well.

Many newspapers use feature material prepared by a number of news feature syndicates. Perhaps best known as distributors of cartoons, they also syndicate columnists, feature writers, and others who might be interested in messages originating with public relations practitioners.

Some newspapers, many of their Sunday supplements, and significant numbers of magazines also use the services of free-lance writers. Most "in-flight" magazines distributed without charge aboard commercial aircraft acquire considerable material through free-lancers. A number of travel magazines also use their work extensively. Some free-lancers also write for more sophisticated corporate publications directed to customers. Directories of free-lance writers are available at most public libraries.

While less amenable to characterization as "mass media," some organizations' employee publications also can be appropriate outlets for public relations. This especially is the case where practitioners represent nonprofit, health-related groups such as the American Heart Association or the American Cancer Society. Employers burdened with fast-rising health insurance costs more and more are opening their employee publications to material that will encourage more healthful worker behavior. They also often will publish material relating to charitable organizations.

MEDIA RESEARCH

Information concerning most of the mass media with which public relations deals is readily available in detailed form. No single source, however, will adequately serve practitioner needs. While several directories are published specifically for the practitioner, other material is equally and occasionally more enlightening. The latter information comes in part from the media themselves and in part from publications prepared primarily for use in the advertising industry.

Practitioners who deal extensively with mass media find it worthwhile to maintain their own reference libraries. Others consult general or university libraries or contact media directly to obtain information. Several sources in most cases are used concurrently to identify media that appear to be (a) most beneficial in terms of public relations objectives and (b) most receptive to material originating with practitioners.

Public Relations Sources

Two sets of informational resources frequently consulted by practitioners are available through Bacon's PR and Media Information Systems of Chicago and Larimi Communications of New York. Bacon, which also provides publicity distribution and clipping services, offers *Publicity Checkers* and a *Media Alert* service consisting of magazine editorial calendars. Larimi publishes radio, television, and cable directories as well as lists of syndicated columnists, news bureaus, and investment newsletters.

Larimi directories. The Larimi broadcast directories provide virtually everything public relations practitioners need to know about the broadcast media. Included are program descriptions, staff listings, names of contact persons, newsroom telephone numbers, audience figures, station data, lead time required for guest bookings, lists of subjects most frequently covered in news broadcasts, and more.

They cover local programming as well as syndicate and network shows in every category. General interest, public affairs, news, religious, business, sports, consumer affairs, life-styles, finance, and science/medicine are among 20 different categories listed for each broadcast outlet.

Larimi's *Television Contacts* lists programs; guest, product, and information requirements; contact names and telephone numbers; program descriptions including show formats; booking and air times; and names of hosts, anchors, and producers. The firm's *Radio Contacts* lists network affiliations, news services, personnel and contact persons, addresses and telephone numbers, program formats, and audience figures. Similar data are provided in *TV News* and *Cable Contacts Yearbook*. Daily updating services are available to subscribers to insure that current information is available at all times.

Bacon directories. What Larimi provides for the broadcast industry, Bacon offers for the print media. Bacon publishes a two-volume *Publicity Checker* for the United States and Canada. One volume is dedicated to newspapers, daily and weekly, while the second covers magazines of every variety.

The magazine directory is organized into more than 150 market groups from "Advertising" to "Welding." It provides complete mailing and contact data and a set of codes indicating types of information in which editors are interested. The codes show interest in new products, trade literature, personnel, events, financial matters, letters, questions and answers, books, contracts, and films. Separate codes show whether publications use publicity photos and whether they charge for cuts.

The newspaper directory lists all of the approximately 1,800 daily newspapers in the United States and Canada with complete mailing information. Editors of 25 different news departments are listed by name. Contact information for more than 7,500 weekly newspapers and weekly publisher groups also is provided. Similar data also are published annually by *Editor & Publisher* magazine in an industry yearbooks. *Editor & Publisher* also prints an annual directory of newspaper syndicates that lists the features they make available to newspapers.

For those in international public relations practice, Bacon also publishers an *International Publicity Checker* for Western Europe. It lists some 10,000 business trade and technical publications and more than 1,000 national and regional newspapers in 15 countries. Magazines are classified by country and market group. Mailing information, telephone, and Telex data are provided and the publicity coding feature includes translation requirements for news releases.

Advertising Resources

Some of the information provided by Larimi and Bacon services, and a great deal more, is available through publications dedicated primarily to the advertising industry. Primary among them are the several directories published by Standard Rate & Data Service (SRDS).

SRDS publishes directories of daily and weekly newspapers, consumer and trade magazines, and radio and television stations. The company also offers several specialized directories. Most recently launched (in 1987) was *Print Media Editorial Calendars*, a service not unlike Bacon's *Media Alert* service. Both signal opportunity to public relations practitioners. Special interest issues enhance potential for acceptance of subject-related materials. SRDS publications, which vary in frequency of issue from monthly to semiannually, also include directories of billboard operators and mailing lists available for purchase. The latter include magazine and credit card lists and often are available by geographic areas. Billboard operators frequently use public service messages and thus are worthwhile contacts for those in public service organizations.

Circulation and audience. SRDS services are designed primarily to provide advertising rate information and mechanical specifications to advertising agencies. Many media listings, however, also provide information of critical interest in public relations. Most important among them, especially where practitioners are seeking to reach a specific audience through magazines, are circulation and audience breakdowns. The value of the data varies with individual circumstances but invariably is helpful to some extent.

Geographic distribution of a magazine's readers may be less valuable when products or services are distributed nationally. Where practitioners' clients or employers operate on state or regional bases, however, they can be most significant. The magazine serving a given industry with the largest circulation may or may not be best covering the state or states in which the product or service is marketed.

Reader data. Readership analyses are helpful in almost any situation. Those provided by SRDS characterize the magazine readers by job title. Where several magazines in a given category are under consideration, the extent to which each is read by individuals in specific job categories can be important in terms of desired results. Detailed circulation data also are frequently provided by the media themselves. Most include results of independent circulation audits in media kits prepared primarily for advertisers.

Where products or services involved are more or less a commodity, as in the case of industrial fasteners or fluorescent tubes, buying decisions most often are handled by purchasing managers or their subordinates. Where heavy equipment is involved, engineers usually are more influential. Decisions concerning professional services are most apt to be made by senior executives, perhaps in concert with in-house counsel.

Total circulation of magazines serving specific industries may or may not be adequate indicators of which will best serve the needs of the public relations practitioner. While one may attract a greater number of senior managers, another may be read by more purchasing managers.

Industry Information

A great deal of additional information of at least marginal value also is available to public relations practitioners seeking to achieve maximum results. Some of the data, especially that contained in academic and professional journals, is highly reliable. Other information, such as the results of market studies conducted by the media themselves, may require closer examination.

Considerable generic information helpful in public relations can be acquired from the pages of *Public Relations Review,* the *Journal of Advertising,* and the *Journal of Marketing.* all of them academic journals. Academic prose often is not readily digested but data presented usually are highly reliable. More practically oriented information is presented by the *Journal of Advertising Research, Public Relations Journal,* and *Advertising Age.*

Statistical material also is published by industry organizations and by independent agencies that audit publication circulation figures. The Magazine Publishers Association and the American Newspaper Publishers Association are representative of the former category; the Audit Bureau of Circulation the latter. Most publishers will provide audited circulation figures on request.

Other Information

Less significant but nevertheless noteworthy are many reports published intermittently by advertising agencies, research organizations, and others. Agency data usually are compiled for clients and internal use and detailed reports seldom are available. Studies by the Opinion Research Corporation and other researchers are published, however, as are data compiled by magazines such as *American Demographics.*

Significant trends in specific industries also are frequently described in considerable detail in the *New York Times,* the *Wall Street Journal, Business*

Week, Industry Week, and other publications worthy of regular reading by public relations practitioners.

IN SUMMARY

The nature of the uncontrolled media and the interests of their gatekeepers and audiences govern the extent to which news releases are accepted for publication or broadcast. Gatekeeper and audience interests essentially are identical. Media content is formulated to attract specific audiences. The primary responsibility of editors and news directors is to increase the sizes of their audiences.

These conditions are rooted in the economics of publishing and broadcasting. With few exceptions, the media are profit-making entities. Their profits are derived from advertising revenues. These revenues are a function of advertising rates, which in turn are governed by the sizes of the audiences that the media command. Media receptivity to information conveyed by public relations practitioners thus is a function of the joint interests of their audiences and managers.

Given these conditions, public relations practitioners must seek out media that, as a result of audience and executive interests, will be most prone to publish or broadcast the information they seek to disseminate. This approach will not necessarily meet preferences of clients or employers. They tend to equate mass media exposure with success on the part of public relations practitioners.

Exposure can be universally equated with success only where clients or employers are more concerned with their egos than with tangible programmatic results. More often than not, the mass media are less than optimally effective in achieving public relations objectives. Public relations deals with specific, precisely defined publics or stakeholder groups rather than with the so-called general public. Even where client or employer products or services appear possessed of more or less universal appeal, their success in the marketplace usually is largely controlled by relatively small percentages of the total population.

Public relations efforts must be directed toward members of those small groups. The media to which they are most exposed thus are of paramount concern to the practitioner. These circumstances require careful analysis of media audiences. They vary significantly within each media category.

Other than in readership, variation among newspapers occurs primarily in geographic terms. They may be distributed nationally, regionally, in metropolitan areas, or in smaller communities. Their total circulations seldom are significant in public relations. Practitioners instead must focus on numbers of prospective users of client or employer products or services within each newspaper's readership.

Depending upon the nature of clients' or employers' products or services, practitioners may find local business or legal newspapers or community weeklies more productive of results than the metropolitan, regional, or national dailies.

The same principle applies in the broadcast sector, and especially in radio. Most major markets are served by multiple radio outlets, each oriented toward a narrowly defined audience. Most broadcasters attempt to attract specific age groups, concentrating primarily on those with the greatest retail purchasing power. The latter factor infrequently is a primary concern of the public relations practitioner since product publicity often is a minor component of public relations practice.

Radio stations also vary considerably in the extent to which their programming formats afford public relations opportunities. At one extreme are a relatively few "news-talk" stations that consume substantial volumes of information and create multiple opportunities for on-the-air appearances by practitioners' clients or employers. At the other extreme, and far more common, are stations that offer little or no news or informational programming, preferring to concentrate on entertainment.

Many television stations, especially independents, also maintain programming formats with little or no informational content. Network outlets traditionally offer local and national newscasts at noon and in early and late evening. News-talk television exists in only a few major markets other than through the Cable News Network. Television news content is oriented to mass audiences and focuses primarily on events amenable to exploitation of the visual component of the medium.

Magazines are considerably more diverse. Some can be categorized as being of general interest but most focus their attention on relatively narrow audience interest sectors. Several usually compete for the attention of each of a near limitless number of special interest groups. The public relations practitioner's primary task in these conditions is to identify magazines that offer the potentially most productive audience.

Information concerning newspaper, broadcast, and magazine audiences is available from multiple sources. Directories produced for public relations and advertising are most informative. Additional information is available from rating services, circulation auditing organizations, trade associations maintained by the publishing and broadcasting industries, and others.

ADDITIONAL READING

Baus, Herbert M. *Publicity in Action*, 2nd ed. New York: Harper & Brothers, 1954.
Canfield, Bertrand R. *Public Relations: Principles, Cases and Problems*, 5th ed. Homewood, Ill.: Richard D. Irwin, 1968.
Center, Allen H., ed. *Public Relations Ideas in Action: 500 Tested Public Relations Programs and Techniques*. New York: McGraw Hill, 1957.
Chambers, Wicke, and Spring Asher. *TV PR: How to Promote Yourself, Your Product,*

Your Service or Your Organization on Television. Atlanta: Chase Communications, 1986.

Goldman, Jordan. *Public Relations in the Marketing Mix: Introducing Vulnerability Relations.* Chicago: Crain, 1984.

Hilton, Jack. *How to Meet the Press: A Survival Guide.* New York: Dodd, Mead, 1987.

Rice, Ronald E., and William J. Paisley, eds. *Public Communication Campaigns.* Beverly Hills, Calif.: Sage, 1981.

Roalman, A. R. *Profitable Public Relations.* Homewood, Ill.: Dow Jones-Irwin, 1968.

Robinson, Edward J. *Communication and Public Relations.* Columbus, Ohio: Charles E. Merrill, 1966.

Schoenfeld, Clarence A. *Publicity Media and Methods: Their Role in Modern Public Relations.* New York: Macmillan, 1963.

9
Scheduling and Budgeting

Scheduling and budgeting in public relations, as in any other business activity, deal with time and cost. Significant differences exist, however, between annual operating budgets developed by public relations departments or consultancies and documents produced in relation to specific programs.

Annual budgets deal in gross numbers, usually providing line item allocations for individual programs. Program budgets are rendered in greater detail. They specify precise cost estimates for each component of each activity and often are accompanied by two "schedules." One is a schedule as such, a production plan specifying which components of each activity will be started, in progress, and completed in each month. The second is an expenditures projection in which total costs are allocated by month for each component of each activity.

Expenditures projections are more common among consultancies than organizational departments since they inform clients in advance of amounts expected to be billed for each period. Projected expenditures often are billed in advance rather than after work has been completed, although billing procedures vary among consultancies. Many if not most of them bill in advance on the basis of estimates and make adjustments in subsequent bills to compensate for differences between estimates and amounts expended. The process is designed to avoid "banking" or financing work undertaken for clients.

Expenditures projections also can be valuable in organizational settings where activities started in one fiscal year ended in another. This especially is the case where governmental entities are involved. Their budgeting procedures often require most or all of unexpended balances be returned to a general fund at year's end. Where this is the case, an annual year-end "spending down" ritual often develops. While varying with specific agencies, it usually involves spending and/or committing remaining funds to preclude their being returned.

Detailed schedules or production plans as well as budgets are essential in these circumstances. They provide executives with knowledge of amounts expended, committed, and uncommitted that is necessary to the spending down process.

Program budgets are nothing more than programs themselves expressed in terms of dollars. The components of each activity are listed. Costs are estimated and assigned to each, producing the basic budget document. Planned expenditures necessarily are made over the duration of the activity. Time projections thus are developed for each activity to create program schedules and these data are combined with cost estimates to create the program expenditures projection.

None of these components of the public relations program, however, is developed in a vacuum. All originate at higher levels. Public relations, for example, may be represented by a single line in the budget of a large organization. The content of that line then is the sum of all items contained in a departmental budget, usually including a single line for each program. Programming and planning processes then expand each line, allocating resources to the several plans within each program and to the multiple activities that constitute each plan. Knowledge of broader budgeting processes thus becomes important to all involved in programming and planning.

BUDGETING ALTERNATIVES

Anticipated productivity and organizational need provide primary guidance in budgeting. The latter is or should be expressed in organizational as well as public relations goals and objectives. Together, they establish priorities for the public relations unit, organizational or consultant. The priorities guide practitioners in developing detailed programs in each practice area: employee relations, shareholder relations, community relations, and so forth.

The process creates a challenge paralleling that which organizations face in addressing the needs of multiple stakeholder groups within relatively rigid economic limitations. Resultant goals and objectives should be reflected in and supported by public relations programming. The relative probable productivity of individual activities then governs their inclusion in specific public relations programs. Applicable activities are listed in order of anticipated productivity and then included in the budget on a "from the top down" basis until available funds all have been allocated.

S. Watson Dunn (1986) calls this the marginal approach to program development and points out that the process is less readily applied than described. Decisions involved must be based on less-than-perfect information, and results of important public relations activities such as research and program monitoring extend far beyond current budget periods.

These circumstances make the term "best budget" somewhat ambiguous. The best budget, in general, is a functional document that produces optimum results and is readily defensible. The latter element requires that funds be allocated for research and monitoring as well as specific programs and activities.

A number of budgeting strategies are available in achieving best results. Prior year's expenditures, availability of funds, percentage, and "zero-based" strategies are most frequently used.

Prior Expenditures

While few would attempt to enter into the budgeting process without reviewing prior years' budgets, they are less-than-reliable guides to budget development. Their primary weakness arises out of several assumptions of doubtful merit.

First, the prior expenditures approach assumes prior years' budgets were logically developed. Second, they assume organizational goals, objectives, and needs remain unchanged. Third, they assume prior years' plans and activities remain most appropriate in meeting those goals, objectives, and needs.

Of the three assumptions, the latter is most questionable. Social and economic changes in the United States have required radical organizational responses in recent years. These, in turn, have produced different sets of public relations needs. The plant closings and massive layoffs of the 1980s, for example, implied potential for substantial deterioration in employee morale and productivity. These circumstances suggested a need for greater attention to employee relations programming than earlier had been the case.

Available Funds

Best use of available funds always is a valid guideline in public relations budgeting. It may be less than adequate, however, where funds are arbitrarily allocated by organizations; where public relations funds are budgeted after other "essential" requirements have been met.

The process again proceeds on the basis of tenuous assumptions. Primary among them is the assumption that senior management has developed a well-thought-out set of priorities and considered public relations needs in establishing each of them. Other assumptions inherent in the process include absence of waste and recognition of long-term organizational needs.

The latter can be especially troublesome. Demographic data compiled by the Bureau of the Census suggest the early onset of significant labor shortages in the United States during the remainder of the century. Few organizations, however, appear to be taking steps necessary to compete successfully in a "seller's market" for personnel.

Fixed Percentages

As the name implies, public relations budgets calculated through the fixed percentage method are based on other components of organizations' financial statements or projections. Fixed percentage budgets most often are found in sales-oriented organizations. Percentages are applied to prior year's or anticipated sales or profits or, occasionally, to the organization's advertising budget.

The fixed percentage method can be advantageous in that budgets expand with sales or profits. Use of prior year's data in calculating amounts, however, is less logical than basing the budget on anticipated sales or profits. This process assumes, as Dunn points out, that "public relations is a result rather than a cause of sales or the other measures on which it is based."

The reverse is equally possible. Declines in sales can result from the absence of an adequate public relations program. Sales of the Audi automobile plummeted during the mid–1980s, for example, when the company repeatedly denied the existence of mechanical problems in the wake of a host of accidents resulting from uncontrolled and uncontrollable acceleration. Communication alone would not have eliminated the sales decline. A skilled public relations practitioner, however, might have counseled management to otherwise handle the problem, limiting damage to the the single model involved rather than to the entire product line.

Zero- and Future-Based Budgets

The most logical and practical approach to budgeting extends strategic planning methods long used in management to the public relations process. Alternatively called zero-based or future-based budgets, they proceed on the basis of contemporary circumstances and anticipated trends or events to generate budgets based on current and future need rather than past history.

The process involved also parallels contemporary public relations practice, which begins with environmental assessment. It then generates programs designed to enable organizations to cope successfully with trends and events that impact their stakeholder groups. The process focuses on long-term organizational need, stakeholder opinion and behavior, and changing environments. As such, it tends to create a greater "comfort level" for those who may be unfamiliar with the fiscal aspects of public relations practice.

More important, this approach links public relations budgeting directly to organizational goals and objectives, rendering the resulting document more acceptable to senior managers. Public relations expenditures can and should be viewed as investments contributing to profits rather than expenses that reduce profit.

At the same time, the future-based process can create difficulties. It literally requires starting at "zero" and creating a budget "from the ground up" in light of contemporary and anticipated need. This process requires considerable information and assumes the prior existence of an adequate environmental monitoring system. Given appropriate information, the process involves a logical series of steps: situation analysis, specifying objectives, developing programmatic alternatives; cost-benefit analysis of each alternative; and documentation of results.

Situation Analysis

Contemporary conditions and those that can be expected to materialize during the budget period and the years immediately thereafter are the raw material of situation analysis. The process is designed to identify current and future problems and opportunities. As indicated above, it requires considerable information that may not be readily available.

Much of the necessary information can be obtained through environmental assessment, a two-part process applicable to organizations' internal and external environments. The process components are scanning and monitoring. The former identifies events that may signal the onset of trends that conceivably might impact the organization. The latter requires tracking those trends to assess timing and magnitude of impact. Public relations practitioners presumably are capable of installing such systems where they do not exist.

Additional necessary information usually is more readily obtained. It comes from senior management and from other departments such as sales, marketing, human resources, and any others involved in any aspect of communication. The goals, objectives, and needs of organizations and their component parts all provide guidance in public relations programming and planning.

Setting Objectives

The key to success in establishing public relations objectives is precision. The process involves more than organizational goals and objectives. It requires attention to all stakeholder groups and recognition of the fact that not all objectives are achievable within a single budget period. Both short-term and long-term public relations goals and objectives are necessary.

Enhanced organizational productivity, for example, can be addressed successfully in the short term by installing appropriate systems and communicating them to employees involved. Recasting traditional management systems to position organizations to compete successfully for diminishing supplies of human resources is another matter. In most organizations, it will require new policies and procedures, retraining of managers and supervisors, and a communication effort extending over several years.

Programmatic Alternatives

Complex, long-term issues almost inevitably require organizational as well public relations response. Programmatic options open to public relations practitioners in these circumstances are circumscribed by organizational policy decisions. Development of on-site child care facilities to assist in recruiting of female personnel, for example, will require different communication strategies than those necessary where staffing problems are first addressed by attempting to reduce overly high absenteeism and tardiness rates.

Public relations practitioners ideally serve as counsel to management as organizations address such issues. They too frequently, however, are not party to decision-making processes. Where the former circumstances exist, budgeting can be a complex and demanding process. Programmatic options may have to be developed on the basis of alternative organizational scenarios. Alternatives in the latter conditions are more limited but all must be considered. Practitioners in each case must specify not only the nature of anticipated programs and activities but the volume of anticipated results.

Cost-Benefit Analysis

Cost-benefit analysis is the principal analytical technique applied in public relations and elsewhere. It involves assessing the cost of public relations programs and activities in terms of the benefits they are expected to generate.

In the case of the absenteeism/tardiness problem mentioned above, practitioners must estimate the extent to which these factors can be controlled and the volume of savings that would result from anticipated improvement. These then must be compared with the cost of achieving desired results.

Where ancillary costs accrue, these must be calculated as well. For example, were senior management to adopt a policy under which a portion of unused sick leave would be converted to vacation time, wages and benefits attendant to the additional vacation time would be part of the cost involved.

Costs also must include all expenses incurred in the public relations unit. These involve, for example, more than printers' charges in producing employee publications. Proportional amounts of staff time must be allocated to the project. Overhead factors also should be included. These indirect costs are quite real but often neglected as "something we have to pay for anyway." Senior managements indeed may view public relations costs in this light but those handling public relations budgeting should include them. At worst, they will impress organizational executives with practitioner sensitivity to cost factors.

Determinations as to which activities should be included in any program then can be made on the basis of cost-benefit analysis. Those most productive, other than in the case of such components as research, are made part of the program for the forthcoming budget period.

Documenting Results

Every component of the contemporary organization is expected to demonstrate a return on investment. Public relations is no exception. Ability to obtain funding for future budgets is a function of prior results expressed in quantitative and/or qualitative terms. The outcomes of every public relations program and, to the extent possible, every activity thus should be documented.

Documentation tends to be a problem only where practitioners fail to anticipate their needs in advance. This is a pitfall readily avoidable where standards for measurement are established and presented as part of the budget proposal. If the proposal projects a predetermined volume of improvement in absenteeism and tardiness, for example, after-the-fact documentation will be readily available from the human resources department.

Other outcomes, such as customer or shareholder perceptions of the organization, are more difficult to measure. Sound public relations practice requires they be assessed before any new program is implemented. Where this is accomplished, reassessment at the program's conclusion or on an annual basis will generate data indicative of change.

As the foregoing should demonstrate, the budgeting process parallels the programming process in public relations. Budgets are nothing more than common, single-use plans. They usually are short-range vehicles, developed in the last three to six months of one calendar or fiscal year to cover the subsequent twelve months. They have significance for public relations managers, however, that extends beyond the numbers involved.

Budget Significance

To a far greater extent than many recognize, budgets express the goals and objectives of organizations and their senior managers. They may or may not be consistent with formally stated goals and objectives. Where inconsistencies exist, the budget logically can be considered the guiding document. It expresses the actions rather than the words of senior managers.

Budgets should reflect priorities established in organizational goals and objectives. Expressed commitments to employee relations and community relations efforts, for example, should be supported in the budgeting process by adequate funding. Where this is not the case, the sincerity of the organization's commitment is open to question.

Competition inevitably exists for organizational resources. Public relations managers' most critical tasks include obtaining a "fair share" of resources for their departments. This requires them to be able to understand organizational financial procedures and function efficiently within them.

This often includes multiple meetings during the budgeting process in which public relations budgets must be defensible. Public relations managers must be prepared to defend their requests by demonstrating their importance in relationship to organizational needs. Arguably among the best approaches to this potential problem is a system described by John A. Koten of Illinois Bell Telephone Company (see Figure 9.1). The system ranks programs in order of priority and provides descriptions of penalties the organization would pay were they to be eliminated.

Budgeting processes in most organizations are decentralized. Budgets originate at the departmental level in the hands of those who will make expenditures and move upward. Typically, divisional budgets ultimately are brought together into a cohesive whole by a budget director or controller for final approval by senior management and the board of directors. In their final form, budgets thus are representative of organizations' real commitments.

COST-SCHEDULING PROCESSES

Decisions taken through cost-benefit analysis as to the sets of activities that will constitute ensuing years' public relations programs are a beginning point in budgeting. Total cost involved readily can be calculated from these data but more is needed. Organizational budgeting processes typically require that information concerning proposed expenditures be presented in two formats. The first summarizes anticipated expenditures by category. The second summarizes them chronologically. Categorical summaries are readily prepared from cost factors listed in connection with each proposed activity. Chronological data require preparation of detailed production schedules attendant to each activity.

Categorical Summaries

Organizational budgets, as indicated earlier, tend to place public relations expenditures in a few broad categories. Most frequently these are limited to wages and benefits, production costs, travel and entertainment, and, perhaps, a miscellaneous category. A capital expenditures line may be included where major equipment purchases are not covered in a separate capital improvements budget. Lines for agency fees and charges may be needed as well. Operating budgets within the public relations unit should be more detailed.

Wages and salaries: Wage/salary budgets, for example, should be broken down into full-time, part-time, and transient personnel with separate lines for wages/salaries and benefits. In large organizations, the wage/salary budget might better be expanded to become a "labor budget," encompassing labor provided by vendors as well as employees. As such, it would serve as a monitoring device indicating to managers those points at which the organization might be better served by adding personnel or subcontracting more of the labor involved.

Overhead: Every public relations organization incurs overhead expenses. These at

Figure 9.1. Illinois Bell public relations budget decision packages. From John A. Koten, "Budgeting," in Bill Cantor, *Inside Public Relations: Experts in Action*, Chester Burger, ed. New York: Longman, 1984. Reprinted by permission.

Rank	Program	Impact If Not Funded	Staff
EMPLOYEE INFORMATION RANKING			
3	Information support of personnel policies and 2-way discussion programs.	Less employee understanding of personnel policies and lack of 2-way communications.	4
2	Employee magazine	Reduced understanding of complex corporate issues; no regular medium to reach retired employees.	5
1	Employee bulletins and phone-in newsline.	No timely employee information on company developments; outside media and rumor mill become primary information sources.	3
MEDIA RELATIONS RANKING			
2	Issue press information on technology advances; respond to media queries on service.	Low-technology image, more competitive losses, more service complaints to regulatory agencies, more adverse coverage on service.	1
1	Provide press information on rates and legal matters; act as spokesperson and coordinate press information.	Poor media representation and less favorable regulatory decisions.	2
ADVERTISING RANKING			
2	Bill inserts to specific customer groups on service matters and dialing changes.	No efficient way to get local service information to customers; more use of 1st class mail; lost sales opportunity.	2
1	Twelve issues of bill insert newsletter to 3.6 million customers.	No recurring way to inform customers statewide of rates, service developments, and new products/services. Lower sales, reduced revenue.	2

Figure 9.1 (continued)

Rank	Program	Impact If Not Funded	Staff
DEPARTMENTAL RANKING			
7	Information support of personnel policies and 2-way discussion programs.	Loss of employee understanding of personnel policies and lack of 2-way communications.	4
6	Bill inserts to specific customer groups on service matters and dialing changes.	No efficient way to get local service information to customers; more use of 1st class mail; lost sales opportunity.	2
5	Twelve issues of bill insert newsletter to 3.6 million customers.	No recurring way to inform customers statewide of rates, service developments, and new products/services. Lower sales, reduced revenue.	2
4	Employee magazine	Reduced understanding of complex corporate issues; no regular medium to reach retired employees.	5
3	Issue press information on technology advances, respond to media queries on service.	Low-technology image, more competitive losses, more service complaints to regulatory agencies, more adverse coverage on service.	1
2	Provide press information on rates and legal matters; act as spokesperson and coordinate press information.	Poor media representation and less favorable regulatory decisions.	2
1	Employee bulletins and phone-in newsline.	No timely employee information on company developments; outside media and rumor mill become primary information sources.	3

minimum include rent, utilities, maintenance, telephone, postage, and a host of other items. These costs should be itemized as line items for accounting purposes and charged to specific programs and activities. Charges can be allocated directly based on usage or on pro rata bases. Percentages of labor consumed in each program or activity provide the most logical basis for pro ration.

Production: Costs associated with production in public relations have escalated rapidly in recent years with the advent of sophisticated audiovisual technology. Satellite-based videoconferencing, for example, can quickly add hundreds of thousands of dollars to budgets. More elaborate programming can cost millions. These costs as well as printing, typesetting, art, design, and photography must be detailed in the operating budget as well as individual program and activity budgets. Only where this is done can managers successfully track costs and make timely decisions as to "outsourcing" versus internal staffing.

Supplies: Considerable variation in supply costs can occur as a result of organizational differences. Where photography, printing, and audiovisual work are handled on an external basis, internal supply budgets will be relatively low. Where these technical functions are handled internally, budgets increase rapidly.

Research: As in the case of technology, research costs at least superficially have increased in recent years. Use of computer-accessed data bases has escalated in preparation of proposals and in programming. Computer costs also have increased in conjunction with communication audits and other research projects involved in program development and monitoring. These costs and those incurred through use of external research organizations must be separately itemized.

Special events: Where handled by the public relations department, special events can be a significant component of the budget. Open houses, anniversary celebrations, and similar activities can quickly drain significant volumes of departmental manpower. Ancillary expenses for a near limitless range of purposes also can be considerable. Even such a seemingly insignificant event as an employee dinner in a small firm quickly can add thousands of dollars to an annual budget.

Travel: Some in public relations tend to relate the term "travel costs" to out-of-town travel. Most organizations and consultancies spend considerably more in their home cities than "on the road." The expenses are incurred in operating automobiles, in taxi charges, and in messenger services. They must be tracked as components of individual programs and activities. In agency situations, they must be compiled for billing purposes as well.

Agency charges: Organizations that retain public relations counsel will want to monitor their charges carefully as well. Detailed invoices should be required in order that purchases made through the agency can be appropriately allocated to specific programs, activities, and budgetary categories.

Other. Other categories that may be necessary in individual organizations include capital investment items for equipment acquisition, equipment maintenance, media costs, rentals of space for news conferences and associated costs, rental of exhibit space at trade shows, and any number of other specialized expenditures.

Chronological Summaries

Most organizations require that their operating entities provide chronological budget projections in order that cash requirements can be successfully anticipated. In public relations, this requires that the timing of all activities be projected for the budget year. Some involve relatively consistent costs in each month of the year. Others vary with project scheduling.

Consistent costs. The bulk of repetitive or consistent costs in public relations organizations occur in the wage/salary, fringe benefit, and overhead areas but others are involved as well. Primary among them are costs involved in producing one or more periodical publications and/or audiovisual reports for diverse stakeholder groups.

Periodical costs are relatively stable on an issue to issue or program-to-program basis. They can readily be projected in keeping with publication or production schedules. Costs of maintaining "hot line" information services to employees, computer data bases for the media, and similar activities also can be successfully calculated on monthly bases.

Inconsistent costs. Other activities produce costs on irregular bases. An annual report or an annual satellite-based audiovisual presentation, for example, will generate high bills from vendors in some months and no bills in others.

In general, bills are payable in the months subsequent to completion of services involved. In the annual report example, then, practitioners should be able to anticipate when they will be charged for photography, design, typography and mechanical artwork, printing, addressing, and mailing.

Chronological budget projections thus must be compiled in order that organizational managers can anticipate significant variation in total costs from one month to another. They are most readily established in light of production schedules.

Other Variables

Several variables can intrude to make a specific activity more costly and time-consuming than otherwise would be the case. They must planned for in advance if subsequent problems are to be avoided. Most relate to the nature of the organization, competitive factors with which it must contend, and the nature of public relations problems addressed.

New organizations. Where organizations or their problems are "new," public relations programming and production can be considerably more complex than otherwise would be the case. From the perspective of managers and clients, for example, a brochure is a brochure. The brochure to be prepared for a new organization or to introduce a new product in fact is considerably more complex than the average.

Most new brochures will require more design work than otherwise would be the case. The new organization may require a logotype or trademark. The new product often requires that similar design elements be created. These factors quickly can complicate the basic task and render it difficult to complete within an earlier established budget or chronological framework.

Competition. Competitive factors can intervene in a similar manner. Where two organizations are introducing competing products or services concurrently, neither can afford to underspend the other significantly. These conditions may force radical revision of public relations budgets.

Unusual problems. Finally, there arise circumstances where the public relations problem at hand may be so great as to require inordinate expenditures. They may range from "disaster" situations such as Johnson & Johnson's problems with Tylenol to circumstances where complexity of the subject at hand demands programming more extensive than otherwise would be the case.

During the mid–1980s, for example, health care costs grew at such rapid rates that many organizations were forced to undertake major revisions in employee health insurance programs. Prior to that era, many had provided "full coverage" programs for personnel. Rapidly escalating premiums forced most of them to change to "participatory" policies, requiring that employees pay part of the cost of care they receive. The changes were complex and organizations found themselves making unusually high investments in employee communications programs during the transition.

PRODUCTION SCHEDULES

Numbers of public relations programs and activities in which organizations may be involved at any time are so great as to require monitoring systems. Potential for error and waste alone demand such systems be used in any organization of significant size.

Production schedules once were maintained primarily on paper in one form or another. The most popular included calendars and elaborate wall charts that dealt primarily with due dates and or flow patterns. With the advent of the microcomputer and its capability to develop and maintain flow charts, these conditions have changed. Due dates and flow patterns remain the primary anchor points for scheduling but much of the management is handled by computer.

Time Requirements

Critical to the process, whether managed by computer, on paper, or mentally, are time requirements that prevail in any complex activity. Process components vary in preparation time. Unless each is available at the required time, the entire project will be delayed.

In the typical corporate brochure, for example, text and illustrations must be near complete before design work can be done. The design must be finished before type can be set. Type must be set and mechanical artwork completed before the printing process can begin. The foregoing may not seem overly complex. Only six components were mentioned. A closer look at one of them, however, may adequately convey the real complexities involved.

Illustration. Illustrations in a corporate brochure can range from simple black and white photos to reproductions of original works of art. None are necessarily as readily completed as they appear. A simple external photograph of a building can be delayed for significant periods by weather. Few organizations are willing to accept bleak winter landscapes in brochures when their summer counterparts are considerably more attractive. This especially is the case when the finished product may be seasonally oriented.

If the brochure is to be used to attract customers to a summer resort, photos of models in and around a swimming pool are difficult to take in midwinter. In practical terms, then, such photos must be taken almost a year in advance even though they may not be needed until a few weeks before printing is to begin.

Similar problems can occur in other situations. In industrial photography, considerable clean-up work often is necessary before photos can be taken. Where original artwork is to be used, even more time may be required. A series of watercolors may require months for an artist to complete. In "worst case" circumstances, some may be unacceptable to clients and/or senior managers and have to be redone.

Technical concerns. Finally, where color printing is to be incorporated into the finished product, the photos or artwork must be available months before delivery dates. Color separations are necessary, and they are neither inexpensive nor quickly completed. This especially is the case where color fidelity is critical, as in the case of food products.

For these and other reasons, major brochure and annual report projects more often than not are developed over as much as a year. Target dates for completion of each phase can best be plotted on a critical path management or similar flow chart and ample time is best allowed for organizational approvals.

Approval Problems

The approval process often is considerably more complex than appears to be the case. In most instances, clients or senior managers will be asked to approve text, proposed lists of illustration, mechanical artwork, and proofs. Again, the list appears short but potential for complications is considerable.

Most prevalent among sources of delay in the process are multiple approvals. Many senior managers prefer to appear nondictatorial. Some are burdened with a level of insecurity. For these or other reasons, approvals may be handled by committee rather than individuals, with time-consuming results.

Multiple experts. The nature of the problem is often most evident early in the production process when practitioners are dealing with text drafts. Most managers consider themselves expert in the use of the English language. Each has his or her own ideas as to precise phraseology. Most importantly, every change, no matter how minor, must be approved by all involved.

These circumstances may force practitioners into multiple major text revisions and an almost endless chain of minor revisions, each of them requiring review by a committee or, worse yet, a half dozen or more managers or executives. Days and weeks early allocated for text preparation thus quickly can become months. Equally significant, early cost estimates quickly may prove grossly understated.

Project control. Many of these pitfalls can be avoided from the beginning where practitioners establish schedules by which specific steps in the production process must be reached. Such schedules then can be submitted for client or senior management approval together with cautions concerning costs attendant to unforeseen delays.

Approved production schedules will not prevent difficulties but constitute a generally adequate defense against later criticism over delays and/or cost overruns. This especially is the case where adequate "paper trails" are maintained. Paper trails most often involve cover memos indicating dates on which materials are provided and acknowledgment notes reflecting the dates on which they finally are approved. Senior managers and clients tend to forget what to them are insignificant delays that can collectively result in deliveries weeks or months behind schedule.

BUDGET AND SCHEDULE MANAGEMENT

Completions of budgets and schedules are starting points in ongoing processes. In the best of circumstances, time and cost factors require adjustment during the budget, program, or activity period involved. At worst, as in the case of the sort of emergencies alluded to above, radical change may be necessary.

The cardinal principle that must govern the activities of counselors and organizational practitioners alike is a simple one: no unpleasant surprises. This, in fact, is the reasoning behind relevant cautions expressed earlier in terms of production schedules and costs. Where production slips behind schedule, one of two results is inevitable: higher cost or delayed delivery. Neither is acceptable where practitioners have failed to notify clients or employers in advance.

For these reasons, both budgets and schedules must be carefully managed on continuing bases. The processes involved are not complex. Monitoring is simply a matter of oversight, involving periodic reviews of budgets and schedules so that financial and temporal goals can be achieved.

Seasoned practitioners learn to handle monitoring as a matter of course, usually through weekly or monthly status reviews. Monthly reviews usually are sufficient in the financial area, especially where adequate record-keeping systems are in place. Adequacy requires that managers stay abreast of financial commitments rather than mere expenditures. Commitment to produce an annual report may account for a significant printing expenditure that will not be reflected in expenditures until the work has been completed. In the interim, the printing budget appears to be underexpended when in fact funds for the annual report have been committed and must be deducted from the fund balance in order to obtain a precise insight into the status of that line item.

Weekly reviews usually are preferable to monthly where production schedules are involved. A week's delay in delivery can be catastrophic, for example, where the finished piece of literature is to be distributed at a meeting of financial analysts that will be conducted on a certain date.

Most busy practitioners who deal with multiple projects for these reasons are prone to use computer-based monitoring systems. These permit entry of base data from which weekly or monthly calendars as well as critical path charts can be created in a matter of minutes. The calendars, generated on a weekly basis, spell out the projected status of each project for the week in question. A comparison of actual to projected project status quickly alerts practitioners to any delays and prompts necessary remedial action. These and other elements worthy of note were set out in some detail in a list prepared some years ago by counselors Gerald Voros and Paul Alvarez (1981):

1. Be sure that the hired agency's budget is completely included in your internal budget and that there is no duplication of expenditures.

2. The agency should be willing and able to document and explain all charges. However, do not have the agency spend an inordinate amount of time in documenting and reporting expenses. The net result can be a waste of money.

3. On monthly progress reports, it may be advisable to have the agency prepare a budget status report similar to your internal budget flowchart. This will help you keep track of spending. You should also consider having the agency submit a written monthly activities report to substantiate invoices and charges for staff time.

4. Be flexible. Allow for a contingency on budget estimates. Many public relations expenses are difficult to predict.

5. Be open to budget revisions. Budgeting is an evolving effort and must be adjusted to the needs of the organization and to new situations.

6. Pay agencies and suppliers promptly. Agency enthusiasm can wane on an account that is constantly delinquent on payments. Prompt payment is good management and good business.

7. Do not ask the agency to absorb or bury costs that are not budgeted or to supply

more services than your budget allows. On the other hand, be sure you get the services your budget deserves.

8. Measure the agency's results, and relate those results to expenditures.

9. When budget cuts are contemplated, warn the agency as far in advance as possible. The agency should be equally prompt in notifying you about possible overages or other problems.

10. Work closely with the agency in developing new programs and in relating them to the budget. Much time and effort can be wasted planning activities you cannot afford.

IN SUMMARY

Scheduling and budgeting in public relations are closely interrelated. The two processes require concurrent attention in that they together permit developing expenditure projections essential in counseling practice and advisable in organizations. Budgets must be prepared for the public relations unit and for individual programs. They require precise cost data for each activity within each program.

Several alternative approaches are used in the budgeting process, which focuses on the relative probable productivity of sets of activities within each program. The alternatives are based on prior year's expenditures, availability of funds, percentages of organizational budgets, and zero-based budgeting.

The prior expenditures approach, in which budgets are modified versions of their predecessors, assume that earlier budgets were adequately drawn. They also assume organizational goals, objectives, and environments have remained unchanged in the interim.

Available funds budgeting assumes a degree of management omnipotence in allocating resources in the absence of well-defined programs and plans. Fixed percentages applied to profits, sales, or advertising assume public relations functions serve almost exclusively as sales generators.

Development of zero- or future-based budgeting parallels strategic planning and public relations processes. It begins with environmental assessment and results in development of programs in keeping with organizational needs. The process is more complex than otherwise would be the case but generally is better accepted among senior managers and public relations clients.

Critical to the zero- or future-based budgeting approach are setting objectives and defining programmatic alternatives. There follow a set of cost-benefit analyses dealing with the alternatives and leading to selection of those that promise to yield best results. In each case, provision is made to generate adequate baseline data for planning purposes and to permit subsequent measurement of what has been accomplished.

When programs and attendant budgets have been developed, two further documents are prepared. The first is a categorical or summary budget in which expenditures are placed in several broad categories. They usually include wages and salaries, overhead, production, supplies, research, special events, travel, and agency charges although others may be added. The second is a chronological summary that projects expenditures within each category by month.

The latter process requires developing a production schedule indicating target dates for completion of each component of the several production processes. This document shows approximate dates on which the organization will pay for each externally produced component. Preparation requires close attention to time factors involved in production to insure that schedules are realistically drawn in keeping with organizational circumstances, especially the nature of approval processes applicable during production.

Budgets and schedules are economic and temporal reflections of public relations programs and plans. They must be managed accordingly. As the former change, so must the latter. Budgets and schedules thus must be monitored on monthly or weekly bases to assure that activities are moving ahead as scheduled.

ADDITIONAL READING

Dunn, S. Watson. *Public Relations: A Contemporary Approach.* Homewood, Ill.: Irwin, 1986.

Koten, John A. "Budgeting." In Bill Cantor, *Inside Public Relations: Experts in Action,* Chester Burger, ed., New York: Longman, 1984.

Shillinglaw, Gordon. *Managerial Cost Accounting.* Homewood, Ill.: Richard D. Irwin, Inc., 1977.

Voros, Gerald J., and Paul Alvarez. *What Happens in Public Relations.* New York: AMACOM, 1981.

10

Releases: News and Feature

News and feature releases appear to many to be the most common communication channels employed in public relations, but these perceptions are inaccurate. Other channels are becoming more dominant and releases are declining in importance with the advent of new technologies and for other reasons as well. News and feature releases remain important to public relations practitioners, however, if for no other reason than they are the most visible aspect of practitioner activities from the perspective of the news media.

These perceptions, and the manner in which they influence media content, are vital in the formation of society's perception of the value of public relations. They also predispose media representatives to treat practitioners with more or less respect and confidence. For these reasons, and to the extent that they remain useful public relations tools, news and feature releases are vital components of public relations practice.

Since news and feature releases are the most visible component of public relations practice to the media, they require considerably more attention on the part of practitioners than otherwise might be the case. Craftsmanship in use of language and compliance with accepted mechanical criteria are necessary but insufficient in developing and distributing releases. They also must reflect exacting standards of professional ethics.

ETHICAL FACTORS

Relationships between news media representatives and public relations practitioners traditionally have been strained. The stresses involved arise out of mutual suspicions. Reporters, editors, and news managers suspect public relations practitioners of attempting to subvert the media; to use them for monetary gain on the part of the commercial interests they represent. Public relations practitioners see themselves in a different light. They suspect media personnel of exploiting their clients and employers in the interests of selling more newspapers or building broadcast audiences. At minimum, they are fearful of what they perceive to be the distortions and inaccuracies that occur in news reporting.

Neither stereotype is wholly accurate. Research has shown that individuals on both sides perceive those with whom they work to be more honest and ethical than others in their respective professions. Considerable honorable performance remains necessary, however, before either group can begin to escape its distorted stereotype. The necessary level of performance requires total integrity, ethical conduct, and mutual understanding.

Integrity

No concepts are more readily understood or more difficult to maintain than integrity and candor. Difficulties tend to dissipate, however, when individuals come to recognize a simple principle: the personal reputations of public relations practitioners and media personnel more than any other factor will influence the levels of personal success they are destined to enjoy.

Career development in both professions largely is controlled by peer opinion. Personal reputation and peer perception are controlling elements in the functioning of informal networks that influence upward professional mobility to a greater extent than many understand. These circumstances require that public relations practitioners adhere to a simple standard: honesty. This does not mean that every media representative's question must be answered on every occasion. There will be times when confidentiality requires that information be withheld. Integrity can be maintained in these circumstances, however, with a simple response: "I can't answer that question." Where answers are provided, however, they must be accurate and complete.

The Unwritten Code

Success in dealing with the news media also requires adherence to an unwritten code in which public relations practitioners occasionally become entangled. It requires that they, as news sources, respect confidences implied in reporters' questions in certain circumstances.

The circumstances relate to subject matter involved. Essentially, the code prescribes that news sources shall not divulge to other media representatives the subject of any news story which a media representative may be seeking. While specifically applicable where feature material is involved, it is best applied in public relations practice to the content of all discussions with media personnel other than in news conferences and other more or less open forums.

Dishonored confidences. To betray the subject of a prospective article that one reporter is seeking to one of his or her colleagues at minimum is considered "bad form." More sensitive journalists might consider such action a form of betrayal, obviously a sin of which no public relations practitioner should appear guilty in the eyes of any media representative. An oft-repeated saying of hazy origin is appropriate here: "Never pick a fight with anyone who buys paper by the ton and ink by the barrel."

The "off the record" side of the ethical coin is another matter. Only by trial and painful error can public relations practitioners ascertain the extent to which reporters may respect their confidences. Most professionals follow a simple rule to guard against potential problems: All statements to reporters are "on the record." They may be used by reporters in their discretion.

This approach occasionally may penalize a reporter who would honor a confidence. It provides the only real protection that public relations practitioners can obtain, however, against embarrassment arising out of untimely disclosure of information provided "in confidence" to members of the media. Public officials, in contrast, incur relatively little risk in providing "off the record" information to reporters. Risk is minimized in their circumstances in that they are highly valued by reporters as news sources. Betrayal of officeholders' confidences can "dry up" news sources without which reporters' work is rendered doubly difficult.

Embargoed releases. One other ethical matter that can create problems for those in public relations involves dated and timed or "embargoed" news releases. "Embargo" refers to the line at the top of the news release that specifies the date and time at which the information may be published or broadcast.

Most media representatives honor release dates and times other than where a competitor breaks the embargo. At that point, all feel free to use the information as they see fit.

Embargoes may be broken by design or accident. Most in public relations tend to ignore the first such breach of etiquette on the part of a reporter. Thereafter, reporters in question may be dealt with in one of several ways. Subsequent releases may not be provided until the last moment or until after the miscreant's deadline. They also may not be provided at all.

The latter approach may be a disservice to clients or employers. Many practitioners therefore arrange for delivery of releases to suspect reporters by messenger services, facsimile equipment, or other mechanisms that assure they are not delivered until immediately before the release date and time.

Equitable treatment. Other than in one set of circumstances all media representatives must be treated equally where news releases are involved. To the best of the practitioner's ability, they must be distributed in a manner that assures that all media have an equal opportunity to print or broadcast the material involved.

The exception applies where media representatives have proven themselves untrustworthy in observing release dates or otherwise. Many practitioners in these circumstances will go to unusual lengths to assure that offenders receive dated releases within minutes of release dates to insure compliance. They will arrange for delivery by messenger or otherwise while releases destined for others are handled by mail.

There are, of course, limits to the "fair treatment" rule. Releases cannot always be timed in a manner that will permit daily and weekly newspapers an "equal break." In addition, events cannot be scheduled in a way that will satisfy all media. Their representatives, however, expect and are entitled to as equitable treatment as possible.

Handling complaints. Equitable treatment should be maintained in the face of all provocations. Even unethical conduct on the part of media representatives must be handled by "turning the other cheek." The "never pick a fight" axiom applies to media representatives individually as well as to the media generally. Complaints to their superiors over broken release dates, mishandling of articles, or even errors of fact in almost every case will be counterproductive. Editors and news directors tend to support their staff members other than in extreme circumstances.

Experienced public relations practitioners handle ethical problems directly with the individuals involved, whether or not the results are wholly satisfactory. The best approach usually involves a telephone call to the individual in question followed by an appointment to discuss the matter. Going over his or her head may bring an admonition from a superior but almost inevitably will poison the interpersonal relationship. In the alternative, pointing out an error in an even-handed manner and taking the matter no further often induces a sense of obligation on the part of the reporter that subsequently works to the practitioner's benefit.

Media guidelines. Many problems can be avoided where practitioners are aware of media policy and procedure, written and unwritten. The print and broadcast media themselves have adopted unwritten guidelines for handling releases of which those in public relations should be aware. In general, stories released for afternoon newspaper editions will be used in noon newscasts while those released for morning editions will be used on late evening newscasts.

Where public relations practitioners find these circumstances unacceptable, only one alternative exists. Releases intended for morning newspaper use can be delivered to all media by messenger after 10 P.M. and evening releases can be delivered after noon.

Concurrent distribution of releases by mail or otherwise usually satisfies the equal treatment requirement. It is not unusual, however, for "special handling" to be accorded those who earlier broke release dates, as indicated above.

Gifts and junkets. Most media today are hypersensitive to any action on the part of an individual that in any way may appear to be an effort to exert undue influence. Gifts to media representatives that once were accepted and, in some cases, expected, are forbidden in most circumstances.

Included in this prohibition are passes to movies, sports events, and other spectator activities. A cup of coffee in most cases is acceptable but meals usually are "off limits." Free trips and subsidized travel, books and records, memberships, and virtually anything else of significant value also are barred.

Some of the media have adopted less stringent rules. The public relations practitioner's best course: If in doubt, ask first. Retrieving unwanted items is time consuming and can be embarrassing as well.

Dealing with Others

The same ethical standards that apply to news media representatives must be used in dealing with clients and employers, present and future. They are readily maintained where information conveyed is what clients or employers want to hear. They must be followed, however, even where the practitioner is a bearer of distasteful news.

This principle is especially important where practitioners are pressed to induce publication or broadcast of information by media to which it is of little or no interest. These circumstances require practitioners to take the time and effort to educate clients and employers as to how the media define "news" (see Chapter 8).

They must also be made to understand that pressure can produce deterioration in relationships between practitioners and media contacts. Since such conduct would place their own subsequent releases in jeopardy, few clients or employers are inclined to press unrealistic demands. Where demands are nevertheless made, practitioners must consider whether they want to put their own reputations at risk. No few jobs and accounts have been resigned over the years as a result.

CRAFTSMANSHIP

The bulk of news and feature releases distributed to the media never are published or broadcast. They may occasionally be pushed aside in favor of breaking news that editors or news directors consider of greater importance to their readers or viewers. The assassination of a president, for example, will drive virtually all other subject matter out of ensuing issues of newspapers and evening newscasts.

News releases more often go unused because of the manner in which they are written, packaged, and delivered. Surveys of editors and news directors suggest they most frequently are discarded because they:

1. contain no news
2. contain inaccuracies
3. fail to conform to appropriate journalistic style
4. are poorly timed
5. are incomplete
6. use improper grammar, spelling, and punctuation

The bulk of these lapses go counter to what should be a basic guideline in preparation of news and feature releases: Make them as easily used as possible. This means limiting use to appropriate occasions and applying media rather than client or employer standards to their development. These practices serve two purposes. First, they avoid burdening editors and news directors with material in which they have no interest. Second, they guarantee closer attention when releases are delivered.

Material received by the media from organizations known for disseminating valueless news releases often is barely read in news rooms to which they are delivered. Where organizations use releases judiciously, or where they always contain information of interest to recipients, the reverse inevitably becomes true. Neither organizations nor those responsible for their public relations programs can afford the former circumstances. The reputations of both are at stake.

Generating News

The weakness most frequently encountered by the media in news and feature releases is absence of information of interest to recipients' audiences. Much of the information organizations attempt to disseminate is indeed of interest to one medium or another. Very little is considered news, however, by more than a few of them. This fact, coupled with a propensity on the part of many to distribute releases with promiscuous abandon, produces what media representatives consider the glut of nonnews releases described above.

Identifying news. This would not be the case were practitioners to prepare and distribute releases with media audiences rather than clients and employers primarily in mind. A simple test almost invariably suffices in determining whether or not to send a news release: Will the content be of interest to the bulk of those who read, listen to, or watch the results? Media content patterns, in other words, are practitioners' best evidence of what will or will not be acceptable by editors and news directors.

Maintaining accuracy. A similar principle applies to the accuracy problem mentioned above. Media methods are based on a system to which successful public relations practitioners must conform. It involves one critical element: dependability.

Time pressures under which media must perform require complete trust and confidence among their personnel. Reporters' articles are accepted as accurate by city editors. City editors' statements are accepted as fact by managing editors, and so on. The speed with which all must work prohibits any effort to double-check every fact in a news article.

Editors and news managers demand the same level of performance from those who submit news or feature releases. The facts must be correct. Names must be spelled properly. Addresses must be accurate. Where inaccuracies are detected, releases become suspect in their totality. Worse, public relations practitioners involved and organizations they represent become suspect.

Where these conditions prevail, even information obviously worthy of publication or broadcast is apt to be delayed if used at all. Editors or news directors involved will consider it essential to be certain it contains no errors beyond those readily detected.

Stylistic weaknesses. Failure by public relations practitioners to conform to appropriate journalistic style is equally likely to create delay or nonuse of releases or feature material. In essence, the value of information provided to the media depreciates in direct proportion to the level of difficulty editors or news directors encounter in preparing it for publication or broadcast.

Basic print, broadcast, and feature writing styles are not difficult to learn. They must be followed with near religious fervor to render resulting releases most readily usable by the media involved. Basic print style, which usually predominates in public relations practice, involves an inverted pyramid format. This begins with a summary lead focusing on the most newsworthy aspect of the material. Other facts follow in order of importance.

While basic style applies to time-oriented or "spot news" releases, feature style is less rigid and focuses on a topic of special interest rather than a newsworthy event. Broadcast style departs from basic print style in that releases usually are written with a "teaser" introduction. This brief statement alerts listeners or viewers to the type of news that follows. This approach is essential in dealing with broadcast audiences in that they cannot "reread" any component of a newscast they may initially fail to understand.

One cardinal writing rule applies in all cases: "Thou shalt not commit literature." Plain, simple subject-verb-predicate sentences will suffice. They are highly desirable, in fact, from the public relations standpoint. The practitioner's purpose is to convey information. Distractions are as readily created by brilliant prose as convoluted sentences and can be equally deadly to the communication process.

Completeness and timing. Incomplete or ill-timed releases also create problems. Public relations practitioners should be knowledgeable as to media news cycles. For best results, they should submit material during the earlier portions of those cycles.

The media do not conform to traditional days, weeks, or months. Among daily newspapers, for example, the "day" for morning editions usually begins about 10 A.M. and ends about 2 A.M. For afternoon newspapers, the news day begins between 4 and 6 A.M. and ends about noon. Sunday editions in part follow "A.M." cycles and in part adhere to weekly cycles. Feature sections conform to the latter pattern. They usually are printed days before main news sections and cycles vary accordingly.

To meet media definitions of the term "completeness," release writers must provide answers to every substantive question that might occur to a reader, listener, or viewer. Where questions are left unanswered, publication or broadcast will be delayed or information may be discarded as unusable.

Packaging News

A set of standards or norms has developed over the years that should be followed in preparing news releases. They cover the format as well as the content of the release. Format considerations may be secondary to content in importance but nevertheless contribute to acceptance rates.

Paper. News releases always should be typed on 8 ½ × 11-inch bond paper. Lighter weight, textured, and erasable papers create problems for editors. Colors other than pastels should be avoided. Darker and brighter paper colors make reading more difficult.

Headings. Headings may be typed or printed. Most professionals use printed headings, which can be beneficial provided content standards always are met. Printed headings in these circumstances signal the presence of material that editors or news directors want to read.

Headings should contain the name, address, and telephone number of the organization involved as well as the names and telephone number(s) of individuals whom editors or news directors may contact for additional information. Since many media operate 24 hours a day, seven days a week, home as well as office telephone numbers (identified as such) are desirable.

Headings also should include dates on which releases are mailed as well as dates and times after which they are intended to be used. FOR IMMEDIATE RELEASE may be substituted for a date and/or date and time where appropriate. Where times are used, time zones also should be indicated, for example, EDT or CST.

Headlines arguably should be included as well. Some contend they appear presumptuous since size and content are in the editor's discretion. Others suggest they provide a quick summary that assists editors in evaluating content.

A dateline containing city of origin and release date, as in MEMPHIS, TN— June 28, 1989, should begin the first lines of releases that are to be distributed to several cities. Editors and news directors otherwise assume they are locally written and apply to local events.

Format. Ample space—25 to 30 percent of the page—should be left below the heading for editorial use. Releases should be written with margins of at least one-half inch at sides and one inch at bottom on all pages. The second and subsequent pages (few releases should extend beyond two pages) should have a one to one-and-one-half inch margin at top. Second and subsequent pages also should carry the name of the organization originating the release and the date of issue at the top. Double or triple spacing is mandatory for ease in reading and editing.

Clear, legible typefaces are essential. Script, old English, and other elaborate typefaces should be avoided. Where releases are written on computers, they should be printed only on letter quality or laser jet printers. Dot matrix printing is unacceptable.

Media Kits

News releases often are used as the primary component of media kits. Once called press kits but renamed in deference to the sensitivities of the electronic media, they are used sparingly today for several reasons. Perhaps most significant among them are media limitations in personnel and equipment that often preclude coverage of news conferences, where kits are most frequently used. In addition, electronic transmission of news releases permits their distribution almost instantaneously after any event.

Where appropriate, media kits usually include basic news releases and fact sheets. Several other items may be enclosed as well. These include photos and biographies of individuals involved in the news at hand as well as descriptive literature where news conferences deal with product announcements. In financial public relations, media kits also may contain copies of annual or quarterly financial statements.

News Conferences

Media kits may be distributed by messenger, at a news conference, or both. News conferences are appropriate only in limited numbers of situations. They are most often used where significant numbers of media can be expected to be interested in the subject, as is the case where a politician announces his or her candidacy. Otherwise, they usually are confined to circumstances where information can not be adequately delivered to media offices.

A public corporation's annual meeting or introduction of a new product would meet the latter criteria. The unveiling of a model of a new high-rise building or a shopping center might qualify as well but some public relations practitioners would be inclined to deliver media kits in the latter case. Models can be photographed and photos should be included in media kits in any event. Captions should accompany photos. They are best attached to the back of the photo with removable cellophane tape.

Media kits also may include copies of speeches to be made during the news conference, a brief history of the organization involved, and any remarks that visiting dignitaries may be invited to make.

Where news conferences are used, a number of factors require early attention on the part of those handling arrangements:

1. Sites and times should be carefully selected. Media convenience should be the primary criterion in both cases.
2. Invitations should be sent a week to two weeks in advance and followed by a telephone check 24 to 48 hours before the appointed date and time.
3. The program should be carefully planned in advance to remain within reasonable time limits, usually 30 to 45 minutes.
4. Electrical outlets needed by the electronic media should be provided for in advance, together with telephones for all reporters if the conference is scheduled close to media deadlines.
5. Media kits should be prepared and labeled for all invited to the conference. They should be delivered immediately afterward to any invitees who fail to appear.
6. Extra copies of the media kit should be mailed to industry and trade publications and, in the case of publicly owned companies, to the financial media as well.

DISTRIBUTION

Distributing news and feature releases for optimum results requires attention to several mechanical functions. They include alternative distribution systems, duplication, distribution lists, and time factors. While of less importance than the elements discussed earlier, each of these factors influences the extent to which content will be printed or broadcast.

Advancing technologies in recent years have produced proliferation in distribution systems. None of them is ideal in all circumstances. All of them can be successfully employed under specific conditions.

Distribution Options

Where delivery in person, by messenger, or by the U.S. Postal Service once were the only options open to public relations practitioners, a multitude of others now are available. Some are nothing more than speedier messenger services. Others involve electronic transmission of releases on direct bases or through any of several distribution networks. Four basic options exist:

1. Duplicating and mailing releases and illustrations with in-house personnel via the U.S. Postal Service.
2. Duplicating and shipping via package express service.
3. Having releases and illustrations duplicated and shipped by a commercial service
4. Having them distributed electronically.

Internal news release production and distribution is time consuming and requires maintaining up-to-date mailing lists. The latter effort, given media personnel turnover rates, is no small task.

Feature material designed for individual media often is produced and distributed by practitioners. Many have been extensive users of express mail services, calling attention to their submittals in the process.

While a "late starter" in the express market, the Postal Service system is used by many due to lower cost and a less cumbersome payment system. The Postal Service uses deposit accounts akin to those used for bulk mailings. Postage can be deposited "in bulk" in advance. Accounts then are debited as mailings are made and users need not cope with a blizzard of individual invoices, as can be the case with competitive services.

Mail Distribution

For large-scale distribution, more and more practitioners are using one of several commercial services. A number of them exist primarily to serve public relations organizations. Among the larger of them is PR Aids, with offices in eight cities across the nation. PR Aids maintains a sophisticated computer listing of editors, reporters, and writers in print and electronic media. The data base includes some 100,000 individual contacts at more than 26,000 media outlets, each categorized by editorial interest. The data base is maintained by a research staff that makes more than 600 changes daily. The change rate reflects the rapidity with which a media mailing list can become obsolete.

PR Aids will design private lists for clients using components of the firm's data base. Users of the service also are free to choose categories of recipients from an order book listing all data-base categories. Under "Congress," for example, users can select Senate, House, House Non-Voting members, or any combination of these categories. They then can specify Democrat, Republican, Independent, or any combination; then Senator/Representative, Chief Aide, Legislative Aide, Press Aide, Committee Aide, Subcommittee Aide, or any combination; then Washington office, home office, or both; and finally geographic distribution by state(s) and/or districts. For those in financial public relations, a similarly detailed securities analyst selection system is available.

Mailings can be addressed to specific media, geographic area, and demographic areas. They can be sent to local media and to local or regional correspondents of national media. Where media are in competition, they can be sorted into sets and sent different releases. Further selections are available by media editorial interests, individual recipient editorial interests, types of text and photo material used, frequency of publication, geographic location, and geographic coverage.

PR Aids is not alone in offering release distribution services although no two are identical. New York-based Media Distribution Services, for example, offers a similar delivery mechanism but places a heavier emphasis on production services than PR Aids. Media Distribution handles virtually any type of printing, from annual reports to autotyped letters, and offers a broad range of direct mail services, including sample and product mailings and fulfillment.

North American Precis Syndicate (NAPS), an editorial promotion service, packages and distributes releases as well as radio and television scripts by mail. The television scripts are accompanied by slides from annual reports or other organizational materials. NAPS writes scripts and guarantees minimum usage levels.

Electronic Distribution

News releases also can be distributed electronically through other vendors such as PR Newswire and Mediawire. New York-based PR Newswire is the industry's leader, offering a Basic News-Line covering some 150 points in 50 cities; Investors Research Wire, reaching leading banks, brokerage houses, and stock exchanges; special circuits serving New England, New Jersey, Florida, and the Western states; and services through affiliates in major cities in the United States, Canada, and overseas. A feature news wire also is offered.

PR Newswire receives releases from clients by mail, messenger, or virtually any electronic transmission system. The firm transmits "immediate release" material within minutes, at a predetermined time, or on further instruction from the originator. The organization uses a computer-based system that renders transmissions compatible with media computers regardless of the type of computer the originator may have used. The system enables PR Newswire to conform to the requirements of any receiving system. Material is transmitted at 1,200 words per minute to AP DataFeature circuits, for example, and handles the formats and computer protocols of the *New York Times*, Dow Jones, CompuServe, and NEXIS with equal ease.

NEXIS is a Mead Data Central data base that also stores information from AP, UPI, Reuters, *Newsweek, Business Week, U.S. News & World Report*, BBC World News, *The Economist, Dun's Review*, the *American Banker*, and a host of other publications. PR Newswire has been the only electronic distribution service with access to NEXIS. Client information is placed in the data base at no additional cost.

Mediawire is a Philadelphia-based affiliate of PR Newswire, offering its own circuits as well as PR Newswire and Business Wire services through offices in Pittsburgh and Philadelphia. Mediawire circuits cover Pennsylvania as well as Delaware, Maryland, West Virginia, Washington, D.C., and other major cities.

A Private Service

One commercial organization has gone so far as to develop its own data base. The 3M Company established "NEWSROOM" on its mainframe computer to make company information more accessible to the media. NEWS-ROOM offers product releases, corporate/financial news, general/background information, technology information, and an interactive mode. Special identification numbers and passwords are issued to media representatives on request.

Broadcast Services

Similar services oriented primarily to the broadcast media are made available to public relations practitioners by organizations such as Audio/TV Features, Inc., Medialink, and Newslink, Inc., all of New York City.

Audio Features transmits radio news and feature material by satellite and the broadcast transmission facilities of the Associated Press and United Press International to more than 2,000 radio stations across the United States. The firm accepts scripts from clients or will write them to order. Professional news announcers are provided and voices of client spokespersons can be included in transmissions.

Medialink and Newslink serve television outlets in the same manner that Audio Features distributes to radio stations, but they provide no production services. Clients produce newsclips and provide broadcast-quality copies to Newslink. They are assembled with those of other clients on a feed tape with appropriate introductory material for transmission.

Newslink transmits descriptions of forthcoming "feeds" to Cable News Network, Satellite News Channel, the Public Broadcasting System's Nightly Business Report, ESPN, and local television newsrooms. Feeds then are made twice during the day to enable all stations to receive them regardless of time zone or limitations of their satellite receiving equipment.

Medialink operates in much the same manner but adds two dimensions that appeal to some users. Medialink provides considerable coverage flexibility. Users may elect state, regional, or national coverage patterns. Medialink also has created an exclusive monitoring system using Nielsen Media Research's VNR Usage. Data generated by the system can be useful to public relations practitioners seeking to document results of their efforts.

Further Distribution

Many public relations practitioners extend the value of news releases by reusing the facts involved and/or resulting clippings and tapes in several forms. Magazine releases are most extensively used. Magazines frequently offer reprints at costs considerably lower than traditional brochures. Reprinted with the pertinent magazine covers, they are considered more authoritative than brochures and often are used as sales literature.

Clippings of published newspaper releases often are reproduced for similar use, especially where illustrated features are involved. Too often, they are used in violation of copyright laws. Most newspapers are copyrighted. While publishers seldom prosecute, it is illegal to duplicate their content for commercial purposes.

Facts contained in articles are not subject to copyright and many public relations practitioners rewrite their content for internal distribution. In some cases, copies of news releases are routinely posted on organizational bulletin boards. In others, they are reprinted—with or without modification—in employee newsletters or magazines. Some organizations, including PPG Industries, provide traveling employees with cassette tapes filled with company-related news for on-the-road listening.

Doing It Yourself

Public relations practitioners who distribute news releases from their own offices also should be sensitive to mailing list maintenance needs. Given personnel turnover rates indicated above, mailing lists quickly become obsolete. While mailing services update theirs regularly, public relations firms and departments—especially the smaller among them—tend to be neglectful.

The process can be handled in one of several ways. Directories that provide frequent revisions, as is the case with Bacon's Publicity Checkers and others, can be helpful where national lists are involved. Bacon issues revisions on a monthly basis. Hudson Associates of Rhinebeck, New York, publishes a "Washington News Media Contacts Directory" updated in April, July, and October. Public Relations Plus, which publishes multiple directories, distributes updates semiannually. Gebbie Press publishes an annual "All-In-One" directory in printed form and on computer discs. Lists of local media representatives usually require in-house revision.

Revisions can be accomplished by mail or telephone. The latter alternative is by far the more preferable of the two. Media organizations' telephone operators usually are most helpful. Their personnel departments also may be willing to assist. Lists should be checked at no less than 90 day intervals for changes in titles as well as names of media contacts.

Failure to revise lists regularly seldom impedes mail delivery. It tells recipients, however, that list users are lazy or inaccurate or both, hardly the sort of impression that professional public relations practitioners should convey.

Fact Sheets

Many news releases are accompanied or preceded in distribution by fact sheets. These are most frequently distributed in advance of events and contain all information necessary to permit media to plan their coverage. All of the essentials of the news release are presented in tabular, "bare bones" form.

Fact sheets in recent years have become increasingly popular with many media. This especially is the case in the broadcast sector and most especially applies where public relations practitioners attempt to use a single release for both print and broadcast media. Releases intended for distribution to print and electronic media too often are written in print rather than broadcast style, requiring rewriting by broadcast news staffs.

These conditions, varying broadcast delivery styles, and a desire by every station to appear "exclusive" encourage news directors to prepare their own newscasts from fact sheets. Research has shown that four of five news directors will select a fact sheet when given a choice between a release and a fact sheet.

IN SUMMARY

Effective use of news and feature releases in public relations practice involves several processes. All of them must be ethically as well as skillfully executed if content is to be printed or broadcast by the media.

Maintenance of ethical practices is paramount. The task is not an easy one in the face of long-standing mutual suspicions but can be successfully accomplished. Most media representatives hold public relations practitioners suspect in general but value working relationships with those they have found to be trustworthy and reliable.

Integrity and compliance with unwritten codes of conduct are essential. Practitioners must respect the confidence of reporters and earn their respect in return. They must take every step necessary to insure that media representatives are equitably treated, even in the face of broken release dates and other perceived offenses. Unethical conduct need not be suffered in silence but must be handled with tact and discretion to produce the best possible results. Contentious relationships between media representatives and public relations practitioners invariably are counterproductive.

Good working relationships can be built over time and usually are highly productive where practitioners meet their professional responsibilities. These include compliance with media standards for news releases: newsworthiness, accuracy, completeness, maintenance of journalistic style, appropriate timing, and proper use of grammar, spelling, and punctuation. Where these criteria are met, results are salutory.

News conferences and attendant media kits today are used with declining frequency other than where circumstances virtually dictate their use. They are generally applicable only where information must be disseminated concurrently to multiple media and where this cannot be practically accomplished through delivery of material to media offices.

Multiple distribution services are available to practitioners. They include the U.S. Postal Service, messenger services, overnight air delivery services, and sophisticated computer and satellite-based distribution systems. Together they constitute a set of resources through which virtually any delivery need can be readily met.

ADDITIONAL READING

Cutlip, Scott M., Allen H. Center, and Glen M. Broom. *Effective Public Relations*, 6th ed. Englewood Cliffs, N.J.: Prentice-Hall, 1985.

Grunig, James E., and Todd Hunt. *Managing Public Relations*. New York: Holt, Rinehart and Winston, 1984.

Nager, Norman R., and Richard H. Truitt. *Strategic Public Relations Counseling: Models from the Counselors Academy*. New York: Longman, 1987.

Newsom, Doug, and Bob Carrell. *Public Relations Writing: Form and Style*, 2nd ed. Belmont, Calif.: Wadsworth, 1986.

Newsom, Doug, and Alan Scott. *This Is PR: The Realities of Public Relations*, 3rd ed. Belmont, Calif.: Wadsworth, 1985.

Nolte, Lawrence W., and Dennis L. Wilcox. *Effective Publicity: How to Reach the Public*. New York: John Wiley, 1984.

Walsh, Frank. *Public Relations Writer in a Computer Age*. Englewood Cliffs, N.J.: Prentice-Hall, 1986.

11

Printing Production

Printing production processes range from the simple to the exceptionally complex. Level of complexity, time requirements, and cost factors vary with types of printing. Each type is appropriate in some circumstances and inappropriate in others.

Level of audience need or desire for information to be conveyed most frequently is the primary determinant in selecting types of printing. Cost and time factors also are significant, and subjective concerns may intervene. Personal ego and social status are among potential intervenors. Black and white photos may be adequate for an annual report, for example, but executives often elect to use color at considerably higher cost.

Printing production proceeds through a logical series of steps after the process has been selected. These steps usually include planning and budgeting, scheduling, copy writing, design, artwork, typesetting, mechanical artwork preparation, image assembly, printing, and binding. Some of these steps are necessary in all situations. Others occasionally are omitted. Many are handled on printers' premises while others are not.

PLANNING AND BUDGETING

Planning and budgeting, scheduling and coordination are the primary responsibilities of the printing buyer. None are as simple as they appear. Planning and budgeting require balancing costs and objectives. Scheduling involves developing rational time frames for development of each project component. Coordination requires bringing the components together smoothly to form the finished product.

Establishing Objectives

With the possible exception of some lithographic prints, every item of printed material communicates. Each is an organizational quality statement. This is true whether the item is a simple instruction sheet or a "coffee table" book. Books inevitably are more expensive to produce but nevertheless may be of poor quality. Instruction sheets usually are inexpensive but can be of high quality. Quality thus may be a matter of form or function as well as content. All of these factors must be weighed in determining how best to produce printed materials.

Other variables that require attention are indigenous to organizations involved. Professional service organizations, for example, tend to express quality by understatement. They often use more expensive papers and production processes but avoid bright colors and exotic designs. The latter are preferred, however, in the travel and entertainment industries. The intent in each case is to attract attention in a manner complimentary to the organization.

Engendering attention. Attention is necessary if messages contained in printed materials are to be delivered. Attention level is not, however, a function of cost. In the case of employee publications, for example, content is the primary generator of attention. Where organizations are open and candid with their personnel, publications are read whether mimeographed or lithographed; whether photos are in color or black and white. Where content is weak, the reverse is true.

Planning and budgeting thus flow from the nature of audiences involved and their predispositions toward information contained in finished products. Printed materials are merely containers for messages. They are utilitarian vehicles that need be no more sophisticated or elaborate than necessary to the audience or audiences involved.

Establishing objectives. Objectives are developed to convey messages and induce audience responses. Responses are the objectives of the communicator. They dictate editorial and graphic content, length and organization of text, and nature of illustrative materials.

Instructional materials, for example, usually involve relatively lengthy texts. Processes and procedures often must be addressed on step-by-step bases. Illustrations most often are simple drawings designed to induce understanding of the steps involved. Sales brochures, in contrast, usually are heavily illustrated with color photographs and contain far fewer words.

Getting Organized

Printing production can be a complex process. It involves multiple components and providers. Some may be found within organizations; others may be vendors. Project organizers in many situations must decide early whether to employ internal or external resources. Their decisions most frequently involve time, cost, and quality factors.

Other than in large organizations, higher quality work often requires outside professionals working at higher hourly rates. These circumstances should not be interpreted as critical of organizational resources. Few require sufficient volumes of high quality printed material to justify maintaining sophisticated production staffs. More often than not, use of outside suppliers requires additional time as well. Project organization therefore is logically carried out by examining each of several variables in context with each project component (see Figure 11.1).

Completing preliminary planning with a document of this sort goes far toward determining what may be practical within existing time limitations. Listing vendors and subsequently obtaining estimates from them also provides guidance as to what is feasible within prevailing economic limitations.

The organizational process should not be confused, however, with planning. Production planning begins with the public relations plan, which provides base information concerning volume of information the product must contain as well as indicators of quantities that may be required.

Planning

Volume of material to be contained in finished products dictates their sizes. Size governs volume of paper required as well as format. Costs are lower where content can be contained in a single folded sheet. Expense increases where multiple sheets must be collated and stitched. Several other factors must be considered, however, before budgets can be prepared. They include number of copies to be printed, paper and ink to be used, and mechanical processes involved.

Quantities. Consumption of printed materials varies with their nature. Numbers of finished items in some cases can be precisely identified. Numbers of copies of employee publications, for example, are governed by numbers of workers. Sales materials, however, are another matter. Demand for product brochures is a function of the productivity of marketing and advertising efforts.

Other than where obsolescence is predictable, as in the case of fashions or automobiles, most promotional literature is printed on an annual basis. Anticipated annual consumption rates, with some exceptions, have proven to be valid quantitative indicators. The most significant exception occurs where prices are subject to change and must be part of the literature. Others involve forms or other materials that seldom are changed. Letterheads and envelopes, for example, may be printed in greater volume except where change of address or telephone numbers is anticipated.

Paper and ink. A virtually limitless number of papers, varying in finish, color, texture, and weight, are available for most projects. Paper prices vary

Figure 11.1. Project planning format for printed materials.


```
                      PROJECT ORGANIZER - PRINT

    Function                    Date     Production  Individual   Source
                              Required      Time     Responsible

    Text
          Select source
          Writing
          Editing
          Proofreading
          Approval

    Layout/Dummy
          Select source
          Rough layout
          Approval
          Comp/Dummy
          Approval

    Typesetting
          Select source
          Specify type
          Mark up copy
          Set type
          Proofread
          Approval

    Illustrations
          Select sources
          Illustrations
          Charts/Graphs
          Photographs
          Approvals

    Production
          Select paper
          Write specifications
          Obtain printing bids
          Select printer
          Approve proofs
          Do printing
          Approve press sheets
          Do binding
          Deliver

    Distribution
          Select method
          Select source
          Obtain Lists
          Address
          Distribute
```

little relative to overall production costs. Better papers for this reason often are used to add quality to the end product at little cost.

Specific types of paper nevertheless are preferable in some circumstances. Hard finishes, as in coated papers, are preferred where color photos are to be used. Ink soaks into softer papers, following the fibers and rendering color photos less "crisp" in finished form. Soft papers are less reflective, however, and often are preferred where material is to be used under bright lights. Reflectivity can be a barrier to reading.

White paper is most often used, especially where full color photos or artwork are to be reproduced. Tinted stock tends to distort colors. Black ink is preferred for text matter because it is most easily read. Other colors can be used but usually are confined to darker shades. Multiple colors also can be used, but only at a price expressed in dollars and time. Multicolor printing requires greater fidelity and may involve multiple press runs.

Mechanical processes. Product design also dictates the extent to which optional mechanical processes are used. Odd sizes, novelty folds, die cuts, embossing, perforating, and other techniques add considerably to the cost of otherwise reasonably priced products.

Some may be appropriate or even necessary to a given project. Die cuts are essential, for example, in producing presentation folders. Perforating is preferable where return cards are incorporated into finished products. In these cases, added cost can be justified.

Other design factors may be troublesome. Unusual finished sizes may require producing custom envelopes at unnecessary cost. Glued products may have to be assembled by hand and their content then manually inserted.

Budgeting

All of these factors must be considered in preparing project specifications. These are essential for two reasons. First, specifications must be provided to printers asked to bid on production work involved. Second, they enable planners to estimate costs accurately.

Preliminary or "ball park" estimates should be approved in advance by clients or employers before printing bids are taken. Bids can be accurately prepared only where all components of the project are enumerated in advance. Many in public relations will use an estimating work sheet similar to the one on page 176 in developing preliminary cost figures.

Most of the items specified on the form are self-explanatory. By special requirements are meant such items as embossing, engraving, special folds, die cutting, and perforating. In writing printing bid requests, items such as these often are specified as "alternates." An alternate is an item that can be added to or deleted from the project to keep total costs within budgeted amounts.

Production time, usually expressed in working days, is the amount of time allowed for printer to complete the work. Rush jobs or those requiring overtime command higher prices. Printing "trade custom" dictates that materials prepared by the printer or the printer's vendors belong to the printer unless contrary arrangements are made in advance. They include color separations,

---

PRINTING PRODUCTION SPECIFICATIONS

Project_____Date_____

Number of copies_____ Date required_____

Finished size (flat/folded)_____

One or two sides_____ Ink colors (front/back)_____

Number of illustrations

     Black and white photos_____ Color photos_____

     Drawings_____ (screened) _____ (line) _____

     Charts or graphs_____ Other_____

Paper weight/color/finish_____

Special requirements_____

Material to be provided to printer:

     [ ] Text [ ] Type [ ] Camera-ready line work

     [ ] B & W Photos [ ] Transparencies [ ] Reflective

Folding_____Other finishing_____

Binding_____Delivery packaging_____

Production time to be allowed_____Date required_____

Ownership of materials_____

---

negatives, and plates. These factors must be taken into consideration in completing budget estimates similar to the example on page 177.

    All of the tasks listed are not necessarily performed by printers. All contribute to project cost, however, and should be included in each estimate. Public relations firms generally make estimates even more detailed. They include, for example, estimated time required for copy writing, including a predetermined number of revisions. Further revisions involve additional charges. The same procedure is advisable in organizational practice. Failure to include staff time in project budgets produces misleading cost data.

    Printers' internal capabilities vary. Some do nothing but printing. They

---

PROJECT BUDGET ESTIMATE

Project_____

Number of copies_____   For delivery_____

Copywriting $_____
Photography
     Black and white_____
     Color_____   _____
Art and design
     Original artwork_____
     Charts/graphs_____
     Rough layout/design_____
     Comprehensive layout_____
     Mechanical artwork_____
Typesetting   _____
Negatives   _____
Plates and printing   _____
Bindery   _____
Sales tax   _____
Packing and shipping   _____

     Total $_____

---

provide no necessary preliminary or "make ready" services such as design, artwork and typesetting. Some subcontract these services to other vendors. Others handle only camera-ready copy. Most subcontract color separation work to photoengraving houses. These and other services can be obtained by public relations practitioners through those same vendors, saving money but incurring potential problems in the process.

Subcontracting involves added costs to printing buyers. Products and services purchased from third parties almost invariably are marked up by printers. At the same time, however, printers assume responsibility for the quality of the finished product. They escape this responsibility where customers handle the process. Any dispute over results, however, then can be troublesome. Dissatisfaction over quality of color photos in a brochure, for example, can pit photoengraver against printer with the customer in the middle.

The Process

The budgeting process usually includes at least two time-consuming steps after planning has been completed. The first involves obtaining a set of estimates. After any necessary adjustments have been made in the scope of the project, quotations or bids must be obtained from all of the vendors involved.

Estimates are merely estimates. They are rough approximations of charges vendors expect to make. Quotations are another matter. They are fixed prices based on precise specifications and binding on both parties. Changes made in printing specifications or otherwise can unduly increase the cost of the finished product.

Avoiding pitfalls. Disproportionate increases in charges resulting from specification changes are common in competitive environments. Many vendors will "low ball" a bid to get a job, counting on increasing profits through excessive charges on "change orders."

The system is not unlike that through which defense contractors provide millions of dollars worth of work for the military. Multiple change orders are expected, especially on developmental projects, resulting in the cost overruns that periodically make headlines across the nation. These problems can be avoided in two ways. First, printing buyers must be aware at the outset of "trade norms." Second, project changes must be kept to a minimum if considered at all.

Trade norms. Virtually every vendor expects to encounter changes between the time a contract is awarded and delivery of finished work. Changes may be moderate or quite costly. It is incumbent on buyers to know in advance what charges may accrue where changes are made.

Photographers may charge on a "per photo" basis. More and more of them, however, charge for time and material. A single extra photo taken at a customer's request thus may add little to overall cost when taken at the same time and place as others. Taken on another day and/or at another location, it is considerably more expensive.

Designers usually charge on a job basis and expect to make minor adjustments. Where changes are excessive or ordered late, costs can escalate rapidly. The same principle applies to typesetting, mechanical artwork, and photoengraving as well as printing. Typesetters correct their errors without cost and anticipate a certain volume of customer changes. Above that predetermined level, additional charges are levied. Those preparing mechanical artwork operate in much the same manner.

Changes in sizes of printed photos can be quite expensive. Photoengraving processes must be repeated in their entirety to reduce or enlarge sizes of color separations where customers demand that finished photo sizes be changed.

Avoiding surprises. Changes of one sort or another nevertheless are made in almost every printed product during the production process. To avoid unpleasant surprises when bills arrive, buyers always should obtain cost figures in advance.

Understandings with vendors also should be reached in advance as to the volume of detail required in invoices, any discounts that will apply, and, as indicated above, the ownership of materials involved in the production process.

COST CONTAINMENT

Understanding vendors and their problems also can be the basis of greater economy in printing production than otherwise would be the case. Savings arise out of two factors: adequate knowledge of the processes involved and a considerate, reasonable approach to vendor as well as buyer needs.

Vendor Relations

Perhaps the most critical elements in the mix relate to scheduling. Production schedules can press vendor resources to their limits or induce a relatively unhurried pace. The former approach tends to be progressively more expensive for customers with each succeeding project. Vendors adjust charges to reflect pressures involved and waste that inevitably develops.

Practitioners who may be tempted to abuse are well advised to think again. Other than in a very few large cities, numbers of vendors qualified to undertake complex printing projects are relatively few. When all have been alienated, practitioners and their clients or employers will pay for the alienation.

An alternative approach eliminates such problems and induces lower costs. It involves giving vendors as much lead time as possible. Jobs that can be put into production far in advance of delivery deadlines can be used to fill the "valleys" in printers' work loads. They become more profitable as a result. Where "the heat is on," the reverse is true.

Printing buyers who make it a habit to schedule as often as possible to meet printers' needs as well as their own earn a valuable bonus. When caught "in a tight," they find printers and other vendors ready to reciprocate for earlier consideration.

Technical Advantages

Careful scheduling and planning also produce direct economies. Where printing schedules are relatively flexible, jobs involving the same ink colors can be run one after another. Press "washups" are reduced in number and portions of the savings can be passed along to buyers.

Flexibility also may produce equipment economies. High-speed presses usually used for high-volume work occasionally become available for shorter runs, creating further potential savings. These are but a few of many techniques that can be used to reduce printing costs and/or enhance the impact of the printed product. Careful use of vendors can produce significant economies. So can repetitive application of some of the components of production. In-house production and care in use of equipment and selection of raw material also can be beneficial.

Multiple vendors. Additional economy can be achieved by developing

working relationships with multiple vendors of varying capability and by plac-
ing significant volumes of comparable work with those vendors.

Few printers or other vendors are equally staffed and equipped for all types
of work. That for which they are most capable usually is produced with
optimum efficiency and lowest cost. Consistent use of vendors also is productive for both parties. They know each other's capabilities and expectations
and work more smoothly together as a result.

Vendor overhead also declines in these circumstances and prices usually
are adjusted accordingly. Repeated patronage reduces costs that vendors
otherwise incur in constantly seeking out new customers.

Multiple applications. Further savings may be realized through repetitive
use of the components of printed material. Designs, illustrations, text, and
even entire products can be used in an assortment of applications.

A basic design adopted by a financial institution in developing a leaflet
promoting one service, for example, readily can be adapted for others.
Changes in ink and paper color with new text in some cases eliminate further
design costs that otherwise would be necessary in producing multiple leaflets
concerning other services.

Illustrations used in employee publications often can be used in promotional
materials. Few photographers take only one view of a subject. Those not
used for one project should be filed for possible use in another. Photographers
occasionally also will sell photos individually or for single rather than multiple
uses at reduced rates. Segments of text material also can be reused, especially
where originals are preserved in electronic form in word processors or computers for ease in revision.

Some organizations use annual reports developed primarily for shareholders and the financial community as part of employee communication programs. They may be supplemented with additional material, which in some
cases has consisted of folios printed on contrasting paper and stitched into
centerfolds.

In-house production. Still further savings may be achieved by bringing
components of the production process "in house" rather than continuing to
use vendors. Organizations that use a great deal of photography often hire
photographers. In-house printing departments are common, and advancing
technologies are encouraging such developments.

A growing volume of type is being set internally using computers and laser
printers. This practice is especially prevalent where some latitude exists in
product quality. Type set through these systems suffers qualitatively in comparison to the product of commercial typographers. It often is more than
adequate, however, for products such as employee newsletters.

An alternative approach to typesetting savings involves using modems
(modulator-demodulators) with computers. They permit transmitting copy in
electronic form to typesetters' computers. Typesetter charges usually are reduced since the material in question need not be rekeyed.

External production. Public relations practitioners usually are skilled writers.

Like others trained in writing, they often consider themselves capable of handling the art in any form. Technically, they may be correct. Pragmatically, a more realistic approach may be beneficial.

Writers, like designers and artists, have nothing to sell but time. Writing necessary in developing any printed product thus must be evaluated in terms of time. Will it take more or fewer hours for staff writers to handle the task than will be the case with outside vendors? Given estimates of numbers of hours and rates involved, intelligent decisions are readily made.

Experience factors must be considered, however, in estimating time requirements. Writers less experienced in particular types of work and/or less knowledgeable in subject matter may require a greater number of hours to achieve comparable quality levels. Research can compensate for knowledge differentials, but only at additional cost.

Art and design. Design and mechanical art services are available from multiple sources. Some organizations maintain in-house art departments and use "clip art" from commercial vendors. Others rely primarily on graphic design houses or free lancers. Still others acquire the bulk of their design and mechanical artwork from "full service" printing companies.

Public relations practitioners often are called upon to supervise the work involved in any of these situations. Successful supervision requires attention to a number of variables. Most important among them are the purposes for which completed material is intended. They should be clearly defined at the outset.

With purposes established, planners must address the nature of audiences involved and the overall impressions or images that completed units are designed to convey. Leaflets advertising drugstore wristwatches, for example, are quite different than those created for designer merchandise sold only in expensive jewelry stores.

When general guidelines have been established based on audiences, technical details can be addressed. These include such matters as typefaces, illustrations, paper, formats, and alternative production techniques. All must be congruent with intended overall impressions.

Matching equipment. Production techniques selected serve as guidelines in choosing potential printers and/or printing equipment. Presses and other equipment come in multiple sizes. Their cost generally is a function of size and complexity. So are rates that printers charge customers for their use.

These circumstances suggest printing jobs be matched to printers and equipment most suitable to them. Use of oversize presses inflates costs. Too small presses may result in deterioration in product quality.

The matching process in part is accomplished by using multiple vendors, as described above, but other factors are involved. In general, presses used should be capable of completing the printing process in one run. Multiple runs are wasteful. Two-color presses, in other words, should be used for two-color work.

Only one exception applies. Some printed material can be successfully "split run." A split run usually involves one long press run, often on one side of a sheet, followed by multiple short runs on the other. The technique often is used by manufacturers in preparing sales literature for multiple dealers. Savings achieved during the long run are prorated among users, reducing costs for all involved.

Buying paper. Paper can be purchased through printers, from wholesalers, or through a beneficial blending of the services they offer. Those who buy paper in large quantities and have adequate and appropriate storage space available may find direct purchases from wholesalers beneficial. Relatively few are in this category, and even they should proceed with caution. Paper is sensitive to temperature and humidity and spoilage can be expensive.

Near equal economy can be achieved by having printers buy paper in bulk and warehouse it until needed. This technique is especially helpful where special or unusual papers are desired. The former category includes custom watermarked paper, which manufacturers will produce economically for those willing to buy large quantities.

Unusual papers include those rarely used in day-to-day printing. Organizations often specify them to achieve an unusual result or gain limited exclusivity, as in using a book paper for letterheads. Little-used papers usually must be ordered in bulk and few organizations have adequate storage facilities. Even where storage is adequate, transporting paper to print shops can be a problem.

Where quantities of printed products number in the thousands, little is to be gained by extensive comparison shopping for paper. More than one usually can be found that will be appropriate for any given project. One may be less costly than another. Cost differences usually are so small, however, that they produce real savings only where tens or hundreds of thousands of copies of a product are needed.

SCHEDULING

Developing functional schedules requires knowledge of optimum and minimum time necessary to complete each step leading to the finished product. By "optimum" time is meant the number of hours or working days required to complete a process under normal conditions. "Minimum" implies the fewest number of hours required with cost no object. A printing job that requires weeks under optimum conditions often can be completed in days, but only at considerable expense incurred primarily in overtime charges by vendors involved.

Alternative processes in some circumstances are available. Type can be set by traditional means or by microcomputer. Steel die engraving can be supplanted by thermography in preparing invitations. Form letters can be mimeographed or lithographed rather than individually typed. Substituting one process for another in each case involves qualitative, economic, or temporal penalties.

Each process requires examination and analysis in terms of these criteria. They include preparation of text and illustrations as well as typesetting, proofing, paste-up, preparation of negatives, printing, and binding. Each can be executed quickly, at high-quality levels, and at low cost. Unfortunately, quality tends to vary inversely while cost varies directly with speed.

Text Preparation

Time required in text preparation usually is the most controllable of the several factors that influence production of printed materials. It will vary, however, with complexity of subject matter and approval processes.

Complexity is the least troublesome of the variables. Relatively predictable amounts of time are necessary in research and/or information gathering prior to writing.

Approval processes are another matter. Necessary approvals usually are quickly obtained where decision making is vested in a single, readily accessible individual. Weeks or months can elapse between completion of a text draft and final approval where several individuals or committees are involved.

Illustrations

Original artwork, design components, drawings, and photographs are the most used illustrations in printing. Time required in their preparation generally ranks them in that order from most to least demanding. There are, however, several significant exceptions. Most important among them is variation in time necessary for photography.

Photography. Photographs can be categorized in several ways. They may be taken indoors, outdoors, or in studios. They can be taken in color or black and white. All are "taken" with a click of the shutter but considerable preparation or waiting may be required before the shutter can click.

"Preparatory" time requirements can range from hours to months. Clean-up work prior to an industrial photograph may entail only sweeping the floor but also may require repainting production machinery. Where outdoor photos are required, the time range can be considerably greater. It may be a few hours until the sun is in the proper position, a few days before clouds dissipate, or a few months before grass turns green in the spring.

Time requirements also vary after the camera work is complete. Color photo reproduction requires color separations; individual lithographic negatives for each basic color. They are made with filters and require considerable precision. Lithographic negatives made from black and white originals, in contrast, can be made in a matter of minutes.

Most organizations use multiple sources for photography. Many have taken advantage of easily-used cameras developed in recent years to generate photos internally for some purposes. In-house photography most frequently is used in preparing material for employee newsletters and other relatively unsophisticated projects. Catalogs, annual reports and sales materials usually require commercial photography.

Original artwork. Watercolors, wash drawings and ink sketches frequently are used in sophisticated brochures. They are most often seen in literature promoting a building or commercial mall and require weeks or months in preparation.

Qualified artists must be found. Their schedules often involve delays before work can begin. The development process then may require multiple pencil sketches before final renderings are undertaken. Finally, color separations must be made.

Other material. Design work on trademarks and logotypes involves the same sequence of events which occurs in developing original artwork. The developmental process requires more research, however, and several sets of preliminary sketches may be required before managers authorize completion of finished material.

Charts and graphs require less preparatory work, especially where gen-erated with computers. Simpler types such as bar and pie graphs can be created by computers from their numerical equivalents in a matter of minutes. Camera ready copy occasionally is provided by printer-plotters or laser print-ers linked to computers. Specialized cameras more often are used to repro-duce computer results directly from cathode ray tubes or screens.

Making selections. One guideline, all other factors equal, should guide selection of graphic materials. Each item used must contribute to the effec-tiveness of the finished product. Material which fails to meet this criterion; which has no functional purpose; should be omitted.

Graphics should be appropriate to the subject and presentation at hand. Each element also should complement the other in creating desired overall impressions. In general, consistency is preferable. Seldom, for example, will a mix of photos and sketches perform as effectively as photos or sketches alone.

Choices between graphic devices are dictated by subject matter. Auto-mobiles and clothing usually are best shown in photographs. Those who consider buying them are looking for relatively precise information as to their appearance. Lawn mowers, on the other hand, are amenable to illustration with drawings. Details of their appearance are relatively unimportant to pro-spective buyers. They are instead interested in utilitarian factors such as po-sitioning of grass catchers, which are readily shown in drawings.

A near limitless number of graphic techniques can be used in any printed item. Their utilitarian characteristics rather than their subjective attractiveness should govern their use. The same circumstances and the same principle apply in selection of type faces.

Type, Composition and Proofreading

Typography and composition proceed relatively rapidly when text is finally approved. These processes can be completed in a matter of hours where accomplished by moving electronic versions of texts through microcomputers and laser printers.

Conventional approaches require commercial typesetting, which produces more precisely defined characters. Text material can be keyed anew into typesetting equipment or input electronically by computer.

Finished type in either case is produced in galley form and must be pasted into final position by a mechanical artist. Mock-ups or dummies of finished items should be provided to guide mechanical artists in the pasteup process. Designers often provide such dummies but only occasionally offer mechanical art services. Where in-house services are not available, public relations practitioners obtain them from commercial artists or printing firms.

Type must be proofread to eliminate errors regardless of source. Most is read by typesetters' proofreaders but finished products seldom are error free. Proofreading is advisable before and after mechanical artwork is completed and should be handled by individuals other than those who write the copy involved.

Final proofreading may be completed at the mechanical art stage or afterward. Printers ultimately bring type and illustrations together to form composed negatives. Images can be transferred to photosensitive paper to produce final proofs of material to be printed in black and white. Where multiple colors are used, negatives are prepared for each. Images then are transferred to light-sensitive sheets of transparent acetate. The sheets are assembled to create "color keys" showing composite images. A "final look" at the project often is added through examination of press proofs.

Changes in a project become progressively more costly as production progresses. They are readily made in typescripts and involve minor additional costs when type has been set. Where the project has progressed to the negative stage, both type and negatives must be modified. When changes are made at the press proof stage, type, negatives and plates must be modified or remade.

Coordinating Activities

Scheduling requires bringing together all the components of the finished printed item in keeping with schedules which permit printing and any necessary bindery work to be completed for delivery on schedule. Total elapsed time varies with project complexity and the factors itemized above.

Most employee publications are relatively simple among printed materials. They seldom involve color photos and, where this is the case, production can be completed in a matter of days. This especially is true where desktop publishing techniques are used.

At the opposite extreme are projects such as annual reports, often considered critical to the economic health of organizations involved. Production usually begins six months or more before the finished product is delivered.

Critical path charts or similar graphic representations of production schedules usually are used by public relations practitioners to track developmental progress. Each component is listed together with starting dates, completion dates, and any other critical junctures in the process.

IN SUMMARY

Printing production follows a consistent pattern regardless of the simplicity or complexity of the project at hand. The principal steps in the process are planning and budgeting, scheduling, copy writing, design, art work, typesetting, mechanical artwork preparation, image assembly, printing and binding.

Planning and budgeting begin with the objectives of the project. Printed products are created to convey messages and induce responses from predetermined audiences. The demographic and sociographic characteristics of those audiences dictate the nature and content of the product.

Printing can be a complex process, involving multiple components and providers. The components are text, layout, type and illustrations. They are brought together in the print shop for production and distribution.

Volume of material dictates sizes of finished products. Quantities are a function of audience size. Most organizations print a one year supply of printed materials in the absence of factors which may create early obsolescence.

Paper and ink are the least costly components of printed products. Their selection is governed by esthetic and utilitarian factors. These are controlled by the nature of the intended audience and the environments in which products will be used.

Audience factors also are major determinants of mechanical processes. Die cuts, embossing and perforating add significantly to cost and usually are used only where they are deemed to add significantly to anticipated response.

All mechanical factors must be considered in preparing project specifications for use in budgeting and bidding processes. Budgets are estimates drawn up for management approval. They are based on mechanical specifications which then are used in conjunction with quantity estimates as a basis for obtaining printing bids.

Some steps in the printing process, including preparation of color separations and sophisticated bindery work, may be performed by third parties. These services can be obtained through printers or on a direct basis. Direct dealing with third party vendors usually results in economies but can create problems. Disputes concerning finished product quality, for example, are difficult to resolve where responsibility is divided.

Printing costs in large part are a function of relationships between printers and their customers. Where the parties work together to create durable, mutually beneficial relationships, costs and quality tend to be better than otherwise would be the case. Printing buyers usually benefit by concentrating work with relatively few qualified vendors.

Further economies often can be obtained through multiple use of printed products and their components. Some savings also can be achieved by performing some "make ready" work "in house." Care must be exercised, however, in estimating savings. Staff time must be included if data are to be comparable.

Scheduling always is a critical factor in printing production. A number of production alternatives permit buyers to save time in such areas as typesetting but quality may deteriorate as a result. Other steps in the process, including photography and design work, seldom can be accelerated without making major qualitative compromises.

Printing is mechanical and amenable to precise control. The major variable involved is coordination. Components of the process must be brought together on a timely basis if products are to be completed on time and at the lowest possible costs.

ADDITIONAL READING

Beach, Mark, Steve Shepro and Ken Russon. *Getting It Printed: How to Work with Printers and Graphic Arts Services to Assure Quality, Stay on Schedule and Control Costs.* Portland, OR: Coast to Coast, 1986.

Bruno, Michael H., ed. *Pocket Pal: A Graphic Arts Production Handbook*, 13th ed. New York: International Paper Col, 1983.

Conover, Theodore E. *Graphic Communication Today.* St. Paul, MN: West, 1985.

Crow, Wendell C. *Communication Graphics.* Englewood Cliffs, N.J.: Prentice-Hall, 1986.

Nelson, Roy P. *Publication Design*, 4th ed. Dubuque, IA: Wm. C. Brown, 1987.

Pickens, Judy E. *The Copy to Press Handbook: Preparing Words and Art for Print.* New York: John Wiley, 1985.

White, Jan V. *Mastering Graphics: Design and Production Made Easy.* New York: R.R. Bowker, 1983.

12

Radio-Television Production

Production processes used in preparing radio and television material in many ways are similar to those employed in the print sector. Words and illustrations remain the primary components of the finished product. They differ only in packaging. Where printed materials are synthesized in ink on paper, broadcast materials for the most part consist of audio- or videotape. The sole exception involves live presentations, which constitute a significant component of broadcast communication in public relations practice.

Live presentations differ from taped materials in one major respect. Words and visuals conveyed in this manner are beyond recall. No editing is possible. Technical personnel and those in front of microphones and cameras must get it right the first time. Preparation for live broadcasts thus requires considerable attention.

INITIAL CONCERNS

Audience-related factors, as in the case of the print media, are the primary concerns of those preparing for broadcast presentations. The nature of audiences and their demographic and sociographic characteristics are of primary importance.

They govern practitioners' basic planning analyses: With whom are we communicating? What do we want of them? How can we establish community of interest? How shall we express the thoughts involved in a manner most conducive to receipt, assimilation, and desired response?

Process Differences

Responses to these questions differ to some extent in accord with the nature of presentations. Where live broadcasts are in prospect, the impact of words and images may be influenced by third parties. These include moderators, interviewers, or interrogators involved in many so-called talk shows, audience members during "call-in" broadcasts, and media representatives at news conferences. The questions they pose and the mental agility of the speaker are major influences on results.

Message control. Originators totally control message content and delivery processes only where they are making speeches and production personnel are employed by them. Problem potential here is perhaps best illustrated by President Ronald Reagan's unfortunate experience in preparing for a radio broadcast. In the relatively relaxed moments before the broadcast, while media technicians were adjusting equipment, he joked about nuclear war. The microphone was open although the broadcast had not begun and his remarks later were subjected to considerable criticism.

Had broadcast personnel involved been employed by Reagan rather than the media, the offensive words doubtless never would have escaped the controlled environment, but environments rarely are totally controlled. Those involved thus must be totally prepared to cope with the unforeseen and choose their words carefully at all times.

Preparation varies in method and extent. Reporters' questions suggest that presidents are expected, perhaps unreasonably, to be masters of multiple bodies of complex information. They therefore prepare extensively for many media "free-for-alls," especially campaign "debates" and news conferences. Preparation usually involves extensive study of "briefing books" compiled by aides on every foreseeable topic. Study often is followed by simulated question and answer sessions in which "devil's advocates" pose the most difficult questions they think they can find.

Expert knowledge. Less preparation is necessary where those being interviewed are specialists rather than generalists. They deal with relatively narrow informational sectors with which they are relatively familiar. School superintendents, for example, usually require little preliminary effort in preparing for news conferences or talk shows. Their work involves the day-to-day problems of their systems. Most questions deal with those problems and are readily answered.

These circumstances are rare where generalists are before the microphone or where individuals involved have been embroiled in controversial issues. Questions tend to be less friendly in the latter circumstances and preparedness in most cases is essential to success. Exceptions arise only where those being interviewed are unusually experienced in dealing with the media. The few who meet this criterion are expert in what might be called the "nonresponsive response." They have the ability to deftly turn aside the most pointed question and speak at length on a topic in which they happen to be more interested at the moment. They confound questioners and leave audiences with the impression that questions have been answered.

Preparedness. Few public relations practitioners are blessed with spokespersons who can or should use this technique. More often than not, the reverse is true. Organizational executives for the most part are ill-prepared to cope with electronic media. They must be trained early by skilled instructors to handle interviews, especially those attendant to crisis situations. Crises often produce a deluge of less-than-friendly questions from media representatives. Any weakness in knowledge or skill on the part of the spokesperson in these circumstances quickly becomes apparent to media representatives and audiences.

A number of organizations that specialize in preparing senior managers to cope with the media have sprung up in major media centers in recent years. Many offer seminars as well as individual training for executives. Their services are worthy of consideration by most organizational managers. The skills they impart are especially valuable in dealing with the electronic media.

Style versus Substance

An understanding of the relative importance of style and substance is especially important in dealing with electronic media. Individual style is insignificant in dealing with print media. Their nature precludes communicating the intangibles involved to readers. The broadcast media, especially television, are another matter.

Style is an all-embracing term that refers to every characteristic of interview subjects, excluding only the information they may impart. It includes demeanor, speaking skills, body language, and any other element that can be seen or sensed by audience members.

One of the most memorable examples of stylistic differences in the political history of the United States involved the 1960 debates between presidential contenders John F. Kennedy and Richard M. Nixon. Both ultimately reached the presidency. Many believe Nixon would have arrived there far earlier had it not been for the debates.

While Kennedy appeared confident, relaxed, and in control, Nixon was none of these. He instead appeared ineffectual and intimidated, perspiring profusely during the course of the interview. Some proclaimed him the winner of the first debate on substance. He was a distinct loser on style, however, and never recovered.

Preparing the Spokesperson

Most organizational executives recognize the media, print and electronic, as profit-making endeavors. With this base to build on, public relations practitioners readily should be able to further educate them. Executives must comprehend contemporary definitions of news, the nature of newsgathering, and the pitfalls that await the unsuspecting in dealing with media representatives.

The pitfalls are especially prevalent in the broadcast media. Statements uttered into a tape recorder or television microphone are beyond recall. The problem is equally if less obtrusively present where print media are involved. Their reporters feel obliged to follow broadcast's lead or risk being "beaten" in competition for audience.

Interviews, as broadcast veteran Jack Hilton (1987) has observed, can be sorted into several categories. In ascending order of handling difficulty, they include entertaining, hard news, in-depth or informational, "how do you feel?," inquisitorial, and ambush.

Entertaining: Late-night talk show hosts are the champions of the "entertaining" interview. They usually are approximately 90 percent fluff and 10 percent substance. As such, they are manageable by virtually any organizational executives who have been even moderately exposed to the medium. It is hoped they will have a few interesting thoughts to express. The thoughts need not be of any great substance, however, in that late-night audiences presumably are not overly bright or less than completely awake.

Hard news: Hard news interviewers seldom proceed beyond the basic journalistic questions: who, what, why, when, where, and how? They often appear at the scene of accidents, fires, and other assorted happenings. Given time constraints imposed by evening newscasts, they seldom ask secondary or more probing questions. Straightforward, concise responses usually are adequate. Reasonably complete information concerning the subject at hand is helpful but circumstances usually are such that reporters will accept ambiguities, for example: "We don't yet know the extent of the damage."

In depth: In-depth or informational interviews often are conducted subsequent to news events and designed to probe deeper into subject matter for more detailed information. "How did the fire start?" "Why wasn't it detected more quickly?" "How are you going to keep the business going?" The interview is not designed to elicit secrets or confidential information, although they occasionally are blurted out in the process. Complete familiarity with subject matter usually is sufficient to keep executives out of trouble. Beneficial results are likely where they also are knowledgeable concerning interview and production techniques involved.

"How do you feel?": Reportorial ineptitude is the primary component of the "how do you feel" interview, although many an individual has been embarrassed by the process. It usually involves an embarrassing incident that has placed the subject in the headlines and often occurs on the courthouse steps. "How do you feel?" is a substitute for an intelligent question that usually elicits a forlorn response. The response later is broadcast in juxtaposition with footage of the reporter's question and dour countenance.

Inquisitorial: Reportorial preparedness turns "how do you feel?" into an inquisitorial interview or inquisition, a technique that television reporter Mike Wallace has turned into a career spanning more than three decades. Wallace interviews on "60 Minutes" remain one of the more feared adventures in television. Inquisitorial interviews seldom produce anything better than a "draw" from the perspective of the victim. Some in public relations counsel against agreeing to participate under any circumstances. Others believe failure to appear produces worse results. Only the most experienced of organizational managers should be permitted to undertake such assignments in the best of circumstances.

Ambush: Relatively little used today, the ambush interview was devised by arguably less-than-ethical newspeople seeking to go one up on Wallace. The tactic involves waylaying the victim on the street and peppering him or her with the same sort of questions used in inquisition interviews. Virtually no victim has come away unscathed. Most are ill-prepared, as ambush perpetrators intend, and at best appear so in resulting programs. Only one tactic has been known to frustrate ambushers: responses so laden with epithets as to preclude broadcast of material involved.

Total preparedness eliminates many of the pitfalls that exist in many of the forms of interview described above. Preparedness consists, however, of more than knowledge. Experience is essential and a knowledge of broadcast media and their techniques can be helpful as well.

Problem Questions

Most who deal frequently with the electronic media ultimately encounter a number of "problem questions," occasionally called "when are you going to quit beating your wife questions." The latter description is overstated but nevertheless signals the extent of the potential danger.

Irrelevant and seemingly innocuous questions most frequently produce the greatest problems. Exemplary of these are some of the remarks of the several presidents of the United States at news conferences that later have been explained away as misstatements by media aides. Organizational executives' public relations personnel have considerably less access to the mass media. Their disclaimers almost inevitably will go unreported.

"What if" questions are another potential trap, especially where the broadcast media are involved. They invariably are well-qualified and complex, requiring lengthy responses. The questions too frequently are forgotten if broadcast at all. Under these conditions, a businessman's comments as to how he might respond to a hypothetical unethical competitor quickly cast him as a villain.

Apparent inconsistencies also can cause problems. Some media representatives do their homework. They delight in finding published statements of years earlier that contradict spokespersons' current positions. Victims of the process find themselves faced with demands for explanations.

These are but a few of the several types of problem questions that ultimately confront most organizational spokespersons. Learning to handle them is a necessity. Learning by experience exacts too high a price. Where executives reasonably can expect to be contending regularly with the media, professional training is advisable.

Content Differences

Significant content differences exist between print and broadcast media. Distinctions between broadcast media, however, are more apparent than real from a public relations perspective. Television is predisposed to visually oriented content because the medium's visual component constitutes its primary audience appeal. Immediacy is the primary criterion of radio news in that radio stations for the most part are not constrained by television's network programming. They seek to exploit this advantage in competing for audience and advertiser dollars.

The broadcast media thus will be considered concurrently here. Their potential in public relations is more a function of content formats than technical differences. News-talk stations thus are most attractive to those seeking to disseminate information. They seek appropriate programming content 24 hours a day. Other stations nevertheless can be valuable outlets in several areas.

Most broadcasters use morning shows of one sort or another. Radio disc jockeys often use information that does not qualify as news. Television talk shows are equally amenable to feature material.

Public affairs programs also exist in both media. Virtually any information of general consumer interest and a great deal of more specialized material is of interest to them. The latter includes crime, children, drugs, education, energy, the environment, the economy, health and fitness, senior citizens, unemployment, and the like.

News versus Features

Broadcasters are as interested in features as in hard news material. The nature of the media and the diversity of public relations objectives are such, however, as to make feature exposure more readily obtainable than news coverage. Information that qualifies as news arises relatively infrequently in most organizations. Feature material is almost unlimited.

Organizational or product exposure on radio and television are most readily obtained where practitioners prepare adequately to meet media informational needs. A media kit and appropriate cover letter are highly desirable unless subject matter qualifies as news.

Media kits should include a news release, a fact sheet, a photo and biography of the spokesperson, background information on the organization and/or product, a list of suggested questions, and reprints of any available clippings or articles relative to the subject. Accompanying cover letters should focus on a single news or feature "angle." News directors and producers are too busy to sort through a broad range of options.

Several additional items should be gathered for prospective use if this material produces an affirmative response. They include photos or horizontal slides of products involved, products themselves if they are readily transportable, and any visuals that might be of interest to the producer. These include props, videotape, models, and so on.

Making the Pitch

Initial contacts with broadcast media usually involve news directors, news assignment editors, or program producers. Each can be contacted by mail or telephone. Initial contacts are appropriately made by telephone where news or other time-oriented material is involved. Mail otherwise is more appropriate.

Manner of approach where feature material is involved is often a function of practitioner preference. Where contacts are known, telephone is the usual choice. Mail otherwise is often used but a telephone follow-up may be advisable as well.

Callers should plan conversations carefully to conserve time and produce best results. They essentially are in selling situations and should begin with a sales-oriented statement. "Perhaps you've seen the article on _____in today's newspaper. I think you might be interested in following up on this national story with a local angle on _____."

Initial rejection need not be readily accepted where callers anticipate such responses. They should follow by mentioning unique aspects of the organization, product, or service. Time-oriented "hooks," relating subject matter to current events, also can be helpful. Safety-oriented organizations, for example, find linkages to holiday weekends a most effective ploy.

Resistance should be expected. Media representatives seek indirect assurance that subject matter will be of interest and that callers will follow up. Concurrently, however, they are looking for material of interest to their audiences and usually will listen to worthwhile suggestions.

Preprogram Interviews

Broadcasters seldom invite individuals and/or organizations with whom they are not familiar to participate in programs. They usually preinterview those involved and occasionally ask to see or hear a tape of a prior appearance. The process is designed to produce a preliminary impression of the individual's personality and ability to communicate. "No unpleasant surprises" is the cardinal rule.

Ability to perform in front of a camera also is important where television is involved. Television guests must be good speakers and comfortable in front of a camera no matter how well credentialed for the topic at hand. While many radio interviews are taped, most television appearances are live. This denies producers the ability to edit what is broadcast.

Follow-up Procedures

Successful broadcast placements do not end with agreement on the part of the media. Client or employer objectives largely may have been achieved at this point, but practitioner goals require more. Those who follow through professionally find subsequent placements readily arranged. Failure to follow up produces the opposite result.

Much of the follow-up involves details and technicalities. Practitioners need to know the approximate length of the segment with which they'll be dealing; whether it's live or taped; the names of individuals involved; and arrival instructions. They also should obtain information as to facilities needed for any demonstrations that may be involved. If tapes of the appearance are wanted, they should be arranged for in advance.

Arrangements should be reconfirmed 24 to 48 hours before the program date with an offer of "any assistance you might need." Media representatives should be notified as early as possible if problems arise and anticipated guests will not be available. Schedule changes often can be arranged if calls are made early and subject matter is of sufficient interest to the media.

Variation in Interviews

Length is the major variable in broadcast interviews. They can range from seconds to a quarter hour or more. Short interviews for news, news features, or short public affairs programs require conciseness and brevity on the part of respondents. Clarity of language also is essential. Resulting broadcast segments may be as brief as six seconds. Audiences must be able to assimilate content within that time span.

Appearances on longer public affairs programs permit more information to be conveyed but require equal diligence in meeting the demands of the medium. Guests should plan presentations carefully. They may have little more time to present their primary points in panel discussion or call-in formats than in brief interview situations. Most find it helpful to concentrate their efforts on no more than three primary points of information.

BROADCAST DEVELOPMENT

Preparation of broadcast content follows a pattern essentially similar to that which prevails in developing material for the print media. It also parallels the public relations process, involving research and planning prior to writing. It departs from the print and public relations patterns, however, in that the end product may take any of several forms. Broadcast content may be unscripted, semiscripted, or scripted. Each form is commonplace and successful public relations practitioners must be familiar with all of them.

Research

The research phase of broadcast production addresses three questions identical to those that arise in public relations planning. What objectives are to be accomplished? What audiences are involved? What messages must be conveyed to those audiences to induce desired responses?

Writers require an overview of these elements in order to design and construct program content. In dealing with clients or employers, they often can obtain necessary information with relative speed by requesting concise answers to similar questions. What do you want to say? To whom do you want to say it? What response do you want of them?

Successful program development requires that the answers be used to design a research agenda involving audience and content. Audience knowledge and interest levels are primary determinants of content. Writers must be knowledgeable in both areas. Only with complete information can they determine how to design an action plan leading to a program that will best meet audience, broadcaster, and public relations needs.

Action Plans

Action plans consist of at least four basic elements: a profile of the audience, a set of programmatic objectives, an outline of program content, and an overall sense of presentation or "treatment."

The action plan is an intermediate step in the developmental process. It alternatively has been called a program proposal, research report, or set of recommendations. It is essential in television and advisable in radio except where brief interviews are involved.

Audience profile. Considerable care is necessary in developing audience profiles. They must address secondary as well as primary audiences. Initial broadcast audiences may be the first of several with which practitioners are concerned.

Secondary audiences fall into two categories. The first, which almost always is of substantial concern, consists of representatives of other media. Public relations processes always are oriented to take advantage of the so-called herd instinct among the media. Subject matter printed or broadcast by one gains in stature among others. Exposure in one medium encourages more serious consideration of subject matter among other gatekeepers.

The second category involves other organizational audiences. Tapes of broadcast presentations are inexpensively obtained by prearrangement and can be used with a host of other groups. Employees and shareholders are most often among them. Content must be tailored to as great an extent as possible to meet their interests as well as those of primary audiences.

Program objectives. Broadcast programming succeeds only where objectives are achieved. Objectives are no more than statements of what programs are intended to accomplish. Each expresses a change that a program is expected to produce in one or more of the audiences involved.

Objectives typically are categorized as informational, motivational, and behavioral. Each requires that audiences become involved in subject matter to be presented although degree of involvement varies with the nature of the objective.

Where objectives are informational, programs usually are straightforward. They apply a presentational style. Content places no demands on audiences, whose responses and actions are not specified. A program describing results of basic research is exemplary of informational programming. Implications of the research may suggest long-term benefits, perhaps even products that ultimately might be offered for sale, but no audience reaction is sought.

Motivational programming, in contrast, requires changes in attitudes that ultimately are expected to produce behavioral change. A program dealing with accident prevention, for example, would include detailed descriptions of circumstances leading to these conditions. Audiences would be expected to avoid behaviors conducive to mishaps. Motivational programs tend to be more difficult to develop than others and results usually are harder to measure. This especially is so where desired responses involve avoidance of specified activities.

The opposite is true where objectives are behavioral. Programs such as training or teaching presentations are designed to produce observable and therefore measurable results. Objectives in these circumstances specify what will be done and how it will be accomplished.

Program content. The nature of objectives and audience characteristics dictate program content. Programming directed toward informational objectives largely is intellectual. Motivational programs tend to be emotional in content while behavioral objectives often require a blending of the two.

Within these general parameters, writers take diverse approaches to engaging their audiences. Some use dramatization. Others employ humor. Still others may use animation techniques. There exist no "right" and "wrong" approaches. Objectives and audience profiles govern major points of informational content. Near total creative latitude exists thereafter.

Mode of presentation. Treatment or presentation of material develops in part through writer creativity and in part through mechanical development. Where no creative concept comes to mind during early developmental stages, as often is the case, audiovisual writers turn to five basic techniques. Van Nostran (1983) described them as talking heads, talking heads with props, visuals with voices, interviews, and dramatizations. Each has its own characteristics.

Talking heads, avoided in most situations, involve the voice and face of a spokesperson. With adequate preparation, many can convey the sincerity and credibility that this presentation method requires. Relatively few manage it well. Talking heads with props, as in the case of television's cooking or home repair shows, create an added dimension for viewers. Results are enhanced in that messages are conveyed visually as well as orally.

The visuals and voices approach removes the face of the speaker from scene. Visuals may include artwork, charts, diagrams, or photographs. "Voices" here are defined to include music or other sound effects as well as the human voice. The combination of oral and visual impressions offers considerable flexibility and often enables writers to compound their individual impact.

Interviews may be an integral part of programs, as most often is the case with talk shows, or may be inserted as vignettes. The on-camera approach places the interviewer as well as the subject before the audience and usually is considered "half scripted" by writers. The latter often excludes interviewers and usually is unscripted. "Half scripted" refers to development and sequencing of questions or discussion points prior to interviewing.

Dramatizations, in contrast to interviews, always are fully scripted. They are most often seen in programs dealing with management of interpersonal relationships. Without dramatizations, the intangible nature of the subject matter would reduce the writer to extensive use of talking heads.

Where dealing with television rather than radio, writers select individual techniques most appropriate to each informational component. They then are placed in chronological sequence together with descriptions of sight and sound as well as participants. Techniques by which transitions from one scene to another are to be accomplished. then are added to complete the treatment—the final element in the action plan.

WRITING FOR EYE AND EAR

Radio and television writing often are viewed as essentially similar, but this is the case only in a very narrow sense. The writing styles are much the same; however, beyond the stylistic component, writers are dealing with different media. Television writing requires thinking in two dimensions, visual and aural. Writers must be adept at visualizing video components that will accompany their words.

The most critical element in television writing is balance: the ability to combine the two basic methods of thought transmission to create a cohesive whole. The "I can write anything" syndrome frequently observed among those trained in any sort of writing can be deadly to the finished product in these circumstances. Few trained in print or broadcast newswriting are readily apt to acquire the skills necessary to achieve critical balance.

As in the case of print media production (see Chapter 11), public relations practitioners have several options open to them. They can attempt the writing themselves, retain free-lance assistance, or turn to professional production organizations in developing audiovisual products. Many do-it-yourselfers who have succeeded in more rudimentary audiovisual formats such as slide/tape or unscripted videotape find professional assistance essential in dealing with full-blown videotape or film production. These factors and others primarily involved in audio and video production for organizational rather than external purposes are discussed in Chapter 13.

BROADCAST PRODUCTION

Potential need for technical support quickly becomes apparent as practitioners address the range of circumstances they may face in preparing material for broadcast. They can be as simple as an on-site interview with a radio reporter requiring no more than a few sentences spoken into a microphone. They also can be as complex as a full-blown television documentary involving studio and location videotaping.

Programming in more sophisticated forms involves practitioners in the technical and procedural aspects of television production. Skilled technical personnel are available to provide guidance but spokespersons must be prepared in advance to participate in often lengthy production processes. They often require multiple rehearsals and involve considerable potential for error.

Rehearsal Procedures

Rehearsals generally fall into several categories: prestudio rehearsals, run-through rehearsals, and dress rehearsals. The term "prestudio" is somewhat misleading. It covers rehearsal meetings usually conducted outside studios and technical rehearsals that necessarily occur in the studio.

Rehearsal meetings: Many television directors schedule rehearsal meetings to conserve costly studio time. They permit production crew members to become acquainted with one another and with anticipated production techniques. Equipment, facilities, and camera sequencing are among matters usually discussed in preliminary form during rehearsal meetings.

Technical rehearsals: The production crew moves to the studio for technical or prestudio rehearsals. These are rehearsals without performers designed to give the production team an opportunity to prepare the set. Furniture and props are arranged. The floor is chalked or taped to indicate positions for performers. Staff members may "sit in" for performers to permit review of anticipated camera shots and timing can be reviewed.

Run-through rehearsals: Performers become part of the process during the run-through rehearsals. There may be one or many. They are held to familiarize performers with their parts, refine production techniques, and enable directors to make technical changes to enhance results. Run-through rehearsals are marked by frequent repetition. A planned shot that does not satisfy the director may be repeated again and again until desired results are achieved.

Dress rehearsals: Unlike run-through rehearsals, dress rehearsals usually are not interrupted. Changes may still be necessary but suggestions are noted for discussion after the rehearsal is completed. Major changes usually are kept to a minimum at this point in the process.

Preparing Performers

Rehearsals can be rather traumatic for clients or employers unless they are thoroughly briefed in advance by public relations practitioners. In the absence of adequate briefings, rehearsals quickly can become traumatic for practitioners as well.

Performers (clients or employers) are thrust into foreign surroundings that can become physically uncomfortable. They may be ordered about by unthinking producers or crew personnel in a manner to which they are wholly unaccustomed. They almost inevitably find themselves making mistakes. Moreover, television lighting tends to be burdensome to the uninitiated.

These conditions can be relatively traumatic for organizational executives who are used to being always in command and expect deferential treatment at all times. They must be anticipated by public relations practitioners.

Performer guidelines. A few simple guidelines provided in advance can make the television experience more palatable to those called upon to perform. Most important among them is punctuality. Considerable money is wasted when television crews are kept waiting. Performer schedules should be arranged around rehearsals and allow ample time for their completion to producers' satisfaction.

Directors should be advised in advance of any special components of planned presentations such as equipment, visual aids, and props. During rehearsals, directors must be aware of performers' whereabouts at all times. Under no circumstances should performers leave the studio without first notifying directors.

Performers must know their parts before rehearsals begin. Questions as to time factors, equipment to be used, prompting techniques, and the like are in order. Other participants cannot be expected to wait, however, while performers learn their lines.

Positive, calm, and cheerful attitudes are necessary at all times. They may be difficult to achieve in studio environments but nevertheless are essential, especially when errors occur, as almost inevitably is the case in rehearsal.

Avoiding mistakes. Performer error is commonplace in rehearsals and to be expected. Organizational executives should be cautioned to look on rehearsals as learning experiences; as opportunities to experience problems and thus learn to avoid them during live presentations.

Most mistakes are commonplace and readily corrected. Most common among them is "being off the mark"—off the assigned floor marks or in the wrong place in the studio. Novices also frequently face the wrong camera, fumble their lines, or "freeze up" on camera. Experience with these problems in rehearsal is the best way to avoid them later.

The process tends to be difficult for the inexperienced but produces favorable long-term consequences. Often organizational executives who have avoided the camera become audiovisual enthusiasts after a few on-camera experiences. As an executive of a teleconferencing company once remarked to a group of public relations practitioners, "he avoided the medium for years, but after a few taping sessions began to fancy himself a TV star."

IN SUMMARY

While production processes employed in preparing broadcast material essentially are similar to those used in the print sector, one significant difference exists in the ultimate product. Much of it ultimately takes the form of interviews or other on-the-air appearances by organizational executives. These circumstances demand special diligence in preparing for broadcasts.

Preparation for broadcast requires special attention to the nature of audiences involved, especially their demographic and sociographic characteristics. Broadcast content must convey information in a manner that will result in receipt, assimilation, and response if public relations objectives are to be achieved.

This objective often must be achieved in the presence of third parties. Interviewers' or moderators' questions require considerable agility on the part of their guests, who essentially lose control of message content to a degree in interview situations. This especially is the case where guests are generalists rather than specialists. Organizations' chief executive officers are expected to be knowledgeable in all aspects of an organization's activities, while many of their specialized subordinates are not.

Preparedness of organizational spokespersons ideally includes specialized training. It is available through organizations formed to provide such services in larger cities and through some trade and professional associations as well. Those who represent organizations also should be knowledgeable as to the workings and motivations of the news media to successfully anticipate many of the questions that may be asked of them.

Broadcast interviews can be categorized as "hard news," "in-depth," "how do you feel?," "inquisitorial," and "ambush." The hard news interview usually deals with journalistic basics: who, what, why, when, where, and how. In-depth interviews address the reasons behind these elements. "How do you feel" interviews usually follow embarrassing events. Inquisitorial and ambush interviews are exemplified by those conducted by the "60 Minutes" and "20/20" television programs.

Content of broadcast interviews differs little from that of the print variety. Television seeks to exploit visually oriented content while radio deals primarily with its time advantage, but content is essentially identical. Both deal in news and feature material. Releases or fact sheets sometimes are used in conjunction with news interviews but complete media kits are necessary in eliciting feature exposure.

Public relations practitioners make initial contacts with broadcasters by mail or telephone depending upon the timelines of the material at hand. Where producers or news directors are interested, preprogram interviews follow. Practitioners then are expected to handle necessary follow-up prior to the appointed broadcast time. The process requires further research based on the audience of the individual station as well as clearly defined objectives. Content then is designed in keeping with those objectives.

Scripts may or may not be used. They never are appropriate in news reports. Interviews usually are semiscripted. Questions are decided upon in advance, however, and usually can be successfully anticipated by those involved. Complete scripts almost never are used in news situations. Where exceptions occur, they can be designed in keeping with criteria for audiovisual programs (see Chapter 13).

Technical requirements for broadcast appearances are handled by the media but spokespersons should be acquainted with procedures. They often involve rehearsal meetings followed by technical, run-through, and dress rehearsals. Spokespersons or performers seldom are involved prior to the run-through phase. Public relations practitioners should brief clients or employers on the mechanics of the processes so that they are appropriately prepared.

ADDITIONAL READING

Blythin, Evan, and Larry A. Samovar. *Communicating Effectively on Television.* Belmont, Calif.: Wadsworth, 1985.

Burrows, Thomas D., and Donald N. Wood. *Television Production: Disciplines and Techniques,* 4th ed. Dubuque, Ia.: Wm. C. Brown, 1986.

Chambers, Wicke, and Spring Asher. *TV/PR: How to Promote Yourself, Your Product, Your Service or Your Organization On Television.* Atlanta: Chase Communiations, 1986.

Gross, Lynn Schafer. *Telecommunications: An Introduction to Radio, Television, and the Developing Media.* Dubuque, Ia.: Wm. C. Brown, 1983.

Hilton, Jack. *How to Meet the Press: A Survival Guide.* New York: Dodd, Mead, 1987.

Kindem, Gorham. *The Moving Image: Production Principles and Practices.* Glenview, Ill.: Scott, Foresman, 1987.

St. John, Tracy. *Getting Your Public Relations Story on TV and Radio.* Babylon, N.Y.: Pilot Books, 1986.

Van Nostran, William. *The Nonbroadcast Television Writer's Handbook.* White Plains,
        N.Y.: Knowledge Industry Publications, 1983.
Weaver, J. Clark. *Broadcast Copywriting as Process.* New York: Longman, 1984.
Wiegand, Ingrid. *Professional Video Production.* White Plains, N.Y.: Knowledge In-
        dustry Publications, 1985.
————. *Broadcast Newswriting as Process.* New York: Longman, 1984.

13

Electronic Production

While radio and television are the most prominent components of the electronic media, audiovisuals are more common in public relations practice. With the advent of videotape equipment, they are achieving parity with the print media in business communication.

Exclusive of radio and television, as discussed here, electronic media include two basic groups. One consists of those traditionally described as audiovisual media. They include motion pictures, multimedia presentations, filmstrips, sound/slide presentations, and audio- as well as videotapes. The second and more diverse group includes telephone and television conferencing, videotext, teletext, facsimile, and computer-accessed data bases. Some are or can be truly audiovisual in nature while others are similar only in that they can be characterized as "electronic."

The basic components of audiovisual communication differ little from those used in the print sector. Most words to be delivered audiovisually are fashioned primarily for the ear rather than the eye. Graphic images appear in transient fashion on screens rather than permanently on paper. Either or both may be accompanied by music in some applications.

Each of the remaining electronic media has advantages and disadvantages but none is common to all of them. Many are a function of the broad range of technologies represented, some still in their infancies in the United States. Videotext and teletext are in this category. Others, such as conferencing systems and data bases, are well-established.

Use of electronic media in any given circumstances must be weighed against a single criterion: cost versus effectiveness. Raw number of dollars involved, as in the print media, seldom is a valid measure of potential. Public relations practitioners instead must be concerned with anticipated return on investment.

Were they practically or ethically able to guarantee clients or employers a significant rate of return, questions concerning cost never would be raised.

AUDIOVISUAL VARIABLES

Audiovisuals in one sense are superior and in another inferior to print media. They are at their best in presenting general information or evoking emotion. They are weak where detailed information must be retained and/ or reviewed. The latter weakness results from absence of audience control. Information is delivered at a predetermined rate regardless of variation in or across audiences.

Visuals and sound effects nevertheless assist audiences in retaining basic concepts. This attribute has led to their extensive use in concert with printed materials in training and educational settings. Film and videotape, especially the latter, are most often used because they present motion as well as sound and images. They also are the most expensive of audiovisual formats but cost is only one criterion by which such materials can be judged.

Other significant factors include the nature of the presentation involved, audience(s) to which it will be shown, locations and circumstances in which it is to be shown, audience perceptions of the media, and degree of flexibility that may permit multiple applications.

Cost Factors

Potential productivity must be considered in assessing audiovisual costs. A $75,000 bill for production of a videotape to train a few dozen service personnel in handling a new product well might be considered exorbitant. Were the same number of dollars invested in a sales tape for use with prospective buyers of 500 new condominiums offered for sale at $500,000 to $750,000 each, cost would be well within reason.

Cost thus can be calculated in raw dollar terms or on the basis of anticipated benefits. Cost per message recipient, as in the case of the broadcast media, also may be a worthwhile measure of effectiveness in some instances.

One or more of these methods almost always is applied in determining whether anticipated production costs can be justified. Justification may involve several variables. They include presentation environments, the extent to which content can be revised or used in multiple applications, anticipated impact, level of retention, and product durability.

Presentation Environments

Potential for successful communication always is limited by the extent to which messages are delivered. Delivery does not assure success but failure in delivery necessarily defeats the process. Those contemplating applying audiovisual techniques thus first must consider the environments in which they are to be used and the audiences to which they are to be directed.

While all audiovisual media are effective in darkened rooms, their effectiveness varies with higher light levels. Light may be necessary where viewers are expected to take notes and may be unavoidable where adequate shades or drapes are not available. Where light levels are high, television receivers and video monitors perform reasonably well. The effectiveness of video projection systems, films, and filmstrips is sharply reduced.

Equipment availability also requires attention. Where audiovisuals are used on producers' premises, necessary playback equipment generally is available. Caution is necessary where they are to be used in other settings. Neither film nor videotape projectors can be assumed to be available, for example, even in larger hotels. Videotape tends to be especially troublesome due to the variety of formats in which it is produced. Available equipment in any location tends to be of a design incompatible with the tape at hand. Compatibility problems also occur in audiocassette recorders and other equipment.

Audio variables. Sound can present parallel problems. Too few meeting rooms are adequately insulated against extraneous noise. Available sound equipment usually is of less-than-ideal quality as well. The impact of programs that rely heavily on sound effects is substantially reduced in these circumstances.

Two other technical factors also require attention. One involves operator skill levels. The other is the complexity of the equipment involved. Unskilled operators may encounter difficulty with the simplest of equipment. More complex varieties tend to suffer mechanical failure at the most inopportune moment.

Operator training always is advisable and should be considered essential for "off premises" presentations. Where programs are of vital importance, backup equipment also should be available.

Audience characteristics. Finally, there is the matter of audience. Two audience characteristics are especially significant: size and affinity for the material being presented. Large audiences experience difficulty in dealing with some audiovisual media. Television monitors and cathode ray tubes are especially troublesome. Some overhead slide projection equipment also is best limited to smaller groups. Content must be readily seen and heard by all involved.

Affinity is another matter. It involves the extent to which recipients feel a need for information being delivered. Attentiveness is to be expected where program content is considered vital to personal success, as in the content of training programs. Where sales material is involved, the reverse is true. High affinity or attentiveness levels can compensate for technological weaknesses to some extent but low levels create major obstacles.

Message Retention

Ability of audiences to retain and respond to messages delivered through audiovisual channels also is influenced by two other sets of variables. Only one set is amenable to control by program developers. It includes the speed and manner in which information is delivered as well as some of the technical concerns itemized earlier. The other involves audience perception of the medium or media employed. Many are predisposed to consider filmstrips and slide presentations as uninteresting or boring.

Some also may be predisposed by background or education to invest print media with greater credibility or reliability than their electronic counterparts. Where this is the case, or where audience members are subsequently expected to apply detailed information or instructions, audiovisuals should be accompanied by parallel documentation. Printed material reinforces message delivery and assists in appropriate application of content.

Message delivery. The pace at which information is delivered must be adjusted in keeping with content. Messages designed primarily to evoke emotional appeals may vary in pace in the discretion of program developers. Those intended to convey information that, is is hoped, audience members will retain require time for assimilation.

Political presentations thus can proceed at any pace while training programs require time for thought and comprehension. These factors may come into conflict with preconceived notions of audiovisual media, compounding programmer difficulties.

Audience perceptions. Whether through overexposure during primary and secondary schooling or otherwise, many perceive slide and filmstrip presentations to be uninteresting. Most audiences tend to be better disposed to film or videotape although they may not be as well suited to specific situations.

Technical training programs, for example, often require slides to be displayed for extended periods while their content is explained and questions are answered. These images can be conveyed by videotape but slides or filmstrips are more appropriate. They permit instructional personnel to vary timing with the needs of individual audiences.

Where procedures such as equipment assembly or disassembly are to be illustrated, videotape or film may be equally efficient. Media selection decisions require attention to all of these points and one other: the extent to which content may be used in multiple applications.

Other Variables

Ease of revision is among the most significant of the variables encountered in evaluating audiovisual channels. Ability to revise easily and inexpensively influences the useful life of the product, which in turn bears directly on cost:effectiveness ratios.

Audiotape is most readily revised and cost is relatively low. Script revisions can be made quickly and rerecording often requires less time than script revisions. Sets of slides are even more readily edited. The new quickly replace the old in the drum or tray.

Revising an audiovisual program requires more work, especially where a professionally produced sound track is involved. Changes must be spliced into the master audiotape and the sound track must be remixed. Resynchronization also is necessary where visuals are changed by sound track audio pulses.

The process of change becomes even more complex with filmstrips, multimedia presentations, videotape, and film. In each instance, additional steps are required. All are time consuming and progressively more costly.

Filmstrips must be remade or spliced and accompanying audio often must be changed as well. Revision in multimedia presentations may require changes in more than one of the media involved. Change in videotape or film requires all of the production steps necessary in producing the original plus splicing.

The extent to which content will be used in multiple applications or with several audiences also has a bearing on the cost of change. Where similar messages or components of messages are to be delivered to multiple stakeholder groups, numbers of modifications and attendant costs require attention before production begins.

AUDIOVISUAL COMPONENTS

Audiovisual components in one sense are identical to and in another quite different from those used in print media. They are identical in that both require words and illustrations. They differ radically, however, in mode of presentation.

The words are contained in a script in which authors also should describe choices in music and visuals. The script ultimately is converted into a sound track accompanied by a compilation of visual materials. These components subsequently are linked together in a predetermined mechanical format for ease of presentation.

Script Development

Those who prepare effective audiovisual scripts universally are aware of and act upon a basic truth: spoken English and written English are so different as to require handling as separate languages. Audiovisual scripts must be prepared in spoken English. They are written for the ear rather than the eye.

Where created to produce best possible results, they are even more demanding than traditional public relations material generated for the electronic media. They require simplicity and austerity in verbiage to produce necessary levels of clarity.

Writing styles. The more words with which an audience must contend, the less likely members are to understand and retain messages they are intended to convey. No concept that can be expressed in a single sentence should be delivered in two or more. No object that can be described in one word should be given a sentence. Smith and Orr (1985) expressed the standard in these words:

The more words the audience hears, the more words the audience has to wade through to reach the major message. If you wade through your scripts first, doing that work for the audience, they'll reward you by retaining your message.

Script writers too often forget that words they reduce to writing will be conveyed aurally; that they are fleeting and ephemeral from audience perspectives. They must be understood and retained as conveyed unless reproduced in accompanying literature.

Scripting options. As is the case in developing print media content, scripts can be written by practitioners, by member of their staffs, or by independent contractors. Many audiovisual presentations can be developed "from scratch" using only organizational resources. While few are equipped to handle motion picture filming, an increasing number have videotape equipment at their disposal

Whether "in-house" production represents the best use of available resources is another matter. Subcontracting components to writers, illustrators, and technicians often is the more practical alternative where resources are available.

Script writing. Preparing an audiovisual script is a far different task than writing a brochure draft. Words on paper require no special pace or rhythm; no specific tone or structure. These components must be present in audiovisual presentations and, moreover, must be consistent in all sound and visual elements. Impressions that the finished product conveys to the several senses must be harmonious.

To insure that the several components are given equal attention, scripts are written in "split page" fashion. The page is divided into two vertical segments. The audio portion typically is written at left while visuals and music are indicated at right. These elements ultimately are brought together in a unitary whole.

Sound Track Planning

With script complete, the next step in the developmental process involves merging narration with music and any special sound effects specified in the writing process. Several variables must be addressed in developing each of these elements.

Narration. Most sound contained in audiovisual presentations involves the human voice. Two sources usually are involved: professional or amateur narrators and the voices of individuals recorded "on location." Narrators usually are referred to as "voice-over" or "on-camera" talent while location recordings are called "actualities" or "sound bites."

Narrator choices are not always easily made. Professionals often can add meaning or drama to words, enhancing their impact. They lend a professional polish to the finished product and usually are far more proficient in script reading. On the other hand, they may experience difficulty in credibly assuming the role of a customer or employee. Amateurs often produce better results where realism is necessary but sound tracks in which they are involved usually require more editing and studio time.

Script flexibility is essential where amateurs are used in audiovisual production. They must be permitted to express the thoughts involved in words with which they are comfortable. This process minimizes their awkwardness and nervousness and softens the amateurishness of the result.

Music. Audiovisual music is more readily but too often illegally handled. It can be taken from commercially produced tapes or records, but only at the risk of litigation. Popular music also creates a potential problem seldom considered by audiovisual producers. By its nature it may become the focus of audience attention, detracting from accompanying words and visuals.

Most commercial production studios offer practical alternatives in the form of music libraries developed specifically for use in sound tracks. They are relatively inexpensive and are produced in components more amenable to sound track use than contemporary music.

Where especially sophisticated production is anticipated, an original music score may be a worthwhile investment. Costs usually are in the thousands of dollars rather than the hundreds involved in using music libraries, but the music can be used in multiple programs to amortize the expense involved.

Where budgets prohibit even a few hundred dollars for music, two alternatives are worthy of consideration. One involves live recording of artists playing compositions on which copyrights have expired. The other entails use of inexpensive background music records. Neither produces the level of finished quality engendered by the other options.

Sound effects. The realities that audiovisuals attempt to convey often can be enhanced through sound effects. These seemingly simple devices often are more complex than they appear; technical assistance may be necessary to achieve desired results.

Sound effects can be enhanced technologically or purchased on inexpensive recordings. They should be used with discretion, however, to minimize undue background noise. Use of assembly-line noise as background for an audiovisual presentation, for example, may better convey the atmosphere of the line but conflict with accompanying narration.

A simple guideline should govern use of sound effects: don't use them for their own sake. They almost always should be enhancers of overall impact rather than "add ons." Overuse of sound effects can destroy the intelligibility of completed sound tracks.

With intelligibility problems there often develops a temptation to "override" the difficulty by "turning up the volume." While technically feasible, the result often is a finished "track" of marginal quality. Qualified sound engineers should be called upon to adjust volume level, frequency response, and signal-to-noise ratio to produce best results.

Developing Visuals

While relatively comfortable in handling script development, many public relations practitioners encounter difficulty in preparing accompanying visuals. The problem arises out of their relative inexperience in visualizing finished products. Smith and Orr prescribed a logical process that assists many in overcoming this obstacle.

The beginning point requires focusing on the finished product rather than any component part. Mental construction of voice and images that appear as audiovisual presentations proceed create a sort of matrix into which available material can be sorted.

Anticipated audiences should be a part of the mental construct. With audience members in mind, brief responses to a set of simple questions can help in planning the visual component of the program. What do you want them to think? How do you want them to respond? What stimuli have been incorporated into the script, and which should be presented visually?

A review of the script and preliminarily specified sound elements then should be undertaken to produce further ideas for visuals. Special attention should be paid to primary message components in light of the questions posed above. Each should be examined mentally as to how the thought involved can be presented in tangible rather than intangible form.

Types of Visuals

Visuals fall into several general categories. They include photographs, graphics, artwork, and so-called computerized visuals. None is uniformly applicable in all audiovisual productions but each can be applied effectively in specific situations.

Visuals should be selected in keeping with the objectives of the audiovisual presentation rather than through personal preference. Types of visuals used in most cases should be limited. Unnecessary change in graphics, as in pace of narration or tempo of music, tends to destroy audience attention to subject matter.

Photography. Studio and on-location photography constitutes the bulk of the graphic content of most audiovisual presentations. This is the case almost regardless of the nature of the medium in use. Graphics dominate only where overhead projectors are used.

Still photography is predominant in slides, film strips, and multimedia presentations, while motion pictures are the primary component of videotape and film. The basic process, however, remains unchanged.

Artwork. Most audiovisual presentations also use artwork in one form or another. It is most common in titles but also is used extensively where photography is impractical, as in the case of a complex piece of machinery in a training film. Diagrams or "exploded views" often are used to show the manner in which components are assembled.

Cartoons, drawings, and other forms of artwork also may be employed to illustrate concepts that are not amenable to photography. Graphic representations of theories or molecular structures are examples of this technique.

Graphics. Text slides, especially of tabular matter, as well as charts and graphs all are classified as graphics. They are most commonly found in informational presentations to shareholder or similar groups.

Graphs and charts most often are used as substitutes for complex verbal descriptions. The content of such descriptions is difficult to understand and retain when presented only in verbal form.

Computerized visuals. Sophisticated graphics programs through which computers generate complex charts and diagrams have added a new dimension to audiovisual presentations. While generally classified as computerized visuals, the products involved range from original designs to conventional material that otherwise would have to be manually drawn.

Computers equipped with color monitors are especially helpful in generating graphs from statistical data. Photography techniques pioneered by Polaroid permit computer screen content to be converted to slides in a matter of minutes.

Computers also can be used to create lifelike drawings as well as abstract designs. They can convert still photos into three-dimensional images or into what appear to be ink drawings. They can change colors and sizes of the objects involved and, because of their ability to "remember," can generate images in multiple variations.

Assembling Visuals

All of the visuals included in any presentation ultimately must be assembled to create a cohesive whole. Decisions as to their use usually are made on the basis of their appearance in context with the finished audiotrack or script. Scripts usually are used where slide-tape or film strips are in production. Audiotracks are used for videotape and film.

Graphic elements usually are first assembled into scenes or series and then reviewed with pertinent segments of the audiotrack or script. Since film and processing are as relatively inexpensive in audiovisual as in print media production, most producers generate double or triple the amount of raw material that ultimately is contained in the finished product.

Other Concerns

At least four other variables also require attention in developing audiovisual programs. They include program design, visual style, clarity, and flow. While primarily technical in nature, they are examined here in that each influences the effectiveness of completed audiovisual programs.

Program design. The term "program design" refers to levels of consistency achieved among program components. Optimum levels of effectiveness are accomplished where consistency is established among visuals and between visuals and words.

Achievement often involves compromise. Two good visuals, for example, are superior to one especially striking visual left overly long on the screen. The underlying principle is simple: consistency breeds attentiveness while variation tends to be distracting. Jarring transitions are to be avoided in all circumstances.

Visual style. Programmatic objectives govern visual style as well as verbal style. Style, in other words, must match purpose. An emotional presentation designed to motivate volunteers for the kick-off of a fund-raising campaign, for example, necessarily differs from an instructional presentation to students.

Training programs require clarity. Information conveyed must be readily understood. The primary objective in dealing with fund-raising volunteers is enthusiasm. High emotional impact is essential in accompanying visuals.

Clarity. The terms "visual clarity" or "fluency" can be applied equally to two components of audiovisual presentations. They necessarily apply in a technological sense. Blurred images, other than in unusual artistic or technical situations, are anathema.

The same concept applies, however, to clarity of meaning. Audiovisuals, as discussed earlier, must be more easily "read" than their printed counterparts. Charts and graphs must be simple and direct in presentation. Lettering must be legible. Captions must be descriptively precise.

The same concept applies to series of visuals or scenes. Relationships among them must be as evident as in the case of successive words and sentences. Communication is obstructed where audience members are forced to struggle to relate one to the next.

Fluidity. Pacing, flow, or "fluidity" refer to sequencing of visual elements and the smoothness with which they are shown. While most noticed when absent in videotape and film, fluidity is essential to other audiovisual media as well.

Fluidity is best evidenced by the absence of "jumps," which are most readily noticed where film or videotape are ineptly spliced, producing the appearance of sudden movement on the part of persons or objects. Jumps also appear, however, where series of views or scenes appear discontinuous. Audiences are "jarred" by these irregular transitions and attention wavers as a result.

The problem is especially troublesome in multimedia presentations where several images are shown concurrently. Producers then must be concerned not only with fluidity in each series of images but across the several series in progress.

All of these factors require attention in dealing with all of the audiovisual media. Some are more important than others, however, to some components of the electronic media category. Some of these communication channels long have been in extensive use. Others probably will grow in usage through much of the twenty-first century.

OTHER MEDIA

Developing technologies have been producing new and enhanced channels of communication at a rate unprecedented in history. Most involve computers or communication satellites and virtually all have been growing rapidly in popularity. Their growth is expected to accelerate as costs decline. The channels involved concurrently will become more a part of public relations practice.

These "new" channels of communication include telephone and video-conferencing, videotex, and computer communication. Technologies permitting telephone and videoconferencing have been available for some time. They have become more popular in recent years with increased competition and declining rates in the telecommunication sector.

Computer-based communication, including electronic mail and videotex services, are growing in popularity but have yet to achieve their forecast potential. Growth in electronic mail potential may be limited by competition from facsimile and overnight express systems but the computer-based media appear destined to become major elements in information transfer.

Videotex and Computer Systems

The term "videotex" has been precisely defined by the International Communication Union to refer only to electronic systems in which modified television sets are used to display computer-based information. "Teletext," in comparison, refers to systems such as those in the United Kingdom that rely on broadcast signals rather than computers to deliver information.

They differ from viewdata systems in that viewdata relies on telephone lines or cables to reach television sets with "interactive videotex" services. Viewdata services can record use of information and answers to questions. They can take orders for merchandise, book airline seats, and provide other similar services.

Videotex and viewdata services differ from systems such as CompuServe and The Source, which essentially are computer utilities. The utilities are computer-to-computer rather than computer-to-television services. They offer considerably greater breadth than videotex and viewdata. CompuServe, for example, provides electronic mail, bulletin board, and computer conferencing services. Utilities serve as host vehicles for multiple special interest groups, and afford users direct access to multiple electronic data bases.

While neither videotex nor viewdata services have become major components of public communication in the United States, the computer utilities have been gaining in subscribers. Declining computer costs and the utilities' ever-expanding range of services suggest they will continue to grow and ultimately become major media in their own right.

Electronic Data Bases

Information retrieval from electronic data bases is increasingly important in public relations practice. The several data bases contain the content of most major newspapers and wire services as well as magazines, newsletters, and a host of other publications.

Published and unpublished news releases are made part of these data bases. Those that are published are contained in files of publication content. Many that go unpublished ultimately become a part of NEXIS, the Mead Data Central utility that regularly receives the content of PR Newswire (see Chapter 10).

CompuServe, The Source, and other computer utilities provide access to limited numbers of data bases. Others, such as NEXIS and DIALOG, are accessible to subscribers on a direct basis by computer. Still others are accessible through so-called gateway utilities, which essentially are wholesalers of information. They purchase "bulk access" to data bases and resell to individual subscribers. Subscribers benefit in avoiding multiple individual accounts and sign-up fees to access individual data bases.

Many of the special interest groups, including the Public Relations and Marketing Forum, accessible via CompuServe, also maintain data libraries containing considerable information of interest to users. Many libraries are open to nonmembers of sponsoring groups and group bulletin boards almost always are conducted on an open basis. Public relations messages can be posted on bulletin boards and, with the concurrence of forum system operators, may become part of data libraries as well. Lists and descriptions of data libraries are accessible by computer. No directory yet has been published other than for individual services such as CompuServe. Creating appropriate distribution lists for public relations use thus would be time consuming but in specific circumstances may prove worthwhile.

Most special interest groups also schedule regular on-line meetings that often are open to all comers. While their motivations doubtless vary, participants in many of the special interest groups are representatives of organizations that act as vendors to members.

Conferencing Services

While computer utilities provide open conferencing services, closed services also are available using telephone and television through a number of organizations. Some limit access to members, as in the case of the American Hospital Association. Others make their services available commercially.

Conferencing services come in three basic formats: computer, telephone, and television. Functional differences among them relate primarily to the visual dimension. They also differ practically, however, in technology, complexity, and cost.

Telephone services. Most telephone services differ little from those of the various telephone companies. Operators bring a predetermined group together at a predetermined time and link the members by telephone line.

Some commercial services offer several "bells and whistles" that telephone companies lack. Darome, Inc., for example, provides on-going monitoring by an operator to assure that all lines are functioning and will provide tape-recorded transcripts. The Chicago-based firm offers multiple telephone conferencing systems and other services. The latter include audio for video conferences and electronic graphics conferencing.

Television services. Most television services are commercial operations. They link sites rather than individuals using microwave transceivers and geo-synchronous satellites of the type used by television broadcasters. Private Satellite Networks, Inc., of New York, for example, uses direct broadcast satellite technology to provide clients with a broad range of services. They include applications development, space segment, receive site surveys and installation, integrated electronics systems, total network operation, and full maintenance.

Television conferencing requires more equipment than the telephone variety to handle voice and picture. Sophisticated productions require extensive studio facilities and personnel. While the technologies involved permit users to select conference locations, economic limitations confine most to fixed facilities. All of the production concerns that apply in television broadcasting are applicable in television conferencing (see Chapter 12).

Computer services. Technology necessary to a computer-based system exists but services have been slow to develop. University Tech-Tel Corporation of Bethesda, Maryland, has been a pioneer in this area with its Tele-writer system. University Tech-Tel has combined personal computer networking with an unusual Optel Communications conferencing system. The Optel system incorporates an "electronic blackboard" that permits participants to "draw" on computer screens.

Relative Merits

Cost and convenience factors aside, television conferencing arguably produces the best results. Participants can see and hear one another, creating circumstances similar to those that obtain in face-to-face group conferences. Studio settings create some differences but functional conditions remain almost identical barring equipment malfunctions.

Videotapes of these conferences can be made at reasonable cost for future use. Virtually all are conducted in black and white, however, and quality usually is significantly lower than that generated by commercial broadcasters.

Telephone conferencing suffers from the absence of visual linkages. Chairpersons especially experience difficulty in that they cannot respond to visual signals from those who wish to speak but want to maintain a modicum of courtesy. The problem tends to compound with the size of the group involved, creating barriers to open communication.

Computer conferencing lacks both visual and aural contact. Only one individual can "talk" at a time but the same practical requirement applies where telephones are used. Vocal inflections also are lost, which creates added constraints, as in the hesitancy of most participants to attempt to inject humor. Generally accepted operating protocols assist chairpersons, however, in conducting meetings in logical fashion.

Systems are configured so that senders' names appear at the start of every line of text they transmit. All others thus know immediately who is "talking." Those who wish to talk need only key in a "?" and press "return" or "enter" on their keyboards. Their names and question marks appear as these "messages" are transmitted, enabling chairpersons to call on them in appropriate order.

One other advantage attaches to computer conferencing. Complete electronic transcripts are made automatically by many computer programs. These can be circulated to people who can not attend and retained in electronic or printed form for future reference.

IN SUMMARY

While the broadcast media are most prominent in the electronic sector, others long have been as extensively used. With the advent of videotape systems and computer utilities, broadcast is but one of a broad range of electronic systems used in public relations.

Other than in conventional broadcast, electronic media include other audiovisual systems and a multiplicity of alternative communication channels. The latter, more diverse group includes telephone and television conferencing, videotext, teletext, and facsimile as well as computer utilities. The utilities provide mail and conferencing services as well as data bases and other resources.

Audiovisual media in some applications are superior and in others inferior to the print media. They excel in presenting general information and evoking emotional responses. They are less productive where detailed information is to be retained.

Audiovisual costs vary considerably. Cost factors are more readily assessed in terms of potential productivity than gross dollar amounts. Cost per message recipient also is a valid indicator of potential worth.

Potential for successful use of audiovisuals is limited by the nature of the several devices available and the environments in which they are to be used. Some, such as overhead transparencies, are best applied with smaller audiences and function relatively well where light levels are high. Others, including videotape and film, are suitable for larger audiences but suffer in brighter environments.

Equipment availability also is a problem where audiovisuals are to be used in multiple locations or away from developers' premises. No generally accepted standards exist for videotape, for example, and sound system quality varies to a significant extent.

Perhaps most important in developing audiovisual materials, however, are the characteristics of audiences. Some have an affinity for one medium but not another. Where homogenous groups are involved, variations in comprehension levels can be significant.

Producers also must consider alternative applications of material in preparation. Revisions are relatively easily and inexpensively accomplished in some audiovisual presentations, such as audiotapes and slide-tapes. They are more difficult and more costly where multimedia and motion picture are used.

Words, illustrations, and background music are the primary components of most audiovisual presentations. Script development tends to be more difficult for many public relations practitioners than is the case with print media texts. Writing styles differ and writers must concurrently anticipate use of audio and video dimensions.

Script writing usually is the first step in the developmental process. Sound track development follows, incorporating narration and music. Multiple music sources exist, varying considerably as to cost. Music prepared specifically for audiovisual presentations usually is superior in producing desired results.

Sound effects often are employed to enhance the realities that audiovisuals are intended to convey. They must be used judiciously, however, to produce best results. Indiscriminate use of sound effects tends to distract audiences rather than enhance overall impact.

Visuals also require care in development. They are most readily developed where practitioners focus their primary attention on the finished product rather than component parts. Concurrent mental construction of voice and image can create a sort of matrix into which visual material can be effectively inserted.

Visuals fall into several general categories. They include photos, artwork, graphics, and computer-generated visuals. Most audiovisual producers prepare double to triple the number of visuals they expect to include in finished products and then select those most appropriate to the script and audience.

The selection process best proceeds under several guidelines. Most important of these is a general rule that suggests that as few types of visuals be used and that changes from one type to another be held to a minimum.

In the overall, developers also must be concerned with program design, visual style, clarity, and fluidity in bringing the several components together. Program design addresses consistency among components. Effectiveness is greatest where consistency is established among visuals and between visuals and words.

Style refers to content in context with programmatic objectives. Emotional styles are desirable where content is motivational. Training programs require more logical presentations.

Visual clarity or fluency also is important both as to images and words. Images must be crisp and clear. Charts must be simple and direct in presentation. Lettering and captions must be precise.

The words "pacing," "flow," and "fluidity" refer to the smoothness in the sequencing of visuals and transitions from one to another. Jarring transitions, such as those that occasionally occur where videotape or film splicing produces a "jump" in the image, also serve to distract audiences and diminish overall results.

These production guidelines also apply to other electronic channels. They include video, telephone, and computer conferencing but are less significant in videotex, teletext, and viewdata systems. Electronic data bases necessarily are somewhat "ragged" due to the nature of message delivery.

Television, telephone, and computer channels are increasing in popularity and computer systems generally are becoming progressively more dominant in public relations practice. The latter conditions arise out of their multiple uses. They include electronic mail and extensive data bases as well as on-line conferencing systems.

ADDITIONAL READING

Castells, Manuel, ed. *High Technology, Space and Society*. Beverly Hills, Calif.: Sage, 1982.

Cornish, Edward, ed. *The Computerized Society: Living and Working in an Electronic Age*. Bethesda, Md.: World Future Society, 1985.

Degan, Clara, ed. *Understanding and Using Video: A Guide for the Organizational Communicator*. New York: Longman, 1985.

Didsbury, Howard F., ed. *Communications and the Future: Prospects, Promises and Problems*. Bethesda, Md.: World Future Society, 1982.

Gross, Lynne Schafer. *The New Television Technologies*, 2nd ed. Dubuque, Ia.: Wm. C. Brown, 1986.

Kaatz, Ronald B. *Cable: An Advertiser's Guide to the New Electronic Media*. Chicago: Crain, 1982.

Lazar, Ellen A., Martin C.J. Elton, James W. Johnson, et. al. *The Teleconferencing Handbook: A Guide to Cost-Effective Communication*. White Plains, N.Y.: Knowledge Industry Publications, 1983.

Masuda, Yoneji. *The Information Society as Post-Industrial Society*. Tokyo: Institute for Information Society, 1980.

Mills, P. J., ed. *Trends in Information Transfer*. Westport, Conn.: Greenwood Press, 1982.

Rice, Ronald E. et al. *The New Media: Communication, Research and Technology*. Beverly Hills, Calif.: Sage, 1984.

Smith, Judson, and Janice Orr. *Designing and Developing Business Communications Programs that Work*. Glenview, Ill.: Scott, Foresman, 1985.

Weaver, David H. *Videotex Journalism: Teletext, Videwdata and the News*. Hillsdale, N.J.: Lawrence Erlbaum Associates, 1983.

14

Special Events

Special events are staged "happenings" through which public relations practitioners obtain favorable exposure of organizations, products, or services to one or more stakeholder groups. Organizations create some special events and participate in or sponsor others.

Created events include open houses and ceremonies attendant to organizational anniversaries, plant or office openings, and the like. Participatory events are those staged by others in which organizations take a major role. They include the various fund-raising and educational activities undertaken by charitable and philanthropic organizations as well as community celebrations and similar activities. Sponsored events range from community health fairs to the rededication of the Statue of Liberty.

Special events vary primarily in the extent of direct organizational involvement they require. Created events are most demanding. Organizational personnel or vendors must handle every aspect of their planning and execution. Participatory events usually are planned by others but involve significant organizational commitments of manpower and/or dollars. Sponsored events often require nothing more than a financial commitment and public relations support.

PLANNING FOR SUCCESS

All special events share one attribute: Their success or failure is a function of organization and planning. Volume of effort is governed by the extent of the organization's commitment and the nature of the event involved but all require planning and coordination to achieve objectives.

Effort, cost, and outcome are the primary variables in special event planning. Each is a function of level of involvement. Benefit potential usually varies, in other words, with resources devoted to the project. Where commitments are limited, as in participatory or sponsored events, benefit potential is reduced proportionately. Public relations practitioners' primary challenge always involves obtaining maximum benefit in relation to organizational commitment.

Their efforts follow a clearly marked path that begins in the planning and budgeting processes (see Chapter 9). Planning and budgeting require examining all available message delivery systems and selecting those that are best suited to the public relations program. Where special events are among them, the process next addresses a simple question: Which are most appropriate to the program?

Selecting Events

Participation in special events should be governed by the same criteria applied in selecting any channel of communication. Each must convey messages designed to induce desired behavioral responses on a cost-effective basis to specific audiences. Anticipated benefits of participation thus must be weighed against the value of results that might be achieved by allocating comparable sums to alternative programs.

Cost effectiveness analyses rely on the same criteria used in planning and budgeting. Audiences or stakeholder groups first must be specified. Alternative communication channels appropriate to each group then must be analyzed as to their relative efficiency. Only where special events generically rank high on the resulting list of alternatives are they worthy of further consideration. Still further analyses are necessary in selecting specific events.

Selection criteria in examining groups of prospective special events include several that are not involved in preliminary decision making. Appropriateness of the event to the sponsoring organization is a critical factor. It would be incongruous, for example, for a hospital or medical association to participate in the annual celebration of auto racing at Daytona Beach, Florida. Sports car manufacturers such as Maserati and Porsche would be equally out of place in sponsoring a community health fair.

Durability of relationship is another major concern. "One-time" events necessarily are more costly than the repetitive variety. Planning and executing a second annual health fair will require fewer hours and be less demanding than the first. Repetitive events such as annual marathons or music fests also may grow in popularity and memorability, compounding public relations benefits.

At the opposite end of the spectrum, the potential impact of special events readily can be lost. Economic disasters of this sort usually occur where events are undertaken without clear-cut purposes or where planning and scheduling are inadequately handled.

Plans and Schedules

Planning and scheduling are among the most complex tasks associated with special event planning. The processes are especially demanding where "events" consist of multiple activities over extended periods of time.

Complex events such as the opening of a new corporate headquarters readily can involve dozens of public relations activities. Preparations can extend over a year or more where this is the case. The event may involve sets of activities undertaken over a period of weeks or months. Follow-up activities can consume additional weeks.

Planning and scheduling processes begin with a decision to proceed and continue through a predetermined series of steps leading to the start of the event. They include establishing dates and schedules, developing budgets, obtaining necessary facilities, planning programs, notifying participants, and organizing staff members and/or vendors to attend to a myriad of details.

ESTABLISHING THE SCHEDULE

Scheduling processes necessary to complex events appear overly burdensome in the early stages. They require detailed backward time projections for each component of each activity. Backward time projections require analyzing activity components. Dates are established by which preparatory work must begin on each component if all are to be in readiness by the scheduled activity date. Multiple progress checkpoints usually are specified as well.

Efforts to secure a notable speaker for a seated banquet, for example, often begin a year or more prior to the specified date. If the dinner is to be followed by dancing to live music, a band must be booked months in advance. Program content must be complete weeks before the event in order to meet time requirements inherent in program printing.

These are but a few of the elements that may be necessary in successfully executing one activity on a list of which may include dozens of them. Complex events thus require exhaustive planning.

First Steps

The scheduling process begins with selection of a tracking system rather than dates and times of activities. Options range from large desk calendars to wall charts, flow diagrams, and computer-based critical path systems.

Many prefer wall charts or computer systems in that both provide current status summaries at a glance. Where major events are planned, entire walls may be covered in white vinyl and blocked off by date in 6 × 8 inch squares. The mechanics are less important, however, than the manner in which they are applied. All activities involved in proposed events and each component of every activity must be listed. So must each step of every preparatory

process. Ample space must be allowed to permit adding activities and components for each date. Few complex events proceed from initial decision to
execution without addition and deletion of activities.

Clearing dates. With a tracking mechanism in place, scheduling can begin.
The first step in the process requires "clearing dates" for all activities. "Clearing" in this context means eliminating any substantive conflicts, a complex
task in itself.

Significant numbers of potential dates can be eliminated early in the process. These include holidays and holiday weekends and the weeks in which
schools and universities schedule commencement exercises. Dates that might
conflict with other organizational activities such as annual meetings, new
product "roll-outs," sales meetings, and the like usually are eliminated as
well.

The "clearing" process also should include contacts with local chambers
of commerce, athletic organizations, schools, and other groups that might be
planning special activities. A telephone call to daily newspapers' city or metropolitan editors also is worthwhile. They often are among the first to know
of major events planned in their communities.

Scheduling activities. Few major events are limited to a single activity. Public
tours of a new building, for example, often are preceded by multiple similar
activities for elected officials, media representatives, customers, and others.
Each activity must be separately listed by date.

Activities also should be subdivided into functional components. Components of an early showing of a new building for customers might include a
series of small group tours followed by a reception and a seated dinner.
Again, each must be scheduled individually.

Activities are best placed on schedules chronologically. Components should
be listed in the order in which they will be required to be ready and/or
operational. Where dedicatory events are planned, for example, programs
may not be required until the last business day before the event but public
address systems should be installed early enough to be available for any
necessary rehearsals.

Establishing Time Frames

Lead time is the critical variable with which planners deal in establishing
temporal frameworks for activities to be undertaken as part of the special
event. Most planners deal with target dates rather than absolute times. By
"absolute" is meant the date on which something must be available or delivered. Target dates fall somewhat earlier, providing a "cushion" against
unforeseen eventualities.

Target dates should be established realistically rather than by adding an
arbitrary number of days to all components of the activities involved. Locally
produced printed material, for example, usually is ordered to be delivered

five to ten working days in advance of need. The ribbon for a ribbon cutting ceremony should not be needed until 48 hours before the appointed time (holidays excluded).

Establishing deadlines. The rationale is a relatively simple one. If a printer encounters difficulties or a last-minute program change is necessary, a week usually is adequate to recover or reprint. If the ribbon is delivered in the wrong color, width, or length, replacements usually are more readily available. Readiness deadlines thus must be established for each component of each activity. These then are entered on the wall calendar or placed in the computer and become the special event schedule.

Where wall calendars are used, 30-day calendar sheets also should be prepared for activity coordinators and others responsible for multiple activities. These should be revised and redistributed as often as necessary during the preparatory period. They always should be accompanied by cover memoranda requiring all involved to report immediately any missed deadline in order that adjustments can be made promptly.

Monitoring vendors. Wall calendar entries are best color coded where vendors are used in order that coordinators can readily differentiate between responsibilities delegated internally and those assigned to vendors. Similar coding can be used in entering computer data to facilitate monitoring processes. Vendor monitoring can be delegated to activity coordinators or handled through a single individual.

Whether vendor-supplied or internally generated, each activity component should be entered into the calendar in detail adequate to assure monitoring. Schedule detail for printed materials, for example, at minimum should include copy, typography, proof, and delivery deadlines.

Budget Monitoring

Special event budgets usually are established in one of two ways. Either predetermined sums are allocated within which events must be completed, or detailed estimates are prepared covering all anticipated costs. In either case, preliminary budgets usually are established before final decisions are made to proceed with the project. Close monitoring is necessary thereafter to insure that each activity as well as the project as a whole remain within prescribed economic limitations.

The scheduling process is a logical first checkpoint in budget monitoring. By the time target dates are established, quantitative factors will have been determined and both vendors and internal suppliers will have been contacted for preliminary cost estimates. These data should be compared to original estimates and requests for budget modifications made wherever necessary.

Numbers and scope of activities to be undertaken in connection with the event as well as budget allocations usually are made final at this point in the process. Planners are well-advised, however, to allow for significant budget flexibility. Special events are prone to "grow" as target dates approach.

Budgets ideally are entered into microcomputers as they are approved. Expenditures should be authorized only by purchase order and resultant data should be entered as well. Event managers thus can monitor the impact of the commitments involved.

FACILITIES AND PERSONNEL

Special events inevitably require extensive resources in the form of facilities and personnel. Every activity must be "housed." Some may require ancillary space for child care, media facilities, parking, and other associated activities. The "personnel" component of the event is no less complex. It may include visiting dignitaries, speakers, entertainers, caterers and their staffs, as well as a host of organizational executives, managers, and employees. All of their needs relative to the event must be anticipated in facilities and personnel plans.

Facilities

Most facilities plans begin with the building or location at which the principal event is to be conducted. Some are dictated by the nature of the event, as in the case of a plant dedication. Others, such as an employee field day or picnic, may be conducted outdoors. None of the sponsor's facilities needs are as simple as they appear.

Plant dedications require more than a location within the complex for the ceremonies involved. Available rest room facilities often are insufficient to handle numbers of individuals expected to participate. Child care often must be provided for guests or personnel who will be taking part in or assisting with the event. Appropriate quarters for media representatives must be provided. Adequate parking must be available.

Where events are scheduled outdoors, rest room facilities are not the planner's only concern. Bad weather must be anticipated as well. A standby facility may be needed or, in the alternative, arrangements must be made in advance to notify all involved of a postponement. Hotel or motel rooms often must be arranged for visiting dignitaries as well as entertainers and others.

Food service needs must be evaluated in all settings. They usually can be readily met where hotel meeting rooms or convention halls are used. Where events are scheduled at other sites, food handling resources may be inadequate. Caterers then may be used or other arrangements made.

The nature of the organization, the event, and the audience also require attention in arranging for necessary facilities. Charitable organizations usually avoid luxurious accommodations, which may raise the eyebrows of prospective donors. Religious and ethnic organizations may have specific criteria as to foods and/or beverages and their preparation.

As prospective facilities are identified, each requires close inspection in light of a set of predetermined criteria. These range from seating capacity to price; from security to power and telephone requirements. Preliminary unannounced visits by event planners are advisable to avoid "best behavior" arrangements on the part of operators. Further visits should be planned when details of the activity are completed and 24 to 48 hours before the specified activity date. Both are intended to assure that planner requirements are being met; that there will be no unpleasant surprises.

Personnel

The term "personnel" is used here in its broadest sense, encompassing all of those who will attend, participate in, or work on the special event. The latter group usually consists of organizational and vendor personnel. The former encompass program participants, speakers, special guests, entertainers, media representatives, and others.

Each must be made aware of all details of any activity in which he or she may be engaged or involved. Organizational personnel and vendors should be given precise instructions as to the nature of their duties and obligations. As reflected in Sperber and Lerbinger's checklist for company dinners and "bashes," these can be extensive (see Figure 14.1).

Tasks assigned to personnel as well as assignments to vendors should be integrated into the master schedule. Copies of original and revised schedules should be provided promptly to personnel, who also should be responsible for regular progress reports. One member of the organization should be assigned to monitor and report on vendor progress.

Those who will participate in activities should be advised as early as possible. Notification should include all necessary information concerning duties or obligations assigned. Special attention should be paid to introductory remarks, speeches, and other activities that may require preparation. Speakers and masters of ceremonies require special attention.

Speakers. Care is necessary in selecting speakers for special events. They must be appropriate to the occasion, available, and affordable. Propriety often is a subjective matter. Availability and cost usually can be ascertained by telephone.

Public relations practitioners usually develop lists of candidates for submittal to clients or employers. Organizational and media contacts frequently are helpful in identifying candidates and determining availability and cost.

Many speakers must be engaged six to twelve months in advance and, especially where governmental officials are involved, even then may cancel at the last moment. This circumstance can be anticipated to some extent by maintaining a list of local substitutes who can be called on short notice.

Figure 14.1. Checklist for company dinners and bashes. From Nathaniel H. Sperber and Otto Lerbinger, *Manager's Public Relations Handbook*. Reading, Mass.: Addison-Wesley, 1982.

Company Dinners and Bashes	Assigned to	Date/Time Assigned	Date/Time Completed
I. In choosing a location, be certain that: 　1. It is convenient for all. 　2. It is large enough. 　3. It has a controllable bar. 　4. It will be comfortable for all.	_____	_____	_____
II. There will be control over impromptu romantic, impassioned, or belligerent situations.	_____	_____	_____
III. There will be sufficient food, and that it will be served on time.	_____	_____	_____
IV. Specific hours are set for the affair.	_____	_____	_____
V. One person will be responsible for giving orders to hotel or establishment personnel.	_____	_____	_____
VI. One person will be responsible for handling the entertainment.	_____	_____	_____
VII. There are personnel assigned as "sergeants-at-arms."	_____	_____	_____
VIII. There is proper accommodation for checking and parking.	_____	_____	_____
IX. Someone will be in charge of emergency situations (e.g., firefighters, nurses, etc.).	_____	_____	_____
X. Proper I.D.'s are used (badges) to eliminate crashers and freeloaders.	_____	_____	_____
XI. Determine whether the affair will be for or limited to: 　1. Direct employees or including employees' families. 　2. Customers or good friends of the company. 　3. Directors. 　4. Principal shareholders. 　5. External service personnel. 　　a. Advertising agency. 　　b. Law firm.	_____	_____	_____

(continued)

Figure 14.1 (continued)

	Company Dinners and Bashes	Assigned to	Date/Time Assigned	Date/Time Completed
	c. Contractors.			
	d. PR counsel.			
	e. Brokerage house.			
	f. Community leaders.			
	6. Press.			
	7. Company photographer.			
XII.	Assign a staff person to assure attendance of CEO, president, chairperson, senior officers, and to:	_____	_____	_____
	1. Provide a "ready room" for head table guests and bring them in all together.			
	2. Provide lectern and microphone(s) for head table.			
	3. Signal for speech time to coincide with dessert eating.			
	4. Allow no table clearing until end of speeches.			
	5. Make certain speeches are not too long.			
	6. If necessary, provide speech hand-outs to press table.			
XIII.	In addition to above, summer outings should have these considerations:	_____	_____	_____
	1. Determine method of assuring employee family attendance and participation in events.			
	2. Be sure park is large enough and has facilities for proper summer events (ball games, etc.).			
	3. Be certain safety factors are under control.			
	4. Assign one person to handle each of the following:			
	a. Food.			
	b. Bar.			
	c. Athletic programs.			
	d. Children's events.			

(continued)

Figure 14.1 (continued)

Company Dinners and Bashes	Assigned to	Date/Time Assigned	Date/Time Completed
e. Entertainment.			
f. Prizes and awards.			
g. Transportation for those without cars.			
h. Transportation for those who should not drive home.			
XIV. Assign a company photographer and employee publication or company writer to prepare promo for distribution within the company.	_____	_____	_____
1. Instruct photographer to be sure to get at least one photo of each person attending, preferably while participating in an event.			
2. Arrange for free, or minimal cost, prints for employees.			
3. Plan to produce a broadside of a montage of the best photos and distribute them to all employees and other selected groups (shareholders, local papers, etc.)			

Invitations to speakers should be issued by the organization's chief executive officer but support from the public relations unit can be helpful. Many in the public arena can be most readily reached through aides who are most understanding of potential political gain and other factors that might be mentioned to induce affirmative response.

Speakers will want considerable information concerning the engagement and should be asked to provide necessary news release information to special event planners. They will want to know the nature of the event, anticipated attendance, the nature of the program, identities of past speakers, and length of the proposed talk. Date and time obviously must be provided as well.

Public relations practitioners will require the titles of proposed speeches, biographical sketches, recent photographs, and authority to issue news releases. As the speech is prepared, drafts may be requested to prepare further news releases.

Chairpersons. The conduct of every activity must be assigned as a primary responsibility to one individual. He or she may be a host, chairperson, or master of ceremonies responsible for seeing that events proceed as scheduled.

Individuals involved must be personable and able to exert a commanding presence while warming up audiences and seeing that unforeseen incidents are handled with aplomb. They should not, however, be so brilliant as to overshadow guest speakers. Outsiders will be selected on some occasions to handle these responsibilities. Members of the organization otherwise handle the duties involved.

Those in charge at any event require a more complete program than is provided to guests. Every step in the proceedings must be spelled out in detail. Where names of those to be introduced are susceptible to mispronunciation, phonetic spellings should be provided. Any "surprise" presentations should be listed as well. Where chairpersons are "personalities" in their own right, biographical sketches and photos should be requested for news release purposes.

Organizational personnel. Organization members who are expected to play a role in any activities associated with the event should be notified early. All should be given detailed information concerning their responsibilities as well dates and times when they will be expected to be present.

Lists of prospective guests and other participants preferably should be provided to them as well. Organization members frequently can assist in early identification of those whose names might otherwise be omitted to the embarrassment of all involved.

News media. When preliminary scheduling has been completed, fact sheets should be compiled and distributed to news media to enable them to plan in advance for any appropriate coverage of the event. These preferably should be delivered in person by public relations staff members who concurrently should obtain as detailed information as possible as to media needs and preferences.

Plans of the broadcast media, especially television stations and networks, require special attention. Their equipment often requires more electricity than readily is available. Supplemental wiring usually can be provided if needs are identified in advance. Seating arrangements in meeting and banquet halls also should be planned to accommodate any planned television coverage. Cameras should be placed as unobtrusively as possible but in keeping with the needs of the medium.

The informal survey of media plans conducted during fact sheet distribution also provides preliminary indications as to what may be required if the event and component activities are to create breaking news. Newsrooms then often must be provided with ample numbers of telephones, desks, chairs, type-writers, and such.

If the event is to be staged at a convention hotel or resort, arrangements should be made to accommodate media representatives as well as guests. They will not accept and should not be offered cost-free lodgings or food. Planners should arrange, however, to see that their needs are met on as convenient a basis as possible. This occasionally requires that rooms be "blocked off" for media use. Where this is the case, media representatives should be notified of any deadlines by which their reservations must be received.

Invitations. Invitations must be sent early to special guests, government officials, and any others whose schedules tend to be set far in advance. Three to six months is preferable for this group. Four to six weeks' usually is barely adequate for others. One to two weeks notice is too short for any guest. Invitations preferably should be extended by letter as well as in formal fashion to special guests.

All organizational executives should be provided with copies of proposed invitation lists in advance to insure against errors of omission. Final lists then can be used to record any acknowledgments requested and as a basis for providing "head counts" to caterers or hotel personnel.

Staffing. Special attention must be paid to staffing needs relative to special events. While quantitative factors vary, special events usually are labor in-tensive and needs tend to be under- rather than overestimated. This especially is the case where plant tours, open houses, and similar events are scheduled. Careful planning, however, can minimize potential problems.

Tours, for example, can be guided or unguided. Significant numbers of personnel will be needed in either event. Organizational representatives should be stationed within sight of each other over unguided tour paths to answer questions and provide assistance to visitors. A quick walk through will indicate how many will be needed. Where tour guides are necessary, their number is a function of (a) numbers of visitors expected, (b) duration of the tour, and (c) sizes of tour groups.

Gross personnel requirements developed in this manner must be adjusted for absenteeism. Further adjustments in numbers of tour guides also may be necessary to cope with unforeseen circumstances. Minor mishaps, lost children, and the like tend to be routine during such events. These are just a few of the factors that require attention, as Sperber and Lerbinger point out (see Figure 14.2).

Other concerns. Additional elements may or may not be a matter of direct concern to public relations practitioners in context with special events. This especially is the case where they are staged in convention centers or large hotels. Security arrangements, exhibit set-up and knock-down, and other factors usually are handled by management in these settings.

Food service arrangements, banquet seating, transportation, and other matters also may be included or excluded from practitioners' scope of operation. Early in the planning the public relations department or agency should establish scope of responsibility in order to guard against unpleasant surprises as the event draws closer.

PUBLIC RELATIONS PLANS

Public relations activities in conjunction with special events are dictated to a significant extent by event schedules. As schedules are developed, parallel public relations plans should be created. The plans should be based on the individual activities that constitute the special event.

Each activity, whether it involves introduction of new products, election of officers, or talks by governmental or industry dignitaries, can be a source of news from the perspectives of organizational stakeholder groups. Each must be considered in context with every activity.

Plan Development

Developing special event public relations plans ultimately involves three components. First among them are organizational public relations goals and strategies. These should include exhaustive lists of stakeholder groups as well as plans and activities oriented toward each of them.

Each activity associated with the special event should be examined in context with goals and strategies and in light of a single question: What information will be generated through or during the special event that should be conveyed to each of these groups?

Some events, such as new product roll-outs, are of near universal interest. Customers, prospective customers, shareholders, dealers, distributors, employees, and the news media all will be interested to a greater or lesser extent. The public relations plan should be responsive to those interests.

All available channels of communication first should be identified through which each group can be reached. Prerequisites to using those channels, usually in the form of lead time, then should be specified. Articles and photos for an employee newsletter, for example, may be needed only weeks before

Figure 14.2. Checklist for plant tours. From Nathaniel H. Sperber and Otto Lerbinger, *Manager's Public Relations Handbook*. Reading, Mass.: Addison-Wesley, 1982.

Plant Tours	Assigned to	Date/Time Assigned	Date/Time Completed
I. Consider establishing a regular program of plant tours.	_____	_____	_____
II. "Isolate" specific areas of interest for the purpose of such tours.	_____	_____	_____
III. Visit and inspect the tour site to mark the limits, lines, and length of the tour.	_____	_____	_____
IV. Obtain permission and agreement from pertinent area manager. Check pertinent employee reaction to proposed tour.	_____	_____	_____
V. Identify target audiences (visitors); i.e., schools, clubs, stockholders, visiting dealers, congressional blocs, other VIP's, trade press. Invite other employees and their families for a first tour.	_____	_____	_____
VI. Recruit guides for the tour from the lower management levels and train them for the task. Write out the tour pattern and have it approved by relevant executives. The final pattern should be memorized by the guides.	_____	_____	_____
VII. Set days and times so there is no interference with production. 1. Prepare stanchions, ribbons, and signs of identification and directions. These become the responsibility of the department from which the guides are recruited. 2. Spot and place directions and signs well before visitors arrive. 3. Keep groups to a manageable size, preferably to between twelve and fifteen. 4. Prepare and distribute a small printed takeaway flyer to each visitor, including other mementos where appropriate. These hand-outs are excellent vehicles for company publicity.	_____	_____	_____

(continued)

Figure 14.2 (continued)

Plant Tours	Assigned to	Date/Time Assigned	Date/Time Completed

VIII. Consider conveniences for people taking tours:
  1. Parking.
  2. Lunch or refreshments, restrooms (especially for groups).
  3. Reception area away from the front door, and near a coat-check area.
  4. Security arrangements to prevent unnecessary incursions, wandering, snooping, and theft.
	_____	_____	_____

IX. Provide badges or name tags for the guests.
  1. Provide identification tags for the guides.
  2. Place signs over machinery or work in progress. Make them simple and explicit.
	_____	_____	_____

X. Distribute press releases with photos immediately to pertinent media.
  1. Arrange for Polaroid shots of guests, and give to them.
  2. Give employees copies.
  3. Give copies to company paper.
	_____	_____	_____

XI. Consider sponsoring an essay contest for school groups. This would include what was seen on the tour. Give a prize to the winner of the best essay.	_____	_____	_____
XII. Write a "thank you" letter to each group leader.	_____	_____	_____

XIII. In case of full tours of entirely new facilities, i.e., new or expanded buildings:
  1. Give employees and their families a special tour before outside groups have visited.
  2. Invite community neighbors and leaders and the press second.
  3. The third group should consist of security analysts, investment group members, and stockholders.
  4. Dealers and customers should be asked fourth.
	_____	_____	_____

the special event. Comparable material for trade or industry publications, however, may have to be prepared and distributed months in advance.

Creating a Schedule

All of this information should be organized in the form of a schedule similar to the master schedule used by event planners. The schedule ideally is first organized by stakeholder group and then restated chronologically.

Stakeholder group schedules specify channels of communication, message content, and technical details pertinent to each activity. In most cases, planning should include advance and follow-up as well as "spot news" releases. Production schedules and release dates should be established for each. Chronological schedules then should be created to show those activities that must be completed on specific dates and insure that messages are delivered as planned.

The latter schedules reflect the needs of individual communication channels to be used in reaching each stakeholder group. Material for use in daily newspapers and the broadcast media, for example, usually is last to be completed. Releases and photos for business and trade magazines must be prepared well in advance. Only in this manner can the organization be assured of maximum impact.

An example. Consider, for example the Apple Computer and IBM new product introductions of 1987. After months of rumors in all media, daily newspapers published the company's announcement that the new line would be introduced the following week, prompting a few speculative articles in weekly magazines and trade papers.

The following week came the introduction-day releases in the daily newspapers and broadcast media. They were followed within the next few days by newspaper columnists' analyses of the impact of the new equipment from stockholder, industry, and user standpoints. The following week, the news weeklies and business weeklies "weighed in" with their more detailed analyses. A few weeks later, the computer magazines were on the newsstands with still more detailed reports designed for computer users.

These public reports were paralleled by extensive dissemination of information by both companies to more specialized groups. They included dealers, peripherals vendors, employees, shareholders, the financial community, and a host of others.

Benefits of planning. Neither the months of rumors preceding the announcements nor the massive media exposure that followed developed by chance. These instead were the products of well-orchestrated efforts to induce the greatest possible volume of affirmative exposure through multiple media directed toward diverse audiences. They were tangible evidence of the extent to which skilled planning can turn simple product announcements into major media events.

The same sort of communication yield can be expected where public relations practitioners apply professional knowledge and skills to special events of virtually any variety. Each of them is an exercise in detailed planning, careful execution, and applied public relations techniques.

OTHER SPECIAL EVENTS

The range of special events in which organizations participate today is virtually unlimited. Level of participation is a major variable. It may involve merely providing large sums of money and a television spokesperson, as in the case of some athletic events. At the other extreme are organizational anniversary celebrations, building openings, and other events that can extend over a period of days or weeks. A close look at some of them indicates the extent to which advance planning and detailed follow-through are essential.

Plant Tours

The plant or office tour is undertaken regularly in some organizations and occasionally in others. Governmental agencies, the news media, and manufacturers of consumer products are among the leaders in regular tour operations. Many organizations conduct open house or open plant events as new facilities are dedicated or as part of anniversary or similar celebrations.

Operators of regularly conducted tours over time manage to establish standard operating procedures that minimize or eliminate many of the problems that occasional tour sponsors encounter. They know through experience the approximate numbers of individuals to expect. Visiting hours in most cases are limited by policy and appointments are required.

They also have provided for ample parking, installed ancillary exhibits, produced brochures or information kits, and taken necessary safety precautions to guard against accident. Those contemplating a plant or open house must address all of these needs and many more (see Figure 14.3).

Among concerns that require early attention are traffic control, rest room and refreshment areas, child care facilities, special insurance for visitors, and additional staffing. The latter component may include additional security personnel and almost inevitably will require tour guides and cleanup crews in abundance. Most of the same considerations must be addressed for dedications and groundbreaking ceremonies but other events can create unusual needs.

Other Events

Anniversaries create significant opportunities for organizations. They can be addressed simply with a banquet for staff, dignitaries, and friends, or in a year-long celebration. Most are confined to relatively limited periods, usually

Figure 14.3. Checklist for exhibits, shows, and seminars. From Nathaniel H. Sperber and Otto Lerbinger, *Manager's Public Relations Handbook.* Reading, Mass.: Addison-Wesley, 1982.

Exhibits, Shows, and Seminars	Assigned to	Date/Time Assigned	Date/Time Completed
I. Assess company budget for exhibitions and shows and determine its realism.	_____	_____	_____
II. Have a cost analysis done for each proposed show.	_____	_____	_____
1. Determine cost of space.			
2. Estimate number of employees, both in preparation and staffing. Figure their costs.			
3. Estimate cost of exhibit materials and other preparation costs.			
4. Check out costs of professional exhibit specialists.			
5. Check all division/department heads for their estimates of values received by having company participation in each show.			
III. Assess effects on company's sales, reputation, new business, recruitment, etc., if any show is dropped from schedule. Estimate effect of smaller exhibit and space in costs and results.	_____	_____	_____
IV. Assign PR staff to cover show.	_____	_____	_____
1. Get report on legitimacy of company participation.			
2. Review guest book or other list of those who see your exhibit.			
3. Check your advertising department for special ads concomitant with the show.			
4. Be sure that you have enough PR staff to man booth and hospitality suite.			
V. Determine show/exhibit target:	_____	_____	_____
1. Recruiting.			
2. Sales.			
3. Prestige.			
4. "Showing the flag."			
5. Dealer relationships and participation.			
6. Platform for new product announcement.			

(continued)

Figure 14.3 (continued)

Exhibits, Shows, and Seminars	Assigned to	Date/Time Assigned	Date/Time Completed
7. Demonstration of "state of the art" and company status in advances.			
8. Springboard for sales meeting.			
VI. Check news releases appropriate to the show. Save a significant release timed for show period.	_____	_____	_____
VII. Determine who is to be responsible for the hospitality suite.	_____	_____	_____
1. Make certain that someone opens and closes and supplies the suite.			
2. Watch out for "freeloaders" and arrange for legitimate admission system.			
3. Make certain that there are available visual aids, samples, press kits, news releases, promotional literature, company annual reports, etc.			
VIII. Decide how leads will be solicited at the exhibit. Make sure they are followed up after the show (within five days).	_____	_____	_____
IX. If seminars are to be held in conjunction with the show, get list of those who will read papers.	_____	_____	_____
1. Read the papers yourself before the show to determine the significance of the releases.			
2. Prepare appropriate news releases about the papers and those who will read them.			
X. Submit a re-cap or summary of the show and your company's participation to pertinent division/department heads and the CEO.	_____	_____	_____
1. Include your reaction.			
2. Get reactions of showgoers (quotes).			
3. Assess cost effectiveness.			
4. Include recommendations for improvement for future shows.			

about a week. They often are accompanied by publication of organizational histories, dinners, honors for long-time employees, and a host of other activities.

Similar festivities may accompany a major technological breakthrough, achievement of a leadership position in an industry, and virtually any other occasion or milestone that management elects to render the set piece of a special event.

Exhibits, shows, and seminars also are often a part of organizational promotional programs. In some cases they are primary components of communication programs. Manufacturers, for example, often expend considerable time and effort in producing such programs for distributors and dealers. In other cases, as with industry trade show participation, they may be a small part of a broader program.

The level of detail necessary in planning remains essentially unchanged, as indicated by Sperber and Lerbinger's checklist (see Figure 14.3).

Sponsorships. While usually little involved directly in their execution, organizations sponsor near limitless numbers of events of all kinds. They include athletic events, cultural and civic programs, free entertainment, research projects, and so on.

Successful sponsorships are not selected capriciously. Those that prove most productive are oriented to either the messages or the audiences with which sponsors are concerned. While especially applicable to those involved in the recreation industry, athletic events also are sponsored by auto manufacturers and others seeking to market goods and services to fans. Newspapers sponsor use of their products in classrooms, museums promote shows, and Holiday Corporation sponsors a team of aerobatic fliers.

Sponsorships also extend to events and organizations such as Thanksgiving Day and New Year's Day parades, McDonald's All American Band, Budweiser's Clydesdales, and Goodyear's blimps. They are selected and developed with all the care necessary in planning and executing any other public relations activity.

Speaking tours. Similarly detailed planning is necessary in orchestrating an activity that only generically falls into the special events category: the management speaking tour. Public speaking can be a valuable communication channel, especially where organizations are caught up in contemporary issues. They also are useful in establishing an organization in the minds of specific groups as an industry leader, an innovator, or a good citizen. Tours require only two basic components: qualified speakers and well-planned itineraries.

Qualified speakers are readily created through appropriate internal training programs where none already exist. Those on any tour must be selected in keeping with predetermined strategies catering to the preferences of forum organizers. Some require speakers to be chief executive officers of their organizations. Others are more interested in specialists in one area or another.

Speeches must address contemporary topics of interest to audiences that involve the organization. They may be written internally but more often are assigned to professional speechwriters.

Audiences are most readily selected from Gale Research Company's *Business Organizations & Agencies Directory*, which lists literally thousands of them. Selections are based on organizational objectives, scope of operation, and other factors.

IN SUMMARY

Special events include a broad range of "happenings" in several categories. They include events staged by organizations as well as participation in and sponsorship of those staged by others. All are designed to obtain favorable exposure of organizational products or services to specific stakeholder groups.

Special events universally succeed or fail in keeping with the quality and volume of planning undertaken in preparing for them. Outcomes vary more with effort than with cost.

Participation in special events should be governed by their ability to convey messages on cost-effective bases to audiences with which organizations are concerned. Their potential can be evaluated successfully only through application of the same standards used in public relations planning and budgeting processes.

Selection processes also must deal with the appropriateness of events. Safety councils, for example, would be far better advised to sponsor campaigns to control drunk driving than auto races. Also worthy of consideration is the extent to which events can be made repetitive. Benefits tend to compound where this is the case.

Planning and scheduling are the most complex tasks involved in developing special events. Most of them involve multiple activities and can extend over days or months. Preparations inevitably require considerably more time.

Planning and scheduling processes begin with clearing dates; insuring that dates selected will not conflict with other events that might detract from that being planned in attendance or otherwise. After dates have been cleared, scheduling systems are established. They may consist of oversize bulletin boards covering entire walls or can be handled by computer. They are necessary to provide planners with a continuing status overview. Schedules usually are published periodically for all personnel involved in planning and developmental work, each reflecting any changes made since the prior printing.

Events and activities of which they are composed are entered into the scheduling system as plans are completed. In each case, they are entered in keeping with lead time requirements for each component. A speech, for example, may require months to a year or more in overall development because major speakers often make bookings 12 to 18 months in advance. Both "ideal" and "absolute" dates are entered. The ideal are target dates established with built-in "cushions" to guard against problems. Absolute dates are those by which specific objectives must be reached. The difference between the two involves the amount of time necessary to correct problems that may arise. A schedule change, for example, may require reprinting a program.

Special events require careful compilation and supervision of budgets. Compilation usually is accomplished by designing programs within a predetermined budget or developing budgets based on anticipated costs. Budgets usually are established before managements make final procedural decisions.

Budget flexibility is essential but planners must guard against a tendency on the part of budgets to "grow" as target dates approach and as a seemingly innumerable number of "good ideas" are offered by individuals involved in the process. Flexibility is especially important in making preparations for facilities and personnel.

Activities must be housed and staffed. Each requires more space than immediately becomes evident. Child care, media facilities, parking, and other needs often must be met in conjunction with each basic activity. Personnel components are no less complex, involving visitors, dignitaries, speakers, and entertainers as well as organizational personnel.

Food and beverage services, hotel and motel accommodations, and a host of other factors must be coordinated to insure that results meet management expectations. Information concerning arrangements must be provided to all involved on a continuing basis to assure that their responsibilities will be discharged as scheduled.

Speakers and chairpersons or masters of ceremonies require special attention. Speakers require considerable information concerning their engagements and must be asked for information and photos necessary for news releases. Chairpersons also may be celebrities and then require similar treatment. More important, however, they must be prepared to discharge their responsibilities. This requires that they be provided with programs far more detailed than the published variety and including every component of the event, including such items as "surprise" presentations.

Equally detailed preparations must be made to meet news media needs. Fact sheets should be distributed to them early, preferably by hand. Practitioners in the process can obtain necessary information concerning their coverage plans and make appropriate arrangements. These extend from such technical details as placement of television cameras to relatively mundane matters such as sleeping accommodations for crew members.

Complete public relations plans must be developed in parallel with event and activity schedules to insure that the informational needs of each of the organization's constituent groups is met. Channels of communication must be identified early in order that material can be prepared in keeping with their production schedules.

The same level of attention to detail must be maintained in handling events ranging from plant tours and open houses to speaking tours. Preparedness produces success.

ADDITIONAL READING

Grunig, James E., and Todd Hunt. *Managing Public Relations.* New York: Holt, Rinehart and Winston, 1984.

Phillips, Charles S. *Secrets of Successful Public Relations.* Englewood Cliffs, N.J.: Prentice-Hall, 1985.

Reilly, Robert T. *Public Relations in Action.* Englewood Cliffs, N.J.: Prentice-Hall, 1981.

Sperber, Nathaniel H., and Otto Lerbinger. *Manager's Public Relations Handbook.* Reading, Mass.: Addison-Wesley, 1982.

Wilcox, Dennis L., Phillip H. Ault, and Warren K. Agee. *Public Relations: Strategies and Tactics.* New York: Harper & Row, 1986.

15

Advertising Production

Boundaries between public relations and advertising have become progressively more difficult to define. Practitioners in both fields historically have produced brochures and other materials for distribution by mail and otherwise. Both also have provided advertising specialties for clients and employers. Public relations practice over the past several decades increasingly has involved institutional, advocacy, or "public relations" advertising in print and broadcast areas as well.

Traditional boundaries between the two disciplines have been further eroded in smaller communities. Where limited professional services are available, practitioners in each area often are called upon to move "across the line." Such moves are especially common where advertising complements other organizational activities.

Advertising in any of several forms can be productive in community relations efforts relating to plant openings and other activities; in supporting employee relations efforts in such areas as safety campaigns; and in promoting organizationally sponsored scholarship programs. It is applicable in any circumstances in which organizations are seeking to sell themselves rather than the products or services they offer in the marketplace.

Use of advertising in public relations seldom creates substantial difficulties for practitioners. Techniques used in print and electronic production in public relations generally are applicable in advertising. Some differences exist, however, and they become significant where practitioners are dealing with advertising specialties, direct mail materials, and the promotion of products and professional practices.

PRINT ADVERTISING

The components of print media advertising are identical to those with which practitioners deal in producing brochures and other printed materials. Words and illustrations must be brought together in an effective fashion to convey messages designed to induce desired reactions among specific audiences. Finished products differ significantly, however, from those obtained with printed materials. They consist of composed negatives and proofs produced to exacting specifications and delivered to the media for reproduction.

Creative Components

Before preparing negatives and proofs, advertisements must be written, illustrated, composed, proofread, and perhaps modified. These steps may be handled within the public relations agency or department or assigned to vendors. The capabilities of personnel involved and the resources of the organization dictate which alternative is preferable in each case.

Words. Few public relations practitioners experience difficulty in creating the verbal component of advertising. Their experience in persuasive writing for the print media, in fact, arguably equips them as well as advertising copywriters in preparing such material.

Many advertising copywriters specialize in consumer or industrial products. Their skills are less amenable to application in institutional or issues advertising than those of public relations practitioners or advertising writers who prepare copy for service organizations. Where copywriting for public relations advertising is to be subcontracted, members of the latter groups most often are selected.

Illustrations. As in the case of printed materials, the visual component of public relations advertising most often consists of photos or drawings. Like the verbal component, they may be prepared by staff members or assigned to contractors.

Quality is all important in either case, and especially where the advertisements are to be used in multiple media. The technical capabilities of the print media are far from uniform. Newspaper reproduction usually is inferior to that of magazines and considerable variation exists within the two sectors.

Precisely focused images and adequate contrast are essential to good reproduction whether photos or other forms of black and white illustration are used. Color density is equally important in process color reproduction.

Preparing Materials

Text and illustrations are prepared in identical fashion regardless of numbers of ink colors to be used in completed advertising. Text drafts usually are completed first and approved by managements or clients together with verbal descriptions of proposed illustrations.

Typesetting. Approved texts then can be set in type immediately where illustrative material can be conceptualized with sufficient detail to permit allocation of space within the advertisement. Caution is necessary, however, in that the best finished illustration may differ from the original concept. Professional photographers and illustrators often conceive of better approaches than those that occur to public relations practitioners.

An interim step in the typesetting process is available to those equipped with appropriate computer equipment. Commercial typesetting is a relatively costly but necessary process in preparing advertising material. The fidelity of type generated by microcomputers is considerably lower than that generated by commercial typesetters. Computer-generated prints from laser jet printers, however, are more than adequate as preliminary proofs. They permit practitioners to "preview" copy in different type sizes and styles before delivering it to commercial typesetting services.

Organizations with established advertising programs often can avoid "trial and error" in typography and design by adapting graphics contained in their commercial advertising. Basic formats, borders, logotypes, and trademarks often can be "lifted" in toto. They are especially applicable in institutional or issue-oriented advertising where content often involves little more than type and trademark.

Graphic designers called upon to bring copy and illustrations together in advertisements seldom want to proceed without copy, graphic elements, and illustrations in hand. Changes are expensive in that designers are paid by the hour. Most clients thus prefer to wait until all content material is available.

Proofs. Advertising usually is proofed at several stages in the production process. Type usually is proofed before and after pasteup. Revisions undertaken after negatives have been made are considerably more costly than those accomplished earlier.

Where multiple ink colors are involved, additional "proofs" usually are inspected in the form of color keys before publishers' negatives and progressive proofs are made.

Color keys consist of sheets of light-sensitive acetate. One is prepared from each of the basic printing colors: yellow, magenta, cyan, and black. They then are superimposed over one another to create a visual composite of the finished product. Color fidelity is poor in that acetate is not totally clear but the result is adequate for final proofing. Negatives of individual colors then can be can be corrected before publishers' negatives are made where any imbalance is detected.

Publishers' negatives made for each of the colors are the primary end product of the preparation process. They are accompanied by progressive proofs. The latter consist of a series of press proofs showing the result as each color is applied. They enable publishers to convert negatives to printing plates as accurately as possible.

Publishers' requirements. Final negatives and proofs must be prepared to publishers' requirements. A number of variables are involved other than the size of the finished advertisement. They include the density of screens or dot patterns in which photos are reproduced, the thickness of negative film, numbers of proofs required, and other factors.

Publishers' specifications are found in Standard Rate and Data Service directories and are available from publishers. They usually are part of rate cards distributed without cost by all publishers. Rate cards often include deadline requirements as well. Publishers require that advertising material be submitted well in advance of publication dates. "Lead time," as it is called, usually is two to three times the publishing interval. For monthly magazines, materials usually are due two to three months ahead of the publication date.

BROADCAST ADVERTISING

Public relations practitioners' involvement in broadcast advertising usually is more limited than is the case in the print sector. Several factors are involved. First, relatively few organizations direct institutional or advocacy messages toward the relatively homogenous audiences attracted by television. Second, where broadcast audiences are appropriate, advertising materials usually are made available without cost through one of several channels.

The latter circumstances apply especially to so-called public service advertising or PSAs, as the spots are called. Many are produced by not-for-profit organizations such as the United Way and the American Cancer Society for distribution by local subsidiaries to stations in their service areas. Others are produced and distributed by the Advertising Council on such subjects as drug abuse and drunk driving.

Local nonprofit organizations such as symphony societies and arts councils occasionally will produce broadcast materials. More often, however, they will induce one or more broadcasters to handle production on a cost-free basis and share the product with other outlets. Commercial television production costs are relatively high and local charitable organizations seldom are able to justify costs involved because of the relatively few stations available to use the product. Radio production is less expensive and more readily volunteered by a station.

Public relations practitioners' activities in the PSA area thus frequently are reduced to writing scripts for radio. Perhaps the only general exception occurs where local nonprofit organizations undertake capital fund campaigns or seek to influence voters in a referendum.

The components of broadcast advertising essentially are identical to those involved in broadcast news releases or audiovisual productions. They include a script, illustrative materials, and music. Detailed descriptions of their development are provided in Chapter 12.

SPECIALTY ADVERTISING

Advertising specialties or novelties are relatively common in public relations practice. The specialty industry originated with imprinted matchbooks, which have declined in popularity in recent years. Imprinted cigarette lighters have supplanted matches to some extent but decline in numbers of smokers has been the primary cause.

Loss of sales among smokers has been more than offset for specialty sales firms by near boom conditions in the clothing sector. Tee shirts have been especially popular but caps, jackets, and other items also are sold in volume.

Total expenditures in the specialty area have grown steadily as more and more manufacturers have entered what has become known as the premium and incentive market. Premiums and incentives are relatively "big ticket" items used primarily as gifts and rewards for performance. They range from travel and lodgings to virtually every manufactured consumer product. They are used in sales contests, as holiday mementos, and as "dealer loaders." The latter is a gift offered to retailers contingent upon their buying predetermined quantities of merchandise from manufacturers or wholesalers.

Specialties versus Premiums

The line between advertising specialties and premiums or incentives is difficult to define other than as to their application. Specialties almost always are given away and usually cost less than $5. They usually are imprinted with the name of the giver or a product.

Premiums and incentives also may be imprinted, however, as has been the case with the face of wristwatches valued at more than $100. They more frequently are a part of public relations efforts than specialty items and usually are components of programs that include brochures, sales meetings, and other materials or events.

Organizations with well-designed trademarks enjoy a distinct advantage where merchandise is to be imprinted. Those that are most amenable to reproduction are executed in one color and are equally applicable in negative and positive form. Buyers then need only provide photostatic prints to vendors in order to be assured of precise reproduction.

Merchandise Applications

Public relations objectives are similar regardless of the cost of the merchandise involved. They almost always include enhanced name recognition and usually are oriented to produce greater sales of a product, a service, or, in political situations, an individual.

Specialties or "give aways" often are popular in political campaigns. The items involved necessarily are inexpensive and usually are utilitarian. They need not be overly durable. Emery boards are popular for women, as are the sort of magnets that hold notes to refrigerators. Golf tees and similar items are popular with men. Virtually anything of a utilitarian nature that can be imprinted is eligible for inclusion in this category.

Premiums. Premiums are another matter. Because of their higher cost, they must be more durable. The utilitarian factor remains strong but place of use also becomes significant, especially where the merchandise involved is used as a business gift rather than for incentive purposes.

The ideal business gift is something that also can be imprinted. More important, however, it should be either utilitarian and conducive to regular use or an item that will remain on top of recipients' desks rather than being taken home for the children to play with.

These criteria are relatively stringent and serve to eliminate the bulk of the merchandise items available. They may be relatively inexpensive but should not be incongruous in the most attractive surroundings. Their color cannot clash with a broad range of office decors. They must be recognizable as being of better than average quality. And they must be amenable to conservative imprinting.

A noteworthy item that met all of these criteria was used during the days of the energy crisis by a public relations practitioner who reported many of them still in use a decade later. They were combination thermometer/barometers fabricated in the form of desktop paperweights by Honeywell. They were gold in color and an anodized aluminum surface permitted their being imprinted with organizational trademarks.

Incentives. A different set of criteria applies to incentives. These usually are merchandise items, although travel and lodgings also are offered through incentive programs directed toward sales personnel, dealers, and distributors. Incentive programs usually are designed to "keep a carrot in front of every participant's nose" for the duration of the program. This requires multiple awards in a relatively broad range of values to keep participants striving to reach next higher reward levels.

Most organizations solve the problem by offering "mini catalogs" designed by incentive sales organizations in different value categories. The best of them include merchandise oriented to women as well as men (small kitchen appliances and hand tools) and to indoor as well as outdoor pursuits (color television sets and patio furniture).

Incentive merchandise seldom is emblazoned with organizational trademarks. Acquisition expenses are apportioned as a component of "cost of sales" and items need not be subsequently identifiable as to source.

Alternative sources. Most incentive merchandise is acquired at prices significantly below retail. Discounts may be as small as 10 to 15 percent where incentive organizations are used and can be as high as 60 percent where buyers deal directly with manufacturers.

Anticipated purchase quantities need not be large to qualify for direct purchase programs. An insurance company in the southern United States with some 200 sales personnel, for example, once entered into an agreement with a major sterling flatware manufacturer to provide place settings in recipients' choice of patterns at a 60 percent discount from suggested retail.

Savings in this instance were sufficient to justify internal administration of the incentive program. Where lower discounts apply, incentive sales organizations often are preferred to manufacturers in that they provide "fulfillment services" as well as catalogs. Fulfillment involves receiving credit slips or coupons issued by sponsoring companies and shipping merchandise direct to winners' homes or places of business.

Manufacturers and incentive sales organizations advertise regularly in premium and incentive magazines. Publishers of magazines such as *Incentive Marketing* produce annual directories of vendors, listing them by name, by types of merchandise offered, and by individual product line.

Other Applications

Use of specialties and premiums in public relations practice is limited only by practitioner imagination. A single case involving a labor relations problem will suffice to illustrate. The problem arose in an Arkansas hospital in the 1970s. Management first became aware of the difficulty when the National Labor Relations Board (NLRB) ordered certification elections in two bargaining units.

Management's primary problem was educational in nature. A great deal of negative information concerning the union existed but educational efforts were hampered by two circumstances. One was the relatively stringent NLRB constraints that then applied to all statements on the part of management personnel. The other was more significant. In adversarial situations, managements seldom are perceived as being as credible as union spokespersons.

The hospital attacked the problem by offering two color television sets as prizes in separate contests. In one, employees guessed the number of strikes in which the union had engaged in the prior 36 months. In the other, they guessed the average dollar value of increased benefits that resulted. Results were announced 48 hours before the date of the representation election.

Advertising specialties came into play on election day. The hospital's public relations firm had anticipated on the basis of prior experience with the union that "union buttons" would appear in the hospital at the last moment. The hospital ordered white lapel buttons printed in red with a single word: "NO." They were distributed by managers in employee parking lots at shift changes before and during election day with a simple statement, "We'll appreciate your support." The hospital won the elections in each of the bargaining units by a handful of votes.

BILLBOARD ADVERTISING

Those involved in the billboard industry prefer to be known as being in outdoor advertising. The word "outdoor" once was quite appropriate but is less so today. Billboards in one size or another now are used in multiple applications and by a far broader clientele than was the case a few years ago.

Billboards conventionally were available in relatively few sizes. They were either painted to papered. Today, they range in size from roadside "spectaculars" near double the size of their predecessors to miniatures affixed to supermarket shopping carts. Between the extreme are found "miniboards" incorporated into bus benches and appearing outside and inside buses as well.

Varied Applications

Similar diversity exists in the application of billboards. Most manufacturing industries, for example, make extensive use of billboards in varying sizes to remind workers of safety records. Others identify their plants as "the home of" various products. Smaller versions frequently appear on employee bulletin boards and elsewhere.

These and other applications of billboard content arguably are more in the province of public relations than advertising. They are designed to communicate specific messages to narrowly defined audiences. User concerns in terms of audiences and messages relate more to public relations than advertising.

Production Requirements

Production requirements for billboards are relatively simple in most public relations applications. As in the case of other materials, their content consists of words and illustrations rendered in paint or printed on paper. Paint is more often used in public relations in that billboard content changes relatively infrequently and paper tends to deteriorate rapidly.

Writers and artists are required to prepare billboard content. Verbiage must be concise. Billboards are observed only briefly, especially where oriented to motor vehicle traffic. Illustrations preferably should be eye catching and message-illustration relationships should be strong.

Billboard design most often is assigned to professionals in the field. Design services are included in the price of board rental in most areas. They usually are purchased by owners of few billboards since the specialized painting or printing services required in execution usually are not otherwise available.

Lists of billboard companies are most readily found through a Standard Rate and Data Service directory of outdoor advertising firms.

"PROFESSIONAL" ADVERTISING

As in the case of some billboards, professional advertising or the promotion of professional practices increasingly is becoming a public relations rather than an advertising function. The canons of ethics of many professionals—attorneys, accountants, dentists, physicians, and others—only in recent years have been modified to permit their use of advertising techniques. The impetus for the change arose out of litigation that resulted in ethical constraints being declared restraint of trade and illegal.

In the wake of these decisions and growing competition in many if not most professions, more and more practitioners turned to mass media advertising. Some persist in larger markets but most professionals appear to be turning to public relations and marketing techniques rather than advertising to build their practices.

Newsletters, brochures, educational programs, and similar devices are common in these programs. Pertinent production techniques are described elsewhere in this book.

COOPERATIVE ADVERTISING

Cooperative promotional efforts originated in the advertising sector and by some are still considered only in this context. Here again, however, the techniques involved are being extended into public relations practice.

Organizational sponsorship of special events is a form of cooperative advertising. More akin to public relations activities, however, are organized efforts to "place" products and services in entertainment media. They have become increasingly popular as the result of Pontiac Firebird sales originating with the Burt Reynolds movie, *Smokey and the Bandit*. Reese's Pieces enjoyed a similar sales surge subsequent to *E.T.*

Several organizations have been founded in recent years to place products from beverages to automobiles in television programs and movies. They do not confine themselves to those products used by the cast. They deal in associated "placements." The choice of which air freight service's truck is parked in front of the robbery scene often is influenced by these firms. So are the aircraft shown in the background during airport arrival scenes. Even the products or services shown on billboards that appear in auto chase scenes are involved.

The same or similar organizations deal with product placement for television's "give away" contests. Public relations practitioners seldom become directly involved in the process. This is not the case, however, where a manufacturer, distributor, or dealer provides products or services for charitable purposes.

Alert practitioners frequently are able to capitalize on usual or unusual public needs through donations that gain media exposure in excess of their value. Results of these efforts most often are seen in context with Christmas basket funds and other charities sponsored by the media.

"Production" seldom is involved. Success instead requires organizational policies and procedures that permit public relations practitioners to act promptly. It is almost invariably the first organization that calls a newspaper or broadcast outlet with a donation that reaps the bulk of the resultant exposure.

ADVERTISING APPLICATIONS

Many organizations fail to achieve optimum returns on their investments in advertising. This most often is the case where the interests and informational needs of their stakeholder groups are not concurrently considered. Any assumption that employees necessarily are familiar with advertising or would have no interest in acquiring a specialty or incentive item made available to dealers is tenuous at best. Experience suggests the reverse is true, especially where stakeholders universally hold the organization and its products or services in high esteem.

Advertising Specialties

In an era in which consumers are willing to pay premium prices for clothing emblazoned with the logotype of the Coca Cola Bottling Company, no organization safely can assume that advertising tee shirts, company uniform jackets, and other merchandise developed for specific audiences is of interest to no others.

Federal Express Corporation, for example, has established what it calls the Company Store to offer for sale components of uniforms and other items bearing its familiar red, white, and purple emblem. Employees buy these items in large quantities for family, friends, and personal off-duty use.

Other organizations encourage use of "trademark clothing" by providing tee shirts and other items without charge to employees participating in community fund raising and other philanthropic activities. At little cost to the firms involved, these items literally turn human beings into two-legged billboards.

Print Advertising

Assumptions that workers see company advertising in business and trade publications or in the financial press is equally open to question. So are suggestions that they are uninterested in such matters. In an era in which employees have been made hypersensitive to the economic condition of their employers, a contrary assumption would be far more logical.

These circumstances suggest advertising prepared for one audience is equally amenable to use with another; that product and service as well as financial advertising is worthy of exposure in employee publications, annual reports, and elsewhere.

Publishing such advertising in media other than those for which it is primarily intended is especially beneficial where this step is taken before rather than after first publication. Mass media production schedules require lead times usually sufficient to permit prior "internal" publication. No significant additional costs are incurred and audiences involved feel more a part of their organizations as a result.

Broadcast Advertising

While more difficult to accomplish on a uniform basis, the same principle applies to broadcast advertising. Audio- and videotapes readily can be used at shareholder meetings. Audiotapes are amenable to being played on organizational public address systems. Videotapes can be shown at orientation and training sessions as well.

Neither print nor electronic advertising should be used ad nauseum with audiences other than those for which they were primarily intended. Incremental advantages in using them on limited bases are considerable, however, in that little or no additional cost is involved.

Billboard Advertising

Miniature reproductions of outdoor advertising units are as amenable as print advertising to reproduction in print media. As in the case of trade journal advertisements, reproductions usually are available well before the billboards go up. They can be applied in several other areas.

Employee newsletters are a logical place to reproduce billboards. Some also might be used in annual reports and promotional materials for dealers or distributors. Their high visual impact also makes them appropriate to posting on bulletin boards.

GETTING IT TOGETHER

While using advertising techniques in public relations is practical and productive, problems can arise. Most of them involve relationships between professionals involved, all of whom tend to be defensive of their "turfs." A number of devices can be used to eliminate or minimize such difficulties, most of them involving organizational structures.

Internally, organizations can place public relations, advertising, and other communication disciplines under unitary control. Clear definitions of advertising and public relations objectives also can be helpful.

In any circumstances, open communication between operating units and/or their consultants is essential. Some organizations require that advertising be reviewed during production processes by public relations staff members. The process can be reversed as well.

The primary objective, regardless of techniques employed, is avoidance of any semblance of conflict. Consistency is essential in organizations' messages to all of their stakeholder groups. Where communication programs operate in a vacuum, risk of conflict compounds. Where it occurs, effectiveness and efficiency decline with predictable results as to productivity.

IN SUMMARY

Advertising in many forms today is a common component of public relations practice. Print and broadcast media are frequently used. Merchandise is incorporated into public relations programs in the form of specialties, premiums, and incentives. Billboard and cooperative advertising programs also are often employed.

Print advertising production in large part parallels steps undertaken in producing printed materials. Words and illustrations are brought together to convey messages designed to produce desired reactions among specific groups. The end product of the process in advertising, however, consists of composed negatives and proofs necessary to print media production.

Practitioners' skills are well-suited to the institutional and advocacy advertising common in public relations advertising. Persuasive rather than merchandising messages are involved and those skilled in product and service advertising often are not well-equipped experientially for the task involved.

The visual component of print advertising in public relations usually involves photos or drawings. High quality is essential to compensate for variation in media reproduction techniques. Focus and contrast are critical, as is color density where process color is used.

Preparation for print media advertising begins with development of text drafts and illustrative material. Texts then are set in type for proofing and approval. An interim step in the process involves using computers and laser jet printers to prepare rough type from texts. This process enables practitioners to "preview" inexpensively a variety of type faces and styles before delivering copy to commercial typesetting houses. Organizations with extensive advertising programs often adopt styles and graphic components from commercial advertising to create design continuity.

Advertising is proofed at several stages in the production process, usually before and after pasteup and again in final form. Finished materials are produced to conform to publication specifications.

Broadcast advertising involves scripts for radio and both scripts and visuals for television. The bulk of broadcast public relations advertising is prepared for radio. Limited television material is prepared by the Advertising Council and nonprofit organizations for use by local affiliates. Local advertising usually is produced by stations involved.

Merchandise applications in advertising once were confined largely to printed matchbook covers and similar give-away items. Matchbooks have lost market share with a decline in numbers of smokers but other items have replaced them. Most cost less than $5 and are imprinted with the name of the giver or a product. Utilitarian items such as emery boards and golf tees are popular in specialty programs.

Merchandise used in gift or premium and incentive programs also may be imprinted but often is free of commercial messages. Items involved frequently are part of broader programs involving brochures, sales meetings, and other materials or activities.

Gift items are more expensive than specialties. They usually are imprinted and are selected for continuing use in business environments. Premium or incentive items, in contrast, seldom are imprinted and most often are used in one of two sets of circumstances. Premiums or "loaders," as they are called, consist of merchandise offered "free" to induce purchase of other items. They commonly are offered by manufacturers or distributors to retailers. Incentives consist of merchandise awards given in recognition of sales or other performance levels.

Premium and incentive merchandise is available through incentive sales organizations and in some cases through manufacturers. Manufacturers usually offer larger discounts but "fulfillment"—the process of getting the award in the hands of the recipient—is the responsibility of the buyer. Incentive organizations usually handle the process for their customers.

What once was considered billboard or outdoor advertising today is often used in public relations in any of several forms. Large outdoor billboards are used to identify plants as sources of products. Others are used at manufacturing sites to encourage in-plant safety. Miniatures of billboards frequently appear on bulletin boards and in employee publications. Billboard content is rendered in paint or printed on paper. Design and production often are included in board rental charges and usually are handled by billboard companies in any event.

Many of these advertising techniques were attempted during the early 1980s by professionals in law, accounting, and other disciplines who had been freed of legal constraints that prohibited their use of mass media. In later years, many of them turned to public relations and marketing to accomplish their practice development goals.

Cooperative promotional efforts involve inducing film makers and broadcasters to use identifiable products in motion pictures and television programs. Several specialized firms have sprung up to promote the use of products in these applications.

Finally, considerable advertising today is being used with multiple audiences. Advertisers increasingly are correctly assuming, for example, that employees are interested in messages disseminated to customers, financial analysts, and other groups. Smaller versions of the advertising in question thus often appear in employee publications in advance of general use. Miniatures of billboards are used on employee bulletin boards as well.

ADDITIONAL READING

Aronoff, Craig E., and Otis W. Baskin. *Public Relations: The Profession and the Practice.* St. Paul: West, 1983.

Cutlip, Scott M., Allen H. Center, and Glen M. Broom. *Effective Public Relations*, 6th ed. Englewood Cliffs, N.J.: Prentice-Hall, 1985.

Dunn, S. Watson. *Public Relations: A Contemporary Approach.* Homewood, Ill.: Irwin, 1986.

Grunig, James E., and Todd Hunt. *Managing Public Relations.* New York: Holt, Rinehart and Winston, 1984.

Newsom, Doug, and Alan Scott. *This Is PR: The Realities of Public Relations*, 3rd ed. Belmont, Calif.: Wadsworth, 1985.

Simon, Raymond. *Public Relations: Concepts and Practices*, 3rd ed. New York: John Wiley, 1984.

16

Production for Other Channels

The term "channels of communication" assumes greater breadth in public relations than in other communication disciplines. It encompasses any and all methods through which messages can be conveyed to selected audiences. Interpersonal and mediated communication both must be included.

Rather than confine themselves to traditional media, public relations practitioners must select those that best meet specific needs. They include meetings of all kinds, telephone applications, personal activities, a host of organizational channels, community events, as well as traditional media. Each requires different handling. Many also function in ways that compound the benefits of other public relations efforts. Their components can be adapted to enable practitioners to better use other channels at their disposal.

Selection proceeds on the basis of a basic principle: Interpersonal communication is superior to mediated communication. Every tool of public relations involves a substitute for face-to-face conversation between two individuals.

MEETINGS

The first "step up" from individual conversation is the small group meeting. Most consider this device primarily applicable in organizations. It has been used extensively in financial public relations, however, and is applicable elsewhere as well.

Meetings of corporate officers and financial analysts constitute the primary application of meetings in the financial sector. They are predicated on the premise that face-to-face communication is superior to mediated communication; that organizational objectives can be better achieved in this context than through news releases, brochures, trade journal articles, and the like.

The same principle applies in many other situations. Primary among them are those in which organizations can deliver information of value to constituent groups in environments conducive to what has been called "counselor selling." This concept involves creating circumstances in which needs can be identified and applicability of organizational solutions pointed out. They readily can be developed by many organizations through educational or training programs.

Training Programs

Manufacturers who market their products through distributor or dealer networks are major users of training programs. Most users of this technique traditionally have focused their efforts on dealers and distributors. Increasing numbers in recent years have extended the concept to end users.

The underlying principle is a simple one: All other factors equal, humans are prone to select products and services with which they are familiar. Sales personnel, in other words, are most likely to "push" those products they know best; with which they are most knowledgeable. End users are most apt to select products that are familiar to them.

Manufacturers of heavy equipment such as industrial boilers thus spend considerable sums in training dealer sales personnel. Some also go to great lengths to provide seminars on equipment applications and maintenance on cost-free bases to existing or prospective users.

Systematic approach. These programs typically involve a more or less standardized approach that includes multiple techniques familiar to public relations practitioners. The first step is need identification, usually carried out through a survey of customers and prospective customers. Surveys are oriented to determining the perceived informational needs of these groups.

When needs have been established, educational materials must be prepared. Conventional printing and audiovisual developmental techniques are applicable. Finally, appropriate forums must be developed. This usually is accomplished by scheduling specific programs and extending invitations to members of groups involved. Those who respond inevitably are prospects for the sponsor's products or services.

Scheduling. Training programs are most beneficially scheduled on "neutral ground," usually in a hotel, for several reasons. Maintaining participant attention requires that all involved be free from day-to-day business concerns. On-premises programs thus are avoided whenever possible. In addition, sponsors find it beneficial to avoid any semblance of a "selling" situation, which some might perceive as threatening.

Half-day or full-day sessions are most frequently scheduled although two- and three-day programs are not unknown. Hotels usually provide appropriate meeting rooms at little or no cost where their food service facilities are to be used. Sponsors need only inspect the premises to assure that facilities are adequate (see Chapter 14).

Provision usually is made to record names, affiliations, addresses, and telephone numbers of participants on registration cards. This information enables speakers to more specifically address participant needs. It also facilitates follow-up by mail or personal calls.

Program content generally is cast in a problem-solution format, using lectures, discussions, audiovisual presentations, and, where appropriate, hands-on demonstrations. Most focus on specific problems indigenous to industries involved but allow ample time to address participants' individual concerns. As the latter are expressed, needs that can be satisfied by applying sponsor products or services are readily identified.

Educational Programming

Content changes little in educational programming but a very different organizational strategy often is applied. Rather than deal directly with customers and prospective customers, educational program sponsors organize their efforts through trade and professional associations that serve virtually every industry.

These organizations are expected to provide educational programs to members in conjunction with conventions, trade shows, and similar events. These events also happen to be major money-making vehicles for the associations. Many gain substantial portions of their operating revenues through admission fees, booth rentals, and the like.

Procedures. Public relations practitioners whose clients or employers are selling to specific industries thus proceed through a simple series of steps. First, they identify informational needs on the part of members of the industry group. Professionals in recent years, for example, increasingly have been using public relations and marketing techniques as practice development tools (see Chapter 15). They then contact the professional associations involved. Physicians, attorneys, accountants, and other professional groups usually are organized on local and state as well as regional bases.

Program developers offer to provide seminars on topics of interest to association members at little or no cost, enabling associations to earn a profit on admission fees. Marketing, public relations, and practice management have been "hot topics" among professional groups in recent years.

Association roles. Associations assume responsibility for promoting programs to members and provide adequate facilities in conjunction with a convention, trade show, or other event. Some will sponsor programs of special interest to members at other times as well.

Association sponsorship adds credibility to speakers and their programs. They are presumed knowledgeable and/or skillful in their subject areas. They are perceived as having been selected by the association to speak on a subject of interest to members although the reverse often is true.

Practitioner Concerns

Training and educational programs are readily arranged and often are used by public relations counselors as well as other professionals in developing new business contacts. Their success, however, is more a function of preparedness than knowledge or expertise. Optimum results require attention to a number of factors:

1. Personnel: More than one member of the organization should be in attendance and available to speak to participants individually during breaks and meal periods.
2. Materials: Brochures describing products and services should be prepared in advance and available in quantity. Reprints of published materials are especially effective.
3. Tracking: Complete lists of participants and their organizations together with addresses and telephone numbers must be obtained
4. Monitoring: Questions posed by participants should be noted for use in follow-up.
5. Follow-up: Thank you notes should be sent to all participants. Where appropriate, literature relative to their individual concerns can accompany the notes. Personal calls and visits should follow to every participant who has evidenced interest in services or products discussed.

Where practical, each session should end with an evaluation process. Appropriate forms should be distributed on which participants can evaluate the program and indicate interest in any other products/services that might be the subject of future programming. Summaries of results then should be provided to association executives, with appropriate expressions of appreciation, to establish bases for subsequent programs.

One element mentioned above is worthy of elaboration. Seminars and other in-person sales opportunities are significantly enhanced where speakers have established themselves as knowledgeable in the industry involved. This is most readily accomplished by publishing feature articles in business and professional magazines. Articles in question can be readily developed as part of public relations programs and serve double duty in this situation.

SPEAKERS' BUREAUS

Reprints also can be helpful as handouts during speaking engagements. These can be arranged individually or through a speakers' bureau, another commonly used approach to delivery of verbal messages to selected groups. The "bureau" need consist of nothing more than a contact person or coordinator within an organization who can schedule talks on specific subjects before interested groups. A bit more effort is required, however, to make the bureau wholly functional.

Speakers' bureaus are commonly formed during fund-raising, election, or other campaigns to bring messages to clubs, organizations, and other groups in the community involved. Most involve a group of individuals knowledgeable in the subject matter who are available to make public presentations. They often are equipped with audiovisual presentations since members seldom are universally well-trained in public speaking.

Coordinators maintain lists of members and serve as contact points for groups interested in presentations. They may assume active or passive roles, the latter of which is more common in public relations practice. In active roles, bureau coordinators actively seek out opportunities for speakers.

Obtaining Appointments

Seeking out processes are the key to bureau success. They entail a simple series of steps to obtain speaking dates with target organizations. The beginning point is an appropriate organization list that can be developed from one or several sources.

Other than in political situations, speakers' bureaus usually are organized to deliver messages to groups that meet predetermined criteria. They may have shared interests, as in chapters of professional groups, or consist of prospects for specific products or services, such as prospective clients for public relations counseling firms.

In the former situation, bureau coordinators seek out exhaustive lists of organizations in specific geographic areas. Telephone directory yellow pages are among several starting points in developing exhaustive lists. Many are found listed under clubs, organizations, and associations. Other lists often are available through community sources such as chambers of commerce, convention and visitors bureaus, and libraries.

The most useful of the lists include names of program chairpersons as well as presidents and provide addresses and telephone numbers as well. Bureau coordinators use these as mailing lists, first sending letters offering speakers and subsequently following up by telephone to schedule appointments.

Handling Bookings

Appropriate "bookings" are readily obtained where community of interest exists. Organizational program chairpersons often experience difficulty in obtaining sufficient numbers of programs of interest to their members in any given period. Most of them have 12 to 52 dates to fill during a year of thankless service and welcome speakers' bureau inquiries.

Bureau coordinators ideally are equipped with several presentations, each accompanied by a list of qualified presenters. As appointments are made, the program involved and the identity of the speaker are entered into a calendar. Each should be confirmed by letter to the program chair with a copy to the speaker. The coordinator then need only follow up 24 to 48 hours in advance to confirm arrangements.

Mechanical requirements for the presentation should be confirmed during initial conversations. This especially is the case where audiovisual presentations are involved. Availability of projectors or videotape equipment is especially important.

TELEPHONE PROGRAMS

Speaking engagements are a small part of a broad range of communication programs that involve the telephone in development or execution. Professionals often use the telephone to solicit business. Membership organizations keep participants aware of activities. Commercial firms use the instrument for sales purposes.

Effectiveness of commercial applications is open to question. Considerable consumer resistance has developed in recent years as a result of sales techniques and technologies. "Boiler room" operations used extensively in the sale of products and services has rendered telephone sales approaches suspect among many individuals.

The advent of "telemarketing" programs employing automated systems using computers and tape-recorded messages has limited the effectiveness of the process as well. Public complaints have become so prevalent that a number of state legislatures in the late 1980s were considering legislation to curb their use.

Eliminating Barriers

The effectiveness of telephone solicitation can be maintained to a significant extent, however, where community of interest exists and sponsoring organizations take adequate preparatory steps. Initial contact by mail, as in the circumstances described above, can serve to clear the way for speakers' bureau telephone calls and others.

Many professionals use techniques similar to those applied in soliciting speaking engagements to obtain new business. They obtain lists of prospects, write introductory letters, and follow with telephone calls to obtain appointments.

This approach is especially productive where callers are well-trained and adequate record-keeping systems are in place. Callers must maintain control of the process at all costs. This requires that they handle conversations with secretaries as well as individuals with whom they are seeking appointments in such manner as to permit affirmative follow up. "Don't call me; I'll call you" responses are to be avoided at all costs.

This requires that callers retain the initiative. Where prospects are out, for example, messages can be left, but always should be accompanied by words such as, "if I don't hear from him/her I'll call again in a few days." Where the prospect comes on the line and is "not interested at the moment," callers should respond with "may I call again in three to six months?"

The key to success is tenacity rather than pressure. Callers never should press for appointments but must make every effort to retain the initiative until they are granted. Courteous and consistent follow-up usually produces desired results and experience suggests such approaches are not only acceptable but successful in a majority of cases.

Organizational Applications

Organizations experience less difficulty in using telephone "networks" to maintain communication with members where time is of the essence. Members are organized into "cells" of perhaps five to ten individuals, each assigned to deliver messages to five to ten others. Where cells consist of five members and each makes five telephone calls, a single message quickly can be delivered to 3,625 individuals.

The key to success again is organization. Reliable callers must be assigned and a coordinator must monitor the system to insure that no message hits a "dead end" because a member of the network is ill, out of town, or otherwise unavailable.

PERSONAL ACTIVITIES

Many organizations reap considerable benefits from the activities of their members, especially their senior managers, in a host of business or professionally related activities. Active membership in associations and special interest groups can be especially significant contributors to sales and profits.

The two types of groups are very different and function in different ways in producing benefits for participants. Active participation in association activities creates multiple contacts within the business or profession. These are valuable in and of themselves but ultimately may place the individual in the role of organizational spokesperson as well.

Participation in special interest groups, even to the extent of creating such groups, can be doubly valuable. This especially is the case where membership is open to a broad range of participants. Owners and operators of retail outlets dealing in computers and associated equipment and supplies, for example, often have established computer "bulletin boards" to serve customers and any others who might be interested. Those "interested" inevitably are computer users who ultimately may become customers.

Computer-based communication channels lend themselves admirably to this form of "networking." CompuServe Information Services, The Source, and others maintain multiple forums open to all subscribers and addressing a broad range of special interests. CompuServe's forums for those interested in computers, for example, cater to users of specific types of hardware and software. Others were organized for writers, entrepeneurs, and educators. Almost any businessperson or professional readily can find one or more groups whose members not only share his or her interests but constitute prospects for products or services.

Success in the latter respect to a significant extent is a function of membership and the familiarity it produces with other members. All other factors equal, humans display a marked tendency to invest those they know with greater credibility than is granted to "strangers." This is the case despite the fact that they never have met in person and that confidence and credibility levels engendered through electronic contact may or may not be justifiable.

The same principle applies in community activities. This has led many organizations in recent years to compensate employees for hours dedicated to working with charitable and philanthropic groups. Compensation often is in time off rather than dollars.

ORGANIZATIONAL CHANNELS

Parallel communication channels often are used within organizations. Many have encouraged participation in quality circles by providing "company time" for meetings and other activities. Computer bulletin boards also are often maintained by individual business organizations. Like the telephone networks that usually are components of organizational communication systems, they appear beyond the reach of public relations practitioners. This only partly is the case. Many organizational systems are accessible and potentially highly productive communication channels. Some are relatively narrow in scope but others permit contact with large numbers of organizational personnel.

Access to these channels requires practitioner understanding of organizational and individual needs as well as changes now occurring in contemporary society. The United States is entering a decade that will be characterized by major shortages of skilled workers. The so-called baby bust generation is coming into the work force. Where the working population recently was increasing at a rate of about 7 percent annually, it soon will be declining. Where people once chased jobs, the reverse soon will be true.

Organizations concurrently are being called upon to make good on their promises of decades past and conform to new standards of social responsibility. They must continue, for example, to employ and provide health insurance coverage for increasing numbers of older workers. To attract and retain qualified personnel, they must offer new services ranging from child care to family and retirement counseling.

These circumstances are inducing them to grant access to internal communication channels to external organizations that a few years ago would have been barred from using them. Virtually any organization whose products or services will make workers healthier, happier, or otherwise more productive today increasingly can gain access. They need only understand employer motivations and the workings of organizational communication systems to produce salutary results.

Employer Motivations

Organizations use communication systems for multiple purposes. Virtually all of them, however, are oriented to provide economic benefits directly or indirectly. Bulletin boards, literature racks, employee newsletters, suggestion systems, and other channels were established to enhance management ability to communicate on topics of organizational interest. Safety, attendance, and other factors that directly impacted the economic welfare of the organization were their primary concerns. Communication channels today are more numerous and more sophisticated but management's objectives are unchanged.

The new channels include employee "hot lines," as well as computer bulletin boards and a host of employee assistance programs, but the old channels continue to function as well. All are amenable to externally generated messages provided a single criterion is met. The community of interest principle long established in public relations must extend to employer and employee as well as message sender.

Community of Interest

United Way organizations long have enjoyed employer support because they serve the interests of organizations as well as their personnel. These community fund-raising groups came into existence to reduce the numbers of individual charitable and philanthropic solicitations with which both groups earlier were forced to contend.

Similar communities of interest since have been established among health care providers, insurers, and employers. Escalating costs forced them to join together to meet mutual concerns, and employers' communication channels now are open to any organization that directly or indirectly encourages cost containment in the health care sector.

The organizations involved are not limited to those listed above. Employers welcome public relations material from virtually any health-oriented organization. Their newsletters and bulletin boards contain releases from health and athletic clubs, family and psychological counseling organizations, recreational facilities, and financial management groups among others.

Some are not-for-profit organizations; others are profit-making. The boundary between the two is rapidly disappearing as they recognize that healthier workers and stronger families contribute to lower costs and greater organizational productivity.

Messages and Origins

These conditions make organizational communication channels receptive to appropriate messages from acceptable senders. Public relations practitioners then need only address message propriety and sender acceptability to insure access. Both requirements can be satisfied in most circumstances.

Resistance and reticence still may be encountered where messages or senders are overtly commercial in nature. Level of commercialism usually can be controlled, however, to the benefit of all involved.

Messages. Points of emphasis in messages almost invariably can be balanced to create acceptance. Balance can be achieved through message synthesis or tactical approaches.

A seller of hearing aids, for example, doubtless would experience difficulty in inducing employers to post copies of newspaper ads on their bulletin boards. They would be more receptive, however, to material relating hearing problems to on-the-job accident risks.

Even greater levels of acceptance could be induced were the hearing aid vendor to offer coupons granting discounts on products or service or cost-free screenings on organizational premises. Organizations necessarily would share the benefits in the eyes of workers. Community of interest, in other words, would have been clearly established.

Origins. Employers in some instances remain resistant even after direct benefits become apparent. Public relations practitioners often can overcome this objection by altering the identity of message originators.

Where a hearing aid vendor may not be an acceptable source, for example, an association of vendors may constitute a viable alternative. While advocating use of hearing aids, the association would not be perceived as commercially oriented as an individual vendor.

A further step backward from commercialism might be accomplished were the vendor to join forces with a nonprofit organization dedicated to solving hearing problems. In either case, the vendor might be individually involved in providing services or in acting as a spokesperson. Pragmatically, he or she would merely be "changing hats" in dealing with the employer.

Many professionals have enhanced their own practices considerably by serving as spokesperson for their associations. Few professional groups, for example, would reject a member's offer to develop and deliver an audiovisual program to community organizations. In these circumstances, the individual literally establishes a speakers' bureau under the flag of the association, reaping a disproportionate share of the benefits by individually presenting many of the resulting programs.

The benefits in part accrue through direct contact with those attending but can be expanded through use of news releases in advance of presentations as well as any news coverage that may result.

Delivery Systems

The same considerations would arise as the hearing aid vendor, having established a functional relationship with an employer, prepared to take advantage of these circumstances. Message content necessarily would have to reflect the nature of the relationship.

News releases for employee newsletters would have to "originate" with the professional association or the nonprofit organization devoted to improved hearing. Brochures for organizational literature racks or posters for bulletin boards would be similarly identified.

A great deal of material appropriate to these applications usually is available from professional associations and nonprofit entities. The American Hospital Association, for example, regularly produces considerable information for use in employee media dealing with a broad range of health issues. So do the many nonprofit associations dedicated to eliminating diseases ranging from high blood pressure to Alzheimer's.

Posters, brochures, audiovisual presentations, and other communication devices similarly are available in quantity. The hospital association and many similar organizations publish catalogs of such materials for sale to nonmembers as well as to members.

COMMUNITY CHANNELS

Community-of-interest approaches in public relations should not end with individual organizations. A near limitless number of events occur in every community that offer considerable potential for alert public relations practitioners, their employers, and their clients. Some are wholly commercial in nature. Others are offered in the "public interest" although the line between the two increasingly is blurred.

The hearing aid sales organization specified above, for example, would find it beneficial to act in context with "health fairs" of the sort that have been springing up across the country. Often sponsored by hospitals, health maintenance organizations, or other components of the health care industry, they often are cosponsored by newspapers, television stations, or other media. Participation always is open to professional and nonprofit groups and for-profit entities may be welcome as well. Here and in other circumstances, the hearing aid vendor need only select the appropriate "hat" and seek out event sponsors to become involved.

Similar events often are staged for the business community by chambers of commerce, industrial development boards, and others interested in stimulating commercial activity. "Business to business" trade shows often are scheduled as well. Each of these creates opportunities for organizations.

They can be especially beneficial to manufacturers and distributors who maintain displays, exhibits, and similar devices for use in business and industry trade shows. These items frequently are used as seldom as twice to three times per year and otherwise are in storage and producing no benefits for their owners.

Commercial Events

While health fairs and business to business shows usually are presented as nonprofit events, similar endeavors often are organized by retail malls and others who use "public service" efforts to generate business. They always are receptive to offers of assistance or participation from outsiders.

Created Events

Where conventional health fairs are not regularly presented, enterprising organizations frequently establish their own. The hearing aid firm, for example, might contact optometrists, podiatrists, and others in the allied health professions to produce "mini-fairs" for shopping center operators or individual organizations.

Larger organizations often sponsor employee health days or weeks on their own premises and welcome participation on the part of virtually any organization that may assist in early detection of health problems. The range of "special events" in which commercial organizations may participate thus is limited only by the alertness and imagination of owners or their public relations practitioners.

Donations

Many neglect potential benefits that can arise through donations to community organizations. They need not involve large sums of money or their equivalent in merchandise in order to be of significant value.

Many libraries, for example, will duly label books and other materials donated by organizations as well as individuals. Where they relate directly to the products or services the organization offers, they can be of lasting value in generating direct inquiries.

Some libraries and many schools often are open to contributions of audiovisual materials. Many organizations capitalize on these opportunities by providing material available at low cost from trade or professional organizations. Some go so far as to produce audiovisuals for this purpose.

One manufacturer of meat products once provided audiovisual and printed materials to schools and designated a public relations staff member to make presentations to home economic classes. Although direct results of such efforts are difficult to measure, sales among young people significantly increased over the ensuing months.

WIDER HORIZONS

Successful use of the channels of communication described above entails more than is immediately evident. In each case, application can and should involve other "tools" of the craft prepared primarily for other purposes. Some of these applications have been mentioned, as in applicability of advertising material in employee publications. Others should be apparent, as in use of product or professional literature during speaking engagements, trade shows, and the like.

With public relations practitioners increasingly held accountable for the productivity of the resources they apply, such multipurpose applications of material are even more important. Costs involved are negligible. Audiovisual programs deteriorate little if at all when used with multiple audiences. Only where modification is necessary do added costs accrue.

Circumstances differ little where printed materials are used. The bulk of the cost in their production is incurred when the first item comes from the printing press or otherwise is ready for delivery. Additional quantities create little added expense. User benefits thus compound disproportionately with extended application.

IN SUMMARY

Channels of communication are not limited to the media. In practical terms, most are substitutes for face-to-face communication. They include a host of other vehicles through which organizations can deliver messages to audience groups. With mass media increasing in numbers and their audiences declining, public relations practitioners more and more are turning to the alternatives. In the process, they are finding some to be considerably more efficient than the mass media. Included in the latter group are meetings in several forms. They are used primarily in training and educational formats designed to create settings conductive to "counselor selling."

Training programs have been used most effectively by manufacturers and distributors of complex mechanical devices such as industrial boilers. Distributors and dealers have been their primary audiences but similar programs now are used to reach end users and prospective users. Seminars on equipment applications, especially where energy savings or greater efficiencies are in prospect, prove highly attractive.

Educational programs are similar but involve a different marketing approach. Rather than offering seminars and workshops on a direct basis, developers market them through business and professional organizations. Trade associations and other groups traditionally have provided "in service" educational programming to members and frequently earn significant portions of their annual revenues in the process. Developers gain the implied endorsement of organizations in the process, which adds considerably to their credibility.

The programming involved can be highly productive where used in conjunction with other public relations techniques and materials. These include brochures, reprints of feature articles, and follow-up procedures to capitalize on leads developed during the programs.

The same materials and procedures also are applicable where organizations turn to speakers' bureaus to reach stakeholder groups. "Bureaus" need consist of no more than an individual who uses mail and telephone to contact stakeholder organizations and offer programs.

Programs based on community of interest but necessarily involving sponsors' products or services are readily "salable" through such approaches. Organizational program chairpersons burdened with from 12 to more than 50 "open dates" each year welcome any and all material that might be of interest to members.

Telephone solicitation systems also can be successfully used on selective bases where similar approaches are applied. Individual letters followed by telephone calls have proven practical approaches to the sale of professional services as well as products usually installed through "custom" application.

The individual activities of organizational personnel, especially senior managers, can be equally beneficial. Active membership in organizations dedicated to objectives of mutual interest is the key ingredient in this approach, generating multiple contacts within specific business or professional sectors.

Within organizations, computer bulletin boards, telephone networks, and other long-used communication channels are being applied with increasing frequency. They are accessible to "outsiders" where, again, community of interest can be demonstrated. This especially is true in terms of activities or programs that tend to enhance employee health and welfare, thereby presumably minimizing absenteeism, tardiness, and other costly organizational problems.

Finally, organizational participation in community events is helping bridge gaps in mass media audiences. They require only a management team sufficiently alert to identify opportunities based again on community interest. Participation in events ranging from health fairs to community festivals is welcomed by for-profit and nonprofit groups alike. These and other activities tend to be especially beneficial where organizations can extend the reach of communication channels developed primarily for other audiences.

ADDITIONAL READING

Aronoff, Craig E., and Otis W. Baskin. *Public Relations: The Profession and the Practice.* St. Paul: West, 1983.

Cutlip, Scott M., Allen H. Center, and Glen M. Broom. *Effective Public Relations*, 6th ed. Englewood Cliffs, N.J.: Prentice-Hall, 1985.
Lovell, Ronald P. *Inside Public Relations*. Boston: Allyn and Bacon, 1982.
Nolte, Lawrence W., and Dennis L. Wilcox. *Effective Publicity: How to Reach the Public*. New York: John Wiley, 1984.
Reilly, Robert T. *Public Relations in Action*. Englewood Cliffs, N.J.: Prentice-Hall, 1981.

Epilogue

Professional public relations practice has been changing at an accelerating rate for the past several decades. Several factors are responsible. One is the extent of social change that has been occurring in the United States and around the world. Changing definitions of social responsibility, family, and worker are exerting pressure on and creating stress within organizations. Another is the changing demographic characteristics of the population. Declines in numbers of entry-level workers and increasing demands for improved working environments are compounding organizational problems. Finally there are two economic transitions, one from a national to a global economy and the other, in the United States, from a manufacturing to a service economy.

CHANGING SOCIAL CONTRACTS

The social responsibility issue probably is most significant from a public relations perspective. The several components of society in the United States of late have been dismantling the "social contract" that long controlled allocation of rewards in commerce and industry. First workers and then middle managers felt the impact of these changes over the past decade and more. Their interests have been sacrificed for the enrichment of senior managers and owners although the latter groups have not been immune from exploitation.

The dismantling process has paralleled the nation's shift away from mass production. In a mass production economy, as Reich (1987) has pointed out, there is no need for mutual trust and confidence. Organizations, workers, and investors simply negotiate the best deals they can find. Contracts spell out each party's obligation to the other.

Economic Differences

Entrepeneurial economies such as that which has developed in the United States in recent years, are inherently different. They arise, Reich says, in fast-changing circumstances where new ideas or inventions render their predecessors suddenly obsolete. These conditions demand "collective entrepeneurialism," which in turn requires mutual investment by organizations' stakeholder groups. More important, those circumstances require mutual trust.

Once relatively common in the United States, trust has become increasingly rare as stakeholder groups pursue their interests at the expense of others. The trend has been most evident in the automotive industry, where pledges of job security in exchange for worker wage and benefit "give-backs" generally have proven valueless, even where companies such as Chrysler have returned to relative health.

Other groups, although less noticeably so, have fared little better. Vendor interests have been capriciously sacrificed by buyers, as when gas pipeline companies abrogated contracts with natural gas producers in the face of declining prices. Investors were abandoned by owners when the Washington Public Power Supply System defaulted on bond payments. Countless communities that granted tax and other concessions to business were left "holding the bag" when successor ownerships closed plants and/or relocated. Reich described the consequences well.

Collective entrepeneurialism depends on commercial trust. Collective gridlock ensues when trust breaks down. The American economy, now in transition, generates countless opportunities for mutual endeavor and joint gains, but at the same time countless invitations to opportunism. Each participant, knowing this and wary of being victimized, forswears trusting collaboration. Thus the system's evolution is stymied. This . . . is the dilemma we face.

Growing Complexities

Pragmatically the problem is even more complex. Contemporary stakeholder groups, especially workers, justifiably are more skeptical than was the case a decade ago. Their suspicions make it doubly difficult for organizations to engender understanding of problems with which they must deal as the industrial age gives way to the information era. These difficulties can only further compound as the "baby bust" generation enters the labor force.

Numbers of workers available in virtually every category will decline through the remainder of the century and beyond. By the year 2010, a "baby boom echo" consisting of youngsters now entering grade school will produce some relief. At least until then, labor rather than capital will be the scarcest component of production.

As the full impact of demographic change is felt, communication inevitably will assume a higher organizational priority. Labor-intensive organizations will find their very survival threatened by mobile and skeptical workers whose scarcity will permit them to dictate terms of employment.

Organizations will be forced to respond, first by recreating viable social contracts and then by convincing workers of their sincerity. Resulting demand for skilled public relations practitioners will be unprecedented in history. By then, however, problems in human resources management will have been compounded by change in channels of communication.

CHANGE IN COMMUNICATION

Communication channels are at once becoming more numerous and more sophisticated. As their numbers multiply, their audiences fragment. The words "mass media" increasingly are becoming mutually contradictory. The results in public relations practice are more than semantic. They challenge practitioner knowledge and skill in seeking to communicate productively with diverse audiences.

The new technologies to some extent are assisting practitioners in meeting these challenges. Electronic distribution services, sophisticated audiovisual equipment, and computers all can be valuable tools. They also, however, can lull practitioners into a false sense of security.

The products of the new technologies are nothing more than tools. They serve for the most part merely to manipulate and distribute messages. They accomplish nothing toward making content more credible or more understandable. Neither do they induce in recipients any greater tendency to accept or act upon messages.

Communication and Behavior

The purpose of communication is behavioral change. Communication has been, remains, and will continue to be controlled by receivers. They must be communicators' primary concern. The most skillfully crafted message is valueless unless received, accepted, and acted upon. Communicator preoccupation with sophisticated technology and message design thus tend to be equally counterproductive.

These conditions collectively suggest that tomorrow's public relations practitioners will have to be more skilled and more knowledgeable than today is the case. They will have to serve as social scientists, diagnosticians, and counselors as well as technicians, in part reversing a trend of recent years that tended to diminish the technician role.

Changing Roles

The new technician role will be different from that of the past. It will involve not only writing for a more diverse set of media but successfully identifying those most appropriate to convey information to specific organizational constituencies.

The identification process itself will not necessarily be more complex. Practitioners will find it necessary, however, to maintain a working knowledge of increasing numbers of media and the groups to which they cater. Media data as well as demographic and sociographic characteristics of audience groups will have to be better known. Until such time as enterprising publishers develop comprehensive directories covering these factors as well as conventional circulation figures, public relations practitioners will be forced individually to monitor the changing channels of communication.

These bodies of information and several others will be applicable in practitioners' emerging roles as diagnosticians. Diagnosis of organizational problems is growing progressively more difficult. Mounting complexities in social and economic spheres are primarily responsible. They create the problems that influence the behavior of organizational constituencies and, in so doing, create both difficulties and opportunities.

Consider, for example, changes in the composition of households that have occurred in recent years. Single parent households have been growing at a rapid rate. More and more of the elderly are being cared for by their children as well. These developments inevitably will increasingly intrude upon organizational environments as workers experience mounting difficulties in finding assistance in caring for children and parents.

First evidence of the problem already exists in the form of rising absenteeism and tardiness rates. Analyses of several organizational personnel complements suggest that these problems are more a function of household difficulties than any casual dereliction of duty. With skilled labor increasingly difficult to find, managements will be forced to act. The nature, timing, and magnitude of their actions will play a major role in molding perceptions of organizations among employees and prospective employees.

Changing Responsibilities

Responsibility for stakeholder perceptions of organizations increasingly is assigned to public relations practitioners. Where this is the case, they inevitably are involved in developing the policies and procedures that shape those perceptions. Successful discharge of these responsibilities requires that they be conversant with the external factors that help mold perceptions of social responsibility as well as the internal workings of organizations.

In the circumstances described above, for example, a number of questions immediately arise. Should the organization provide child care facilities? Might such facilities be equally amenable to caring for elderly but still ambulatory parents? What cost would be involved in providing them, or in not providing them? How should these costs be allocated?

These questions quickly lead to others. What are the organization's current absenteeism and tardiness rates? What is the employee turnover rate? Are the rates increasing? To what extent are child and/or parental care problems contributing to difficulties in attendance? To what extent would they diminish were a care center to be established? What expense is the organization incurring through absenteeism, tardiness, and turnover? What portion of the costs might be saved if these problems could be significantly reduced? What advantages might the existence of a care center mean in recruiting new personnel? In retaining existing personnel?

Many of the answers would not be readily available. Human resources and other records might require examination to pinpoint costs. A bit of formal survey research might be necessary to precisely establish the extent to which costs might be contained. Industry associations and professional journals could yield information on the experience of similar organizations.

With all data as to the scope of existing and prospective problems and their associated costs in hand, a memorandum to senior management delineating alternatives and recommending a course of action then would be appropriate. All of this would have been undertaken under the ever-broadening umbrella called "public relations."

Other Problems

Were this the only emerging problem with which organizations must deal, practitioners would enjoy a far more relaxed atmosphere than will be the case for the remainder of the century and beyond. Organizational problems are legion. How should they respond to growing difficulties surrounding drug abuse and acquired immune deficiency syndrome (AIDS)? These problems ultimately will impact every organization. How will they handle health care for retirees, which soon may be required by the federal government? What of toxic waste, clean air, and clean water? Overseas competition?

The list could go on and on, and every item listed would constitute a potential problem for one or more of the organization's stakeholder groups. Most successful public relations practitioners therefore will be among those able to identify emerging problems, forecast their potential organizational impacts, and offer well-researched action alternatives to management.

IMPACT ON PROGRAMMING

The process involved will constitute the heart of public relations programming. No longer will public relations practice involve receipt of a predetermined organizational position with instructions to make the most of it.

Practitioners instead will be expected to anticipate problems and provide appropriate professional counsel to management. Counsel will cover not only the action alternatives but the manner in which stakeholders can be expected to respond to each. Anticipated responses often will be major concerns in management decisions. The nature of management decisions then will guide practitioners in programming; in developing plans and activities necessary to convey information to stakeholder groups.

Counseling and programming thus will be the dominant components of public relations practice in the years ahead. Communicating in writing will remain a vital requirement at the entry level but will decline in importance thereafter, ultimately becoming a minor practice component for most members of a growing industry. Other forms of communication, however, can be expected to occupy a larger role.

Organizational Changes

The impending human resources shortage promises to induce major change in organizations. A host of books have been written concerning what long has been an obvious need for managers to take a larger part in communication processes. Relatively few contemporary managers are adequately trained, however, in interpersonal and small group communication. Their training well may become part of public relations practice. Multiple counseling firms as well as more specialized consultancies in larger metropolitan areas already are engaged in this sector.

Finally, and most importantly, some in the communication industry suggest that the public relations and human resources management will become a primary source of senior executives in larger organizations. While little evidence supports this view at the moment, history and logic lend credibility to the thesis.

Boards of directors historically and logically have promoted to leadership those equipped with the knowledge and skills necessary to handle the most pressing of organizational problems. Over the years, production, research and development, and finance at different times have been the most popular source of chief executive officers. Developing human resources problems and attendant communication needs suggest that these disciplines next may come into favor.

Both functions have been moving up typical organizational hierarchies in recent years. Senior practitioners in each discipline more and more report to chief executive officers and rank at the vice-presidential level and above. As such, they increasingly are seen and heard in the board room, where senior executives are selected.

In the Board Room

Once within the board room, these executives tend to be more noticeable than others due to their academic and experiential backgrounds. Both necessarily are "people oriented." Both usually are the product of liberal arts rather than business or technical curricula. They tend to take a broader view of their organizations and the worlds in which they must function.

Public relations practitioners additionally are or should be equipped with adequate backgrounds in management, marketing, and other business disciplines to "speak management's language." Those now graduating from undergraduate programs in public relations almost universally are so equipped. Most of their senior colleagues have gained equivalent knowledge through years of experience.

For these several reasons, the 1990s and the decade beyond well may become the golden age of public relations. Need for public relations skills never will have been greater. Practitioners never will have been better educated to meet contemporary challenges. Whether they capitalize on these opportunities, however, remains to be seen.

Professional Responsibilities

As an emerging profession, public relations only now is beginning to recognize and accept the responsibilities that professionalism imposes. The Public Relations Society of America, after years of discussion, debate, and study, only in 1986 began seriously to contemplate the need for mandatory continuing education among its members. Whether the society will act and, if it acts, the rigorousness of its requirements, remain to be seen.

The absence of such requirements, however, does not relieve professionals of their obligations to their employers and themselves. Employers, whether organizations or clients, have a right to expect those they hire or retain to be equipped with state-of-the-art knowledge of public relations as well as industries with which they deal. Practitioners have an even greater need to maintain levels of knowledge and skill necessary to meet their professional obligations.

Those who act accordingly—who invest adequate time and effort in professional development under compulsion or otherwise—will rise to positions of prominence in their organizations and their profession. Adequate professional development programs maintain skill and knowledge levels, especially the latter, in several areas.

Staying Abreast

First, practitioners must stay abreast of contemporary knowledge in public relations. This can be accomplished through reading and by both attending and participating in professional meetings and the organizations that sponsor them. Participation is especially rewarding in that the research it necessarily requires adds to the body of professional knowledge.

A similar pattern readily can be followed in terms of any organization or set of organizations with which practitioners are involved. Business or industry journals and trade meetings are major sources of information.

Finally, a more "global" body of knowledge is required. It embraces all of the suprasystems and subsystems of which organizations on the one hand are a part and on the other of which they are constituted. It requires extensive environmental assessment, and scanning to identify emerging trends and monitoring their progress and potential organizational impacts. While collectively burdensome, these activities are necessary to successful public relations practice and essential to those who aspire to organizational leadership.

IN SUMMARY

Public relations has been changing at an accelerating pace in keeping with the evolution of the environments in which it is practiced. Social and demographic changes have been primary causal factors and the trends involved will continue during the remainder of the century and beyond.

The United States is in the process of redefining "social responsibility." Expectations of organizations on the part of all of their stakeholder groups are in a state of flux. To date, behavioral standards that once governed intergroup relationships largely have been dismantled. Construction of new norms, however, appears to be only now beginning.

The reconstruction period will be rendered doubly troublesome by economic change. The nation now is part of a global society and must learn to compete as such. Successful competition will require joint efforts by organizations and their stakeholder groups, which require mutual trust and confidence. The latter elements today are rarities in the United States. They have been destroyed by what the parties perceive to have been multiple betrayals over the past decade. Organizations thus must create new social contracts and then convince workers and other stakeholders of their sincerity.

The latter objective will involve considerable time and effort. Prevailing levels of distrust first must be overcome through behavioral change as well as communication. Channels of communication have become more numerous. Their audiences have become more diverse, and techniques required in their use are more sophisticated than was the case in earlier years.

These conditions are redefining what once was looked down upon in some quarters as the "technician role" in public relations practice. Where technicians dealt primarily with writing, they now must be expert in channel selection and in the technologies involved.

The same conditions also are expanding practitioners' roles as diagnosticians. Changing environments in which stakeholder groups function induce behavioral change, which creates difficulties as well as opportunities for organizations. Responsibility for monitoring these environments increasingly is part of the public relations function, which compounds practitioner involvement in senior management.

Increased exposure in the management suite and the board room coupled with increasing human resources problems well may induce governing boards to turn increasingly to public relations for senior managers. Those who stay abreast of developments in the profession and the world around them thus will find ever broader opportunities in the months and years ahead.

ADDITIONAL READING

Reich, Robert B. *Tales of a New America*. New York: Times Books, 1987.

Selected Bibliography

Adams, J. Michael, and David D. Faux. *Printing Technoloqy: A Medium of Visual Communications*. North Scituate, Mass.: Duxbury Press, 1977.

Alkin, Glyn. *Recording and Reproduction*. Boston: Focal Press, 1981.

_____. *Sound with Vision*. New York: Crane, Russak, 1973.

_____. *TV Sound Operations*. Boston: Focal Press, 1975.

American Society of Magazine Photographers. *Professional Business Practices in Photography*. New York: American Society of Magazine Photographers, 1981.

Andrews, Patricia H., and John E. Baird, Jr. *Communication for Business and the Professions*, 3rd ed. Dubuque, Ia.: Wm. C. Brown, 1986.

Arnold, Edmund C. *Ink on Paper 2: A Handbook of the Graphic Arts*. New York: Harper & Row, 1972.

Atwan, Robert, Barry Orton, and William Vesterman. *American Mass Media: Industries and Issues*, 3rd ed. New York: Random House, 1986.

Barwick, John H., and Stewart Kranz: *Why Video*. Park Ridge, N.J.: Sony Corporation, 1975.

Beach, Mark. *Editing Your Newsletter*. Portland, Ore.: Coast-to Coast Books, 1982.

Berryman, Gregg. *Notes on Graphic Design and Visual Communication*. Los Altos, Calif.: William Kaufman, 1979.

Bird, David. *From Score to Tape*. Boston: Berklee Press, 1973.

Birren, Faber. *Creative Color*. New York: Van Nostrand Reinhold, 1961.

Bland, Michael. *The Executive's Guide to TV and Radio Appearances*. White Plains, N.Y.: Knowledge Industry Publications, 1980.

Blythin, Evan, and Larry A. Samovar. *Communicating Effectively on Television*. Belmont, Calif.: Wadsworth, 1985.

Borwick, John, ed. *Studio Recording Practice*, 2nd ed. New York: Oxford University Press, 1980.

Breyer, Richard, and Peter Moller. *Making Television Programs (A Professional Approach)*. New York: Longman, 1984.

Budd, John. *Corporate Video in Focus, A Management Guide to Private TV*. Englewood Cliffs, N.J.: Prentice-Hall, 1983.

Bunyan, John A., James C. Crimmins, and N. Kyri Watson. *Practical Video: The Manager's Guide to Applications*. White Plains, N.Y.: Knowledge Industry Publications, 1978.

Bureau, William H. *What the Printer Should Know About Paper*. Pittsburg: Graphic Arts Technical Foundation, 1982.

Burton, Paul. *Corporate Public Relations*. New York: Reinhold, 1966.

Carter, David E. *Corporate Identity Manuals*. New York: Art Direction, 1985.

Click, J. W., and Russell N. Baird. *Magazine Editing and Production*. New York: Watson-Guptill, 1971.

Cogoli, John E. *Photo-Offset Fundamentals*, 4th ed. Bloomington, Ind.: McKnight, 1980.

Connors, Tracy Daniel. *Dictionary of Mass Media & Communication*. New York: Longman, 1982.

Craig, James. *Designing with Type*. New York: Watson-Guptill, 1983.

Crawford, Tad. *Legal Guide for the Visual Artist*. New York: Robert Silver Associates, 1985.

Cummings, Paul W. *Open Management: Guides to Successful Practice*. New York: AMACOM, 1980.

Daniels, Tom D., and Barry K. Spiker. *Perspectives on Organizational Communication*. Dubuque, Ia.: Wm. C. Brown, 1987.

Dennis, Ervin A., and John J. Jenkins. *Comprehensive Graphic Arts*. Indianapolis: Howard W. Sams, 1974.

Deutsch, Arnold L. *The Human Resources Revolution: Communicate or Litigate*. New York: McGraw-Hill, 1979.

Dondis, Donis A. *A Primer of Visual Literacy*. Cambridge, Mass.: MIT Press, 1973.

Douglas, Philip N. *Pictures for Organizations: How and Why They Work as Communication*. Chicago: Ragan Communications, 1983.

Dravov, Paul, Louise Moore, and Adriene Hickey. *Video in the 80s*. White Plains, N.Y.: Knowledge Industry Publications, 1980.

Druck, Kalman B., Merton Fiur, and Don Bates, eds. *New Technology and Public Relations: A Guide for Public Relations and Public Affairs Practitioners*. New York: Foundation for Public Relations Research and Education, 1986.

Duck, Steve. *Human Relationships: An Introduction to Social Psychology*. Beverly Hills, Calif.: Sage, 1986.

Durbin, Harold C. *Printing and Computer Terminology*. Easton, Pa.: Durbin Associates, 1980.

Ehrenkranz, Lois B., and Gilbert T. Kahn. *Public Relations/Publicity: A Key Link in Communications*. New York: Fairchild, 1983.

Fulmer, Robert M. *Practical Human Relations*, 2nd ed. Homewood, Ill.: Richard D. Irwin, 1983.

Gold, Ed. *The Business of Graphic Design*. New York: Watson-Guptill, 1985.

Goldman, Jordan. *Public Relations in the Marketing Mix: Introducing Vulnerability Relations*. Chicago: Crain, 1984.

Gottschall, Edward M. *Graphic Communication '80s*. Englewood Cliffs, N.J.: Prentice-Hall, 1981.

Graham, Walter. *Complete Guide to Pasteup*. Philadelphia: North American, 1975.

Graphic Arts Guild. *Handbook of Pricing and Ethical Guidelines for Grpahic Artists.* New York: 1984.

Gray, James G., Jr. *Managing the Corporate Image: The Key to Public Trust.* Westport, Conn.: Quorum Books, 1986.

Greenberger, Martin, ed. *Electronic Publishing Plus: Media for a Technological Future.* White Plains, N.Y.: Knowledge Industry Publications, 1985.

Grode, Susan. *The Visual Arts Manual.* New York: Doubleday, 1984.

Gross, Edmund J. *101 Ways to Save Money on All Your Printing.* North Hollywood, Calif.: Halls of Ivy, 1971.

Gross, Lynne Schafer. *The New Television Technologies*, 2nd ed. Dubuque, Ia.: Wm. C. Brown, 1983.

————. *Telecommunications: An Introduction to Radio, Television, and the Developing Media.* Dubuque, Ia.: Wm. C. Brown, 1983.

Heath, Robert L., and Richard A. Nelson. *Issues Management: Corporate Public Policymaking in an Information Society.* Beverly Hills, Calif.: Sage, 1986.

Henderson, Madeline M., and Marcia J. McNaughton, eds. *Electronic Communication: Technology and Impacts.* AAAS Selected Symposium 52. Boulder, Colo.: Westview Press for the American Association for the Advancement of Science, 1980.

Holmes, Nigel. *Designer's Guide to Creating Charts and Diagrams.* New York: Watson-Guptill, 1985.

Hudson, Howard Penn. *Publishing Newsletters.* New York: Scribner's, 1982.

Hurlburt, Allen F. *The Grid, a Modular System for the Design and Production of Newspapers, Magazines and Books.* New York: Van Nostrand Reinhold, 1978.

Johansen, Robert, Jacques Vallee, and Kathleen Spangler. *Electronic Meetings: Technical Alternatives and Social Choices.* Reading, Mass.: Addison-Wesley, 1982.

Jones, Clarence. *How to Speak TV: A Self-Defense Manual When You're the News.* Marathon, Fla.: Video Consultants, 1983.

Jones, Gerre L. *How to Prepare Professional Design Brochures.* New York: McGraw-Hill, 1976.

Kagy, Frederick, and J. Michael Adams. *Graphic Arts Photography.* Belmont, Calif.: Wadsworth, 1983.

Kneller, George F. *The Art and Science of Creativity.* New York: Holt, Rinehart and Winston, 1965.

Laing, John. *Do-it-Yourself Graphic Design.* New York: Macmillan, 1984.

LaRae, H. Wales. *A Practical Guide to Newsletter Editing and Design.* Ames, Ia.: State University Press, 1978.

Latimer, Henry C. *Production Planning and Repro Mechanicals for Offset Printing.* New York: McGraw-Hill, 1980.

Lazar, Ellen A., Martin C. J. Elton, and James W. Johnson, et al. *The Teleconference Handbook: A Guide to Cost-effective Communication.* White Plains, N.Y.: Knowledge Industry Publications, 1983.

Lefferts, Robert. *Elements of Graphics: How to Prepare Charts and Graphs for Effective Reports.* New York: Harper & Row, 1981.

Lem, Dean Phillip. *Graphics Master 3.* Los Angeles: Dean Lem Associates, 1983.

Lindegren, Erik. *ABC of Lettering and Printing Typefaces.* New York: Greenwich House, 1982.

Lockhart, Ron, and Dick Weissman. *Audio in Advertising: A Practical Guide to Pro-*

ducing and Recording Music, Voiceovers, and Sound Effects. New York: Frederick Ungar, 1982.

Londgren, Richard E. *Communication by Objectives: A Guide to Productive & Cost-Effective Public Relations & Marketing.* Englewood Cliffs, N.J.: Prentice-Hall, 1983.

Lovell, Ronald P. *Inside Public Relations.* Boston: Allyn and Bacon, 1982.

Lowman, Charles. *Magnetic Recording.* New York: McGraw-Hill, 1972.

Maas, Jane. *Better Brochures, Catalogs and Mailing Pieces.* New York: St. Martin's Press, 1981.

McGregor, Georgette F., and Joseph A. Robinson. *The Communication Matrix: Ways of Winning with Words.* New York: AMACOM, 1981.

McLeish, Robert. *The Technique of Radio Production.* Boston: Focal Press, 1978.

Marlow, Eugene. *Managing the Corporate Media Center.* White Plains, N.Y.: Knowledge Industry Publications, 1981.

Martin, James. *Future Developments in Telecommunications.* Englewood Cliffs, N.J.: Prentice-Hall, 1977.

Marting, Elizabeth, Robert E. Finley, and Ann Ward. *Effective Communication on the Job: A Guide for Supervisors and Executives,* 8th ed. New York: American Management Association, 1963.

————. *The Wired Society.* Englewood Cliffs, N.J.: Prentice-Hall, 1978.

Matthews, Arthur. *Radio Production Handbook.* Downers Grove, Ill.: Meriwether, 1982.

Meyer, John W., and Richard W. Scott. *Organizational Environments: Ritual and Rationality.* Beverly Hills, Calif.: Sage, 1983.

Mintz, Patricia Barnes. *Dictionary of Graphic Arts Terms.* New York: Van Nostrand Reinhold, 1981.

Munce, Howard. *Graphics Handbook.* Westport, Conn.: New Light, 1982.

Murphy, Robert D. *Mass Communication and Human Interaction.* Boston: Houghton Mifflin, 1977.

Nelson, Roy Paul. *Publication Design,* 4th ed. Dubuque, Ia.: Wm. C. Brown, 1983.

Nisbett, Alec. *The Technique of the Sound Studio,* 4th ed. Boston: Focal Press, 1979.

O'Donnell, Lewis B., Philip Benoit, and Carl Hausman. *Modern Radio Production.* Belmont, Calif.: Wadsworth, 1986.

Overman, Michael. *Understanding Sound, Video and Film Recording.* Blue Ridge Summit, Pa.: Tab, 1978.

Peake, Jacquelyn. *Public Relations in Business.* New York: Harper & Row, 1980.

Pesman, Sandra. *Writing for the Media: Public Relations and the Press.* Chicago: Crain, 1983.

Printing Ink Handbook, 4th ed. Harrison, N.Y.: National Association of Printing Ink Manufacturers, 1984.

Rice, Ronald E. et al. *The New Media: Communication, Research and Technology.* Beverly Hills, Calif.: Sage, 1984.

————, and William J. Paisley. *Public Communication Campaigns.* Beverly Hills, Calif.: Sage, 1981.

Rosen, Ben. *Type and Typography.* New York: Van Nostrand Reinhold, 1976.

Rothman, Jack. *Using Research in Organizations: A Guide to Successful Application.* Beverly Hills, Calif.: Sage, 1980.

Runstein, Robert. *Modern Recording Techniques.* Indianapolis: H. W. Sams, 1974.

St. John, Tracy. *Getting Your Public Relations Story on TV and Radio.* Babylon, N.Y.: Pilot Books, 1986.

Saltman, David. *Paper Basics.* New York: Van Nostrand Reinhold, 1978.

Salvaggio, Jerry L. *Telecommunications.* New York: Longman, 1983.

Sanders, Norman. *Graphic Designer's Production Handbook.* New York: Hastings House, 1982.

Saumarez, Maurice de. *Basic Design: The Dynamics of Visual Form.* New York: Van Nostrand Reinhold, 1983.

Schramm, Wilbur, and Donald F. Roberts, eds. *The Process and Effects of Mass Communication.* Urbana: University of Illinois Press, 1971.

Silver, Gerald A. *Graphic Layout and Design.* New York: Van Nostrand Reinhold, 1981.

————. *Professional Printing Estimating.* Philadelphia: North American Publishing, 1975.

Simon, Raymond. *Public Relations: Concepts and Practices,* 3rd ed. New York: John Wiley, 1983.

Smith, Judson, and Janice Orr. *Designing and Developing Business Communications Programs that Work.* Glenview, Ill.: Scott, Foresman, 1985.

Stern, Edward L. *Printing and Graphic Arts Buyers Directory.* New York: Hilary House, 1984.

Stettinius, Wallace. *Management Planning and Control: The Printer's Path to Profitability.* Arlington, Va.: Graphic Communications Center, 1976.

Stevenson, George A. *Graphic Arts Encylopedia.* New York: McGraw-Hill, 1979.

Stockton, James. *Designer's Guide to Color.* New York: Chronicle, 1983.

Strauss, Victor. *The Printing Industry: An Introduction to Its Many Branches, Processes and Products.* New York: R. R. Bowker, 1967.

Strong, William. *The Copyright Book.* Cambridge, Mass.: MIT Press, 1984.

Thom, Randy et al. *Audio Craft: An Introduction to the Tools and Techniques of Audio Production.* Washington, D.C.: National Federation of Community Broadcasters, 1982.

Thompson, Tom. *Organizational TV News.* Philadelphia: Media Concepts, 1980.

Tremaine, Howard. *Audio Cyclopedia.* Indianapolis: H. W. Sams, 1969.

Treweek, Chris, and John Zeitlyn. *The Alternative Printing Handbook.* New York: Penguin, 1983.

Turnbull, Arthur T., and Russell N. Baird. *The Graphics of Communication,* 4th ed. New York: Holt, Reinhart and Winston, 1980.

Van Uchelen, Rod. *Pasteup Production Techniques and New Applications.* New York: Van Nostrand Reinhold, 1976.

Walsh, Frank. *Public Relations Writer in a Computer Age.* Englewood Cliffs, N.J.: Prentice-Hall, 1986.

Weaver, J. Clark. *Broadcast Copywriting as Process.* New York: Longman, 1984.

————. *Broadcast Newswriting as Process.* New York: Longman, 1984.

Weil, Ben H. *Modern Copyright Fundamentals.* New York: Van Nostrand Reinhold, 1985.

Whetmore, Edward J. *Mediamerica,* 3rd ed. Belmont, Calif.: Wadsworth, 1987.

White, Jan V. *Editing by Design: A Guide to Effective Word and Picture Communication for Editors and Designers.* New York: R. R. Bowker, 1982.

Williams, Frederick. *Technology and Communication Behavior*. Belmont, Calif.:
     Wadsworth, 1987.
Winter, Elmer. *Complete Guide to Preparing a Corporate Annual Report*. New York:
     Van Nostrand Reinhold, 1985.
_____. *Mastering Graphics*. New York: R. R. Bowker, 1983.
Zettl, Herbert. *Sight, Sound and Motion*. Belmont, Calif.: Wadsworth, 1973.

Index

About the Author

E. W. BRODY teaches public relations in the Department of Journalism at Memphis State University in Tennessee and maintains a public relations consulting practice in Memphis.

Public Relations Programming and Production is his third book. *Communicating for Survival: Coping with Diminishing Human Resources* and *The Business of Public Relations* both were published by Praeger in 1987.

Dr. Brody's articles on public relations have appeared in *Public Relations Journal, Public Relations Quarterly, Public Relations Review, Journalism Quarterly, Legal Economics, Health Care Management Review,* the *Journal of the Medical Group Management Association, Modern Healthcare, Hospital Public Relations,* and other publications.

He holds degrees from Eastern Illinois University, California State University, and Memphis State University and is accredited by the Public Relations Society of America and the International Association of Business Communicators.